Kinship in the Household of God

Kinship in the Household of God

Towards a Practical Theology of Belonging and
Spiritual Care for People with Profound Autism

Cynthia Tam

FOREWORD BY
John Swinton

☙PICKWICK *Publications* · Eugene, Oregon

KINSHIP IN THE HOUSEHOLD OF GOD
Towards a Practical Theology of Belonging and Spiritual Care for People with Profound Autism

Copyright © 2021 Cynthia Tam. All rights reserved. Except for brief quotations in critical publications or reviews, no part of this book may be reproduced in any manner without prior written permission from the publisher. Write: Permissions, Wipf and Stock Publishers, 199 W. 8th Ave., Suite 3, Eugene, OR 97401.

Pickwick Publications
An Imprint of Wipf and Stock Publishers
199 W. 8th Ave., Suite 3
Eugene, OR 97401

www.wipfandstock.com

PAPERBACK ISBN: 978-1-7252-7441-9
HARDCOVER ISBN: 978-1-7252-7442-6
EBOOK ISBN: 978-1-7252-7443-3

Cataloguing-in-Publication data:

Names: Tam, Cynthia, author. | Swinton, John, foreword.

Title: Kinship in the household of God : towards a practical theology of belonging and spiritual care for people with profound autism / by Cynthia Tam ; foreword by John Swinton.

Description: Eugene, OR: Pickwick Publications, 2021. | Includes bibliographical references and index.

Identifiers: ISBN 978-1-7252-7441-9 (paperback). | ISBN 978-1-7252-7442-6 (hardcover). | ISBN 978-1-7252-7443-3 (ebook).

Subjects: LCSH: Theology, Practical. | Autism. | Theology—Ecclesiology. | Baptism.

Classification: BV3 T36 2021 (print). | BV3 (ebook).

08/16/21

Scripture quotations are taken from the Holy Bible, NEW INTERNATIONAL VERSION®, NIV® Copyright © 1973, 1978, 1984, 2011 by Biblica, Inc.® Used by permission. All rights reserved worldwide.

Contents

List of Figures | vi
Foreword by John Swinton | vii
Preface | ix

   Introduction: Loving One Another | 1
1 Rethinking Autism | 11
2 Problems with Inclusion: Strangers in God's Household | 28
3 Belonging and Becoming: Concerted Efforts of the Circle of Friends | 45
4 From Rejection to Belonging | 62
5 Created in Love to Be with and for Others | 79
6 Covenantal Kinship Community | 104
7 Entering and Growing in Life Together | 129
8 Practicing Kinship Solidarity | 159
   Conclusion: Proclaiming God's Holiness in Community Life | 174

Bibliography | 179
Index | 189

Figures

1 Progression of Belonging in Red Hill and The Cross | 65
2 Changes in Perspectives Resulting from Intentional Engagements | 76

Foreword

John Swinton

WHAT DOES IT MEAN to be a church for everyone? It is, to state the obvious, to suggest that church communities are not always as welcome and loving towards those whom they consider to be "strangers." Despite the fact that the central doctrine of the Body of Christ informs us that we should be a community where difference is present, but never divisive, many congregations still struggle to include people with particular forms of difference. Time and again we find stories of people with disabilities being excluded from congregations and being asked to leave church buildings. It's difficult to imagine Jesus behaving in such ways. There is a difficult tension between the theological demand for inclusivity and belonging, and the actual practice of the church. The church has become a place of struggle rather than welcome. That is not to say that people are deliberately being unpleasant. Often it is a combination of anxiety, not knowing what to do, and a desire to avoid things that may disrupt our lives and force us to re-think certain key theological practices. In a word-oriented theology, the wordless find it difficult to secure a place. In a worship context that requires a certain understanding of order and relies on inflexible liturgical structures, the presence of people who see and act slightly differently can provoke anxiety. When we are anxious, we become fearful. When we are fearful, we tend to push away the things that scare us. When that happens, we create spaces of struggle wherein those who are weaker and have a quieter voice, can easily find themselves overpowered and excluded. We need faithful guides who will help us (all of us together) to see and understand one another more fully and in so doing enable us to practice community more faithfully.

In this rich, deep, and profoundly person-centered book, Cynthia Tam offers to be our guide as we journey into the complexities of communities-of-difference and develop the kinds of theologies that sustain our practices of welcoming and belonging. At heart the premise of the book is very simple: *How do we become the loving family that God has called us to be?* Of course, like all "simple" things, the answer to such a question turns out to be much more complex than it might at first seem. Through a rich and thick description of two people living with autism—Ellen and Dylan, Dr. Tam presents a powerful re-imagining of what it means to be a church family within which people with autism can find safety, acceptance, and love. In teasing out the theological implications of Ellen and Dylan's stories and the stories of other families, she provides us with fresh and new ways of thinking theologically about church and autism, and potential models for engagement with families in ways that bring about love, healing and belonging. It is certainly the case that the church has a long way to go before it can claim truly to be Jesus's body. But every journey needs to begin somewhere. This book is a good place for us all to begin the journey of rethinking our theology and practice in relation to church and autism, and together, move on to develop the kind of sacred space where God is truly worshipped by the fullness of the human community. This is an important book which has the potential to do excellent work. My hope and my prayer are that we can listen, learn, and begin to change.

Preface

In 2006, I held the first support group meeting with parents with children with various disabilities at my church. At the time, I was an occupational therapist working with children and youth who depended on technologies for writing and speaking. These technologies are undoubtedly helpful and necessary, but the young people I worked with told me that technologies have their limits. They could only help if people want to befriend these young people and interact with them. Unfortunately, instead of finding friends, young people with disabilities often experience rejection and isolation in society.

At the first support group meeting, family after family shared stories about the rejections they had experienced in church communities. Many families had switched churches to find acceptance, and some families struggled for over ten years to find a welcoming church. What touched me most was the hunger that these families expressed for God. They taught me that meeting their spiritual needs was as important, if not more important, than merely supporting their day-to-day needs. What I experienced at the support group subsequently led me to pastoral ministry, doctoral study, and then, this book.

Over the years, as I sought to understand the spiritual needs of people affected by disabilities, I have come in contact with many who live with the effects of autism. These interactions changed my medically shaped understanding of autism and helped me see their yearnings for friendship and community. Their difficulties in being accepted by church communities challenged me to look into the reasons behind the rejection. These thoughts led me to rethink who and whose we are as a church and what it means to be united as one in Christ with different members.

The ideas percolated over the years began to translate into a theological understanding of the church as a covenantal kinship community in my doctoral study. I am indebted to my supervisors: John Swinton and Léon van Ommen. To Professor John Swinton, thank you for your wise and gracious advice that always challenge me to think deeper. I am very grateful for your patience, wisdom, affirmation, and unwavering mentorship. To Dr. Léon Van Ommen, I am thankful for your insightful direction and encouragement. Your trust meant a lot to me. I am also grateful to Dr. Thomas Reynolds and Dr. Kenneth Jeffreys for their comments, critique, and direction that sharpened my ideas. Thanks also go to Jared Siebert and Jonathan Fuller for taking the time to read through an earlier draft on sections of this book. They offered valuable feedback and opinions from the field that brought the book to its current form.

In this long journey of thinking through the questions on belonging, I am much obliged to many sisters and brothers in various church communities I affiliated with. Their love and prayers helped me appreciate belonging to a Christian community as a precious gift from God. As always, I am eternally grateful to my family. To my brothers and sisters (including the in-laws), I thank you for your never-failing love and trust in me. To my son, Bernard, daughter-in-law, Susan, and my adorable grandsons, Jedidiah and Joshua, thank you for your love and encouragement. You are indeed a constant source of confidence, especially in my many moments of self-doubt.

More than anything, I am thankful to Jesus, who accepts me as a member of his body, and gives me the experience of what it means to belong to a loving church community.

Introduction: Loving One Another

> A new command I give you: Love one another. As I have loved you, so you must love one another. By this everyone will know that you are my disciples, if you love one another.—John 13:34–35

My friend Teresa and her husband, James, live in a rural area in Canada and attend a small local church there.[1] Two years ago, Teresa heard about a church in a nearby suburban town that offered a support program for families with children with disabilities. James and Teresa have a son, Michael, who is a young adult with severe autism. Learning of such a support program led them to think that their son would be better integrated into the life of that suburban church community. Therefore, they made the switch. Regrettably, soon after they started attending this suburban church, Teresa and James were advised by the church leadership that Michael could not worship with the congregation in the sanctuary because he was making too much noise! They suggested that Michael worship with the families of young children in the "cry room." He was invited to join the special Sunday school where children and young adults with various disabilities are grouped together on Sundays. But Michael was discouraged from participating in any of the adult fellowships. Teresa and James were very upset about the church's lack of acceptance of Michael. They returned to the rural church where Michael's presence was, in Teresa's words, "tolerated."

In Canada, with legislation stipulating access to community buildings, churches are increasingly opening their doors to people with disabilities. However, in Michael's case, we can see that as necessary as the inclusion policies are for bringing people like Michael into the church, these policies are not enough for them to be accepted into the fabric of church life. The

---

1. All names, including names of churches and places, are pseudonyms.

refusal of Michael to worship in the sanctuary and participate in the adult fellowship indicates a troubling issue of rejection of people who look and act differently to the majority of people at church. It is a concern because the church should be the body of Christ in which all members, regardless of their abilities, feel that they belong (1 Cor 12:15–20). Paul's exhortation to the Corinthian church then, and us now, is that Jesus's followers should strive to live out the oneness in Christ, recognizing that all members of Christ's body are indispensable.

From Inclusion to Belonging

With legislation mandating acceptance of people with disabilities in community activities, inclusion is a buzz word. Most individuals will agree that people with disabilities should be included in their organizations or communities. Therefore, there should be no surprise when the Lifeway Research found that "nearly every pastor (99%) and churchgoer (97%) says someone with a disability would feel welcomed and included at their church."[2] However, Aaron Earls, the Lifeway researcher, noted, "fewer are taking active steps to make sure this is the case."[3] Earls's observation is substantiated by Jeff McNair's survey of church attendees. McNair wanted to understand how church attendees' views on "persons with mental retardation [sic]" might translate into actions.[4] His findings identified the same disconnect between recognizing the need for inclusion and acting on it.[5] Remarkably, both researchers use the availability of specialized programs or ministry for people with disabilities as the indicator of the church's willingness and concrete actions for including people with disabilities in the church.

From Teresa and James's decision to switch to the suburban church that provides a specialized program for individuals with disabilities, we can see that even families will consider the provision of disability programs as an indicator of the church's commitment to inclusion. However, as Michael's experience illustrates, more needs to be done than merely providing specialized programs. In the case of the suburban church that Michael and his family attempted to switch to, offering specialized programs meant that he was separated from the body of the church. The autistic behaviors Michael exhibited were considered disruptive. His lack of communication abilities disqualified him from participating in the young adult fellowship. Where

---

2. Earls, "Churches Believe," lines 6–7.
3. Earls, "Churches Believe," lines 2–3.
4. McNair, "Christian Social Constructions," 57.
5. McNair, "Christian Social Constructions," 60.

Michael was deemed suitable was the areas specifically designated for people with disabilities of all ages. Being separated from fellow Christians, to Michael's family, was worse than being "tolerated" but present in the same room with others. Therefore, the family returned to their former church. However, this does not mean that Teresa and James were happy with this rural church's treatment of Michael. They initially wanted to switch to the suburban church because they were looking for a church that would love Michael as their own. Put differently, what this family wanted was a people that loved Michael and welcomed him into the church life and not a church building where Michael could attend physically.

Michael and his family's experience highlighted the struggles of the church's efforts of inclusion. Using the language commonly used in the education system, Brett Webb-Mitchell points out that churches use both inclusion strategies: segregation (as in the example of the suburban church) and mainstreaming (as found in the rural church), depending on available resources. Regardless of which approach is adopted, Webb-Mitchell finds that churches that actively serve people with disabilities tend to create a category of disability ministry or organize specialized programs to separate people with disabilities from the main body of the church.[6] As such, church ministries *for* people with disabilities are outreach and service type of ministries that view them as objects of charity. Evident in Webb-Mitchell's description of the church's inclusive approach is the emphasis of the church's doing *to* and *for* people with disabilities, versus being *with* them in relationships. These two prepositions represent a power differential and a divide within the church along the ability line. Ministering *to* is a gesture of the carers exercising power and acts of care to the care receivers. This gesture diminishes the human dignity of people with disabilities. It also reduces them to a passive role in the church, thus restricting the full provision of gifts by the Spirit.

Moving from inclusion as a ministry for people with disabilities to belonging as one body in Christ requires more than programmatic changes. Talking from her experience as a church consultant in the disability field, Jennie Weiss Block comments on the limitations of inclusionary practices. She says,

> No laws, bishop's letters, human services paradigms, or parish accessibility committees will ever truly provide access to people with disabilities. Liberation and real access to the community

---

6. Webb-Mitchell, *Beyond Accessibility*, 116.

will only be realized through personal relationships that develop into genuine friendships.[7]

Although allowed to be present in the church buildings, many people with disabilities remain strangers to the community. They are excluded from relationships by an invisible wall that separates the unwelcoming church as *us* from *them*, the disabled. This invisible wall prevents *us* from gaining a deep understanding of people with disabilities. The separation makes *us* feel indifferent or even hostile to those who look, act, or think differently from *us*.

Thomas Reynolds calls the church that sets up social boundaries between the abled and the disabled, the "cult of normalcy."[8] "Normalcy," according to Reynolds, is a "cultural system of social control."[9] It presumes a certain bodily appearance and the ability to be representative of a community's identity. As such, it marks out who can and cannot belong to the community. To belong, *they* have to be like *us*. With this way of thinking, Michael and others with autism, who cannot change who they are, do not belong. They are welcomed to come into the church building, but they can only stay on the church's margins.

Paul teaches that the worth of each member of the body of Christ is not based on their bodily strengths or intelligence. Instead, each person is valuable, and each bears the Holy Spirit's gifts for the good of the community (1 Cor 12:7). As such, each member of a Christian community is a valuable bearer of the Spirit's gift for the community. Each is indispensable for the community to receive the fullness and richness of God's gifts. The church is a community in which we minister *with* each other and supporting each other in serving Jesus, the head of the church. The recognition that we, autistic or not, need each other is what creates a yearning to come together as a community. Doing *for* or *to* divides the church into carers and cared for. Being *with* looks forward to belonging together as one body in Christ, with each member exercising their gifts for the good of the body.

Thus, this book seeks to reflect ecclesiologically on the questions brought about by the inclusion of people with profound autism. It is the burden of this book to show that to be faithful and truthful to God's call; the church needs to live out what it means to be the family of God united in Christ. As I will explain in chapter 6, Christians give witness to the holy God by how we live as a family brought together by God's faithful fulfillment of the covenantal promise established with Abraham. Christians are

---

7. Weiss Block, *Copious Hosting*, 158.
8. Reynolds, *Vulnerable Communion*, 59–60.
9. Reynolds, *Vulnerable Communion*, 49.

incorporated into God's family in and through Christ. Being children of God, who is love, we strive to love one another as God has loved us (1 John 4:16, 19). Viewing each person through the lens of God's love enables us to see each other as a beloved child of God. We welcome each other, loving one another, and valuing each person as a sibling. We also acknowledge that each sibling, autistic or not, is given to the family as a gift. Before describing how this concept is laid out in the book, a word concerning the focus on people with profound autism is in order.

Autism as a Magnifying Glass

With inclusion being widely adopted by churches, we begin to see some indicators on how well people with disabilities are participating in church life. In their study, Melinda Jones Ault and her research team reported that persons with disabilities participated in fewer church activities than their peers without disabilities. The level of welcome and support provided by churches was not adequate to enable them to participate in the full range of church activities. Among the different disability groups, Ault et al. found that individuals with autism were the least likely to receive welcome and support in the faith communities.[10] Similarly, by examining the data of church attendance in the American National Survey of Children's Health over the ten years ending in 2012, Andrew Whitehead discovered that young people living with autism were consistently the least likely to be attending a church.[11]

Looking at possible factors contributing to their limited congregational participation, Ault et al. pointed to the behavioral characteristics and limited communication associated with autism as a major barrier for social interactions. Unwelcoming attitudes and lack of supports to enable participation in church programs turned families away from the church. Additionally, the doubt that people with autism can get anything out of participating in the church meant that the church might be reluctant to include them in discipleship programs.[12]

Autism covers a vast range of human experiences. Some individuals with autism can function independently. Many of them can make friends outside of the church. They can also participate in various community activities. The more significant the effects of autism are on a person, the more the person will be dependent on others for care. They may also have more significant behavioral manifestations of autism. In this book, I use the term

10. Ault et al., "Congregational Participation," 58.
11. Whitehead, "Religion and Disability," 387.
12. Ault et al., "Factors," 192–203

"profound autism" to describe individuals who require very substantial support in daily living because of autism. They also commonly have communication difficulties in both writing and speaking.

If behavioral characteristics and limited communication are the reasons for the rejection of people with autism, then we can expect to see more substantial issues with the church's welcome of individuals with profound autism. Therefore, their experience can serve as a magnifying glass to examine how well the church is practicing its belonging with different members to form a united body. The understanding that comes from real-life experiences is what I will take to reflect theologically on the issues and consider how we should faithfully belong with each other as the church of Christ.

As a relational concept, belonging requires a desire from both sides of the relationship to engage with each other. People with autism are commonly portrayed as people living in their own world, not interested in social relationships, and unable to empathize with others' emotions. As this book proceeds, we will see that this way of understanding autism is constructed based on societal norms for acceptable behaviors. Once we understand how the perception of people with autism is socially constructed, examining how we currently belong as a church with the lens of profound autism will show sharply the societal norms that have crept into the church. Instead of valuing all members of Christ's body, the church has adopted societal standards such as independence, productivity, physical appearance, and appropriate behavioral etiquette in how we welcome and value each other.

Moving forward, what is required is a theological approach for understanding the personhood and values of people with profound autism to the church. Discovering how we perceive and receive members with unique differences will also cause us to re-examine the nature of the church and how we belong as a community. The ultimate goal is to reimagine the Christian community as God's loving family in which members, regardless of differences in abilities, stand in solidarity with each other.

Reimagining the Loving Community

When we confess that God is love (I John 4:8), there is no question that we should regard love as the basic premise of our faith. Jesus tells us that the first and greatest commandment is to love God, and the second is to love our neighbors as ourselves (Matt 22:34–40). If we have been Christians for some time, we have probably heard these biblical teachings cited regularly. However, how well are we doing in loving God and all our neighbors? Specifically, what does it mean to love people with profound autism as ourselves?

In his deliberation on what love might look like for people with autism, John Swinton states that for some people with autism, "loving relationships are not marked by warmth, empathy, and mutuality as conventionally defined, but rather by concrete actions."[13] For a person with autism, a concrete expression of love may be making sure that the refrigerator always holds the items his loved ones need every day![14] Swinton's observation raises a crucial point. Loving one another does not always involve the kind of expressions that society regards as loving actions. Although stocking up the refrigerator is not always an expression of love, or at least not in a romantic sense, sending roses or hugging one another is also not the only way to express love. What we need to do is to rethink Christianly about love. Our love for each other should be grounded in the love of God and not based on societal practices. If we believe that the divine love is impartial, we will know that God loves every person, autistic or not, in the same way. Learning to love each of our siblings with the love of Christ means that our love for one another should not be dependent on how others express their love or want to be loved. We love because God first loved us (1 John 4:19). When we can come into the love of God together as the body of Christ, we can become the loving community that God desires for us to be.

With this in mind, this book uses a practical theological approach to critically and theologically reflect on the church's practices of belonging. Practical theological reflection has its starting point in human experiences and concrete situations.[15] Therefore, readers can expect to see the experiences of people with autism, their family, and church communities being highlighted throughout the book. The thesis of the book is that we belong first and foremost to God. Our belonging with each other flows out from our identity as children of God. My hope is to offer perspectives and insights that will enable the church to faithfully practice our belonging as one in Christ with different members.

Understanding the experiences of people with profound autism begins with an appropriate understanding of autism. Medically, autism is considered a neurological condition. However, autism should not be the only description of the person. In chapter 1, I explain the issues of allowing the medical model to dominate our understanding of autism. While unintended, defining a person with the medical diagnosis of autism often leads the public to see the person with autism as "deviant," thus not belonging to the community of "normal." Engaging thinkers from different disciplines

---

13. Swinton, "Reflections on Autistic Love," 267.
14. Swinton, "Reflections on Autistic Love," 267.
15. Swinton and Mowat, *Practical Theology*, 13.

and the autistic community, I demonstrate how the concept of autism is often socially constructed. Autistic people are regarded as people who want to stay in their own world. However, if we listen to the voices of people with autism published in recent years, we will hear that they do want to have social relationships with others. More often than not, we, people in society, are responsible for the communication breakdown and the failure to connect with those living with autistic experiences.

To see how the social concepts of autism have affected the church, I draw on a series of qualitative research interviews I conducted in two churches from September 2016 to November 2017.[16] I introduced two individuals with profound autisms, Dylan and Ellen, to these churches: Dylan for The Cross and Ellen for Red Hill. A Circle of Friends was formed in each of the churches to help Dylan and Ellen's integration into their community. In chapter 2, I follow Dylan into The Cross. Dylan's experiences highlighted the pervasive effects of the defective view of autism. With a culturally biased view against autism and epilepsy, Dylan's family limited his interactions with people outside of the family. Although Pastor George and his wife, Martha, welcomed Dylan to join the Awana program, church members would not invite him to participate in the group's activities. Compounding the situation was the pastor's non-intervention approach. However, Dylan's experiences also demonstrated the power of love from a small circle of friends. Their efforts helped Dylan gain better acceptance at The Cross.

Following Ellen's journey of belonging in chapter 3, we see a different picture. As a church with a vision to become an inclusive community and a leadership dedicated to supporting Ellen, Red Hill shows us the possibility of turning inclusion into belonging. The collaborative approach used by the Circle friends and the family is how Ellen could feel at home at Red Hill by the end of the year. However, Red Hill's experience also exposes the issues of a church that functions like a community center. The social nature of relationships in this church was not deep enough for members to care about Ellen and her family beyond Sundays and Ellen's needs for discipleship.

When I put the experiences of The Cross and Red Hill together in chapter 4, we can see the issues that have limited Dylan and Ellen's belonging. The first thing we see is that when church members avoided or rejected Ellen and Dylan, they were left as invisible beings sitting on the church's margins. The Circle friends' intentional efforts to bring them into relationships with some church members helped Dylan and Ellen be more involved

---

16. Selected quotations from these interviews are included in this book with the pseudonyms assigned to protect the participants' identity. The participants included two individuals with profound autism, their mother, and Circle of Friends. Transcripts of the interviews are stored in the secured hard drive at the University of Aberdeen.

with the community. However, neither of these two churches reached the point of recognizing Dylan and Ellen as members of the church family. Their collective experiences indicate three issues: 1) These two churches have allowed societal values to influence their understanding of people with profound autism's personhood and values. 2) The relationships among members of Red Hill and The Cross were superficial and social in nature; 3) Church leaders have not addressed the specific spiritual needs and discipleship pathways for Ellen and Dylan to belong to Christ's body and participate in the church as contributory members.

Looking at the concepts of humanity and personhood, I show in chapter 5 that humanity is created as a community in relationship with the triune God. As such, our understanding of personhood must include the individual and collective aspects of humanity. Guided by the theology of Dietrich Bonhoeffer, I argue that every person, autistic or not, has intrinsic value because each of us is created lovingly by God. Additionally, I demonstrate that personhood is not a static concept. As a collective being that receives our new humanity from Christ, we encounter each other in relationships, thus learning about each other in Christ. These encounters facilitate our growth into the fullness of our humanity individually and collectively. They also allow us to acknowledge each other as the persons we were created to be. If our relational encounters are essential for our recognition of others' personhood, there is a need to better grasp how we should relate with each other as members of Christ's body.

Applying Paul's teaching, I identify, in chapter 6, that Christian relationship is covenantal in nature and kinship in expression. Our relationship is covenantal because God, with untiring fidelity, fulfills the covenant promise established with Israel in and through the work of Jesus Christ. Believers of Jesus are joined to the lineage of Israel by incorporation into the body of Christ through baptism. Being members of the body of Christ, the New Covenant church share in Christ's sonship, thus belonging to the Divine as children in God's household. It is in Christ and by the power of the Holy Spirit that Christians relate with each other as siblings. The covenantal nature of Christian relationship means that we are committed to love God and love each person that God brings to us as a sibling. Ellen and Dylan are valuable because they are gracious gifts of God for the community. Our faithful response to God's grace is to love and honor them as beloved siblings and support them to be members of the family that exist with and for each other.

Further, I demonstrate that welcoming Ellen and Dylan into the church without baptizing them and teaching them to obey Jesus is a disobedience of the Lord's commands to his church (Matt 28:19–20). Therefore, in chapter 8, I argue for Dylan and Ellen's need to receive baptism or confirmation to become members of the body of Christ. I point out the issues in Christian traditions that emphasize faith as an intellectual assent. Supported by Dietrich Bonhoeffer's baptismal theology, I contend that faith is a gift of God given to the church community. The church community carries the baptizands by faith in the rite of baptism. The community is also responsible for preparing the candidates for baptism while crucially acknowledging that the Spirit of God works in people's hearts to bring them to Christ. As such, cognitive capacity is not relevant and should not be used as a hindrance to the baptism of anyone longing to come to God. Having advocated for Ellen and Dylan to be accepted as members of the church through proper preparation, I show that for the body to have the fullness of gifts that God intended for the church, we need every member God brings to us. Ellen and Dylan are indispensable members because their presence enriches our understanding of God's gifts for the church. Their uniqueness and giftings deepen our knowledge of God. Their presence, as we would see in the experiences of Red Hill and The Cross, worked to release the gifts of other members, thus bringing their communities closer together.

For these theological concepts to inform the church's faithful practices of belonging, I explain in chapter 8 that belonging together as one body with different members requires that we follow Jesus's examples of being with and for his people. Christ's love opens the doors of our hearts to welcome each other in and be sincerely present to each other. When we live together as siblings in the household of God, Christ is present among us. His presence connects us, helps us care for each other, and share in each other's sufferings and joy. This deep connection is what brings us into solidarity with each other in the kinship community.

I conclude with the proposal that the church cannot claim to be a faithful community of Christ without rejoicing over the differences that exist in the church as God's gifts. Living as a community of loving siblings is not only the right thing to do as Christians. It is also an expression of God's holiness. Our love for each other that includes people with profound autism testify to God's righteousness and compassion to those forgotten and oppressed by the world. A loving community of God also reflects God's kingdom of shalom, beckoning people to live harmoniously and lovingly with each other.

I

Rethinking Autism

"Neither this man nor his parents sinned," said Jesus, "but this happened so that the works of God might be displayed in him."—John 9:3

SINCE LEO KANNER'S DETAILED descriptions of eleven children with autism, the information on autism has increased exponentially. The seemingly rising prevalence and the significant impact of autism on individuals and their families' lives make autism a research priority. Much research efforts have been poured into identifying the causes and cure of the condition. Yet no conclusive findings have been reported to date. The vast heterogeneity in the spectrum makes it difficult to draw any definitive conclusion and gain a full understanding of autism. Within the autism spectrum, some are socially awkward but highly intelligent; others have significant communication difficulties and intellectual disabilities; many have scattered abilities and difficulties. The heterogeneity is why there is a common saying that "if you have met one person with autism, you have met one person with autism."

In the Introduction, I use a magnifying glass metaphor to suggest that human differences presented by autism can help us reimagine the church as one body with many members. Before we can look clearly into the church, the first step is to clean our glasses. Therefore, the task of this chapter is to gain a proper understanding of autism. To do so, I engage with different conceptions of autism proposed by thinkers of various professional disciplines and the autistic community. The goal is to demonstrate how these different ways of conceptualizing autism may affect how people interact with those living with autism. While I am offering critiques on these various views of autism, it is essential to note that I am not suggesting that they have no value. My intent is to show that these prominent views on autism are not necessarily the best for Christian reflection, especially for shaping a counter-narrative of the belonging of people with autism to the community.

Autism as a Disorder

Medically, autism is formally known as Autism Spectrum Disorder (autism in short for the rest of this book). It is classified as a neurodevelopmental disorder in the fifth edition of the Diagnostic and Statistical Manual of Mental Disorders (DSM-5).[1] What this means is that there are neural mechanisms in the brain that cause autism. However, the exact mechanisms have not been identified. Autism is diagnosed based on behavioral criteria grouped under two main categories:

a. Persistent deficits in social communication and social interaction across multiple contexts.

b. Restricted, repetitive patterns of behavior, interests, or activities.

In the compilation of DSM-5, researchers collapse the previous four separate diagnoses (autistic disorder, Asperger's syndrome, childhood disintegrative disorder, and pervasive developmental disorder not otherwise specified) into the umbrella term of autistic spectrum disorder. As such, the spectrum covers a wide range of behavioral manifestations and varying levels of severity in symptoms. As evident in the behavioral definition of autism, what holds this broad range of human experiences together is the social-communicational behaviors. However, the range is so broad that communication difficulties could mean anything from being socially awkward to very limited speech and language abilities. The level and type of restricted behaviors also vary from individual to individual. Additionally, many people with autism have comorbid neurological diagnoses (e.g., epilepsy) or psychiatric diagnoses (e.g., anxiety disorder), which may contribute to the vastly different presentations within the autism spectrum.[2] Intellectual disability is common, but the extent of it depends on the associated neurological conditions.[3] The heterogeneity within the autism spectrum makes it a very complex phenomenon.

Aided by technological advancements in neuroimaging and genetic studies, clinicians and researchers began to explore the neurobiological

---

1. American Psychiatric Association, *Diagnostic and Statistical Manual*, 299.00 (F84.0).
2. Rapin, "Introduction," 5–9.
3. Dykens and Lense, "Intellectual Disabilities and Autism," 264.

basis of autism since the 1970s.[4] However, the complexity and ambiguity in our understanding of autism remain. Although there is a general consensus that autism is caused by atypical connectivity in the brain, when and how the connective pathways are affected remain unknown.[5] In the genetic studies, hundreds of gene variants in autism have been revealed, but no specific genetic marker of autism can be identified.[6] The high heterogeneity makes it challenging for these study findings to be duplicated and refined to pinpoint the neurobiological mechanism of autism.[7]

When Kanner first described autism, he classified it as an affective disorder because he observed that the eleven children in his study showed "extreme aloneness from the very beginning of life, not responding to anything that comes to them from the outside world."[8] Kanner also commented that "there are very few really warm-hearted fathers and mothers" in these eleven families and questioned if the parents' lack of warmth contributed to their children's autism.[9] As we will see further down in this chapter, despite the advance in the knowledge of autism in recent decades, the characterization of people with autism as people who have no interest in interacting with others persisted. Medical researchers have since refuted the "refrigerator mother" theory and affirmed the neurobiological basis of autism.[10] However, the classification of autism as a neurodevelopmental condition, while helpful, does not change, and in some ways, reinforced the defective view of autism.

As the goals of medicine are to cure diseases and restore functions and abilities, the medical model considers disability as an undesirable condition that needs to be removed or corrected. With the belief that early intervention has the potential to maximize brain plasticity and improve treatment outcomes, the medical community stresses the importance of having children screened for autism as early as possible.[11] Along with the emphasis on early diagnosis and the need for therapeutic intervention came a rapid rise in many pharmaceutical and behavioral interventions.[12] According to Sven Bölte, a pediatric neuropsychiatrist, empirical support

4. Anagnostou and Taylor, "Review of Neuroimaging," 1.
5. Ralph-Axel and Fishman. "Brain Connectivity and Neuroimaging," 1103.
6. Vorstman et al., "Autism Genetics," 375.
7. Persico and Bourgeron, "Searching for Ways Out," 356.
8. Kanner, "Autistic Disturbances," 249.
9. Kanner, "Autistic Disturbances," 250.
10. Rapin, "Introduction," 4.
11. Dawson and Zanolli, "Early Intervention," 255.
12. Rapin, "Introduction," 8–9.

for many of these interventions is limited, and their claims for cure are debatable.[13] However, driven by the hope for a cure, some desperate parents of children with autism are willing to try even the "dubious, and often risky" therapy strategies.[14]

What we have seen in the medical description and the search for a cure highlights the pervasive issues of the medical model of autism. When autism is described with a list of "defects," the implication is that people with autism are "defective" and in need of cure and therapy. To be clear, I do not deny the importance of medical and therapeutic interventions. As an occupational therapist, I recognize that some therapy modalities and interventions help people with autism learn to regulate their sensory inputs and control their bodies. My point is that when cure is the focus, the medical model ignores the lifelong effects of autism on people living with that identification. The medical model also cannot address the pressing needs to find ways to enable persons with autism to live as respected members of society.

The increasing research interest in the causes and cure for autism, combined with the public's concerns over the apparent epidemic status of autism, caught the media's attention.[15] Journalist Steve Silberman alleges that the movie *Rain Man* released in 1988 caused "an unprecedented surge of interest" of the mainstream media in autism.[16] According to Silberman, the number of stories on autism published by major newspapers or portrayed on television and movies quadrupled a year after the release of *Rain Man*. The media's efforts have promoted public awareness of autism, but unfortunately, their portrayals of autism have also created unintentional adverse effects on how society views people with autism.

I hasten to clarify that I am not suggesting that the media is providing inaccurate information on autism. My concern is the lack of balance in what is being presented. There is evidence that much of the media's portrait of autism followed the DSM-5 definition. For example, Anders Nordahl-Hansen and his team of educators examined an international sample of four TV series and twenty-two films against the definition of autism in the DSM-5.[17] They confirmed that the media's portrayals of autism aligned very well with the DSM-5 diagnostic criteria. However, this means that the media's depictions focused on the social-communicational behaviors associated with

---

13. Bölte, "Is Autism Curable?" 930.

14. Shute, "Desperate for an Autism Cure," 80.

15. Concerned with the apparent increasing rate of diagnosis of autism, the Canadian government set up the National Autism Spectrum Disorder Surveillance System to monitor the situation in a way quite similar to monitoring an epidemic.

16. Silberman, *Neurotribes*, 411.

17. Nordahl-Hansen et al., "Mental Health on Screen," 351–353.

autism. The strength of people with autism was underreported, while savant skills were slightly overrepresented. Nordahl-Hansen's team concluded that the media did successfully promote awareness of autism. However, by highlighting the defective aspects of autism without balancing it with the strengths and contributions of people with autism, the media has created or reinforced the stereotypical understanding of people with autism as people with undesirable social behaviors.[18]

Medical ethicist Jennifer Sarrett was concerned about how the consistent portrait of autism as something undesirable might influence people's reception of individuals identified as autistic. Therefore, she set out to compare the portrayals of children with autism in the 1960s with those broadcasting in the 2000s. She found that, over the years, the media had continued to portray children with autism as children with "behavioral abnormalities" who live in their own world and are "withdrawn from reality."[19] Having a person with autism in the family is usually depicted as a tragedy that breaks up the family and makes life miserable.[20]

Sarrett's concerns were not unfound. Families with children with autism confirm the existence of public stereotypes. In a study conducted by Sydney Kinnear and her team, families of individuals with autism reported that "the public believes that a person with ASD cannot be a good friend, that individuals with autism are mentally ill, are dangerous or a threat to others."[21] These negative images of autism created fear for people with autism. The experiences of isolation, rejection, and exclusion significantly added to the challenges that people with autism face in managing the effects of autism on their lives.

Dawn Eddings Prince, an anthropologist diagnosed with Asperger's disorder as an adult, offers a profoundly moving and reflective account of her own and her son's lives with autism. She begins by commenting on the common perceptions that the general public seems to have on autism:

> When most people think of autism, they think of violent, unreachable people in worlds entirely of their own making, worlds without keys, feeling no empathy, lacking imagination, and unavailable to the deepest of human needs for contact and love. Having autism is the worst fate parents can imagine befalling their children, and they dread its impact on their families.[22]

18. Nordahl-Hansen et al., "Character Portrayals," 635–636.
19. Sarrett, "Trapped Children," 144.
20. Sarrett, "Trapped Children," 145.
21. Kinnear et al. "Understanding the Experience," 946.
22. Prince, "An Exceptional Path," 58.

Prince attributes the rejection that she and her son experienced in life to these negative ideas about autism. She states, "the chief danger and distance . . . is that people can tell you that what you are isn't what you should be."[23] Without attempting to get to know Prince and her son as persons with unique characters and personalities, the public associated them with the stereotypical images of autism and assumed that these images represented who they were and avoided them.

In the defect model, persons with autism can only be accepted into society if their autistic behaviors can be removed or, at least, controlled. The onus is on people with autism to make the changes and become "normal" before they are welcomed into society. When this demand becomes the dominant voice, even people with autism themselves feel that they are the ones who need to make the impossible changes. In her book, *I Am in Here*, Elizabeth Bonker, a woman with profound autism, expresses her sadness and loneliness. She asks her neurologist for help to stop her behaving in ways that scare people away from her.[24]

Internalization of the stigma of autism does not only impact people with autism but also their caregivers. When the public views their children's behaviors as socially unacceptable, parents are often left feeling humiliated, judged, and socially excluded.[25] Unfortunately, these negative perceptions and reactions do not only come from the public but also their friends and families. A protection mechanism of the families is to isolate themselves from the eyes of the community. The public's reactions to autism could also lead caregivers to blame themselves for their children's behaviors. In some cases, the internalization of stigma can translate into rejection, anger, punitive actions, or control of the child's behaviors at all costs.[26]

In recent years, few would argue that autism is related to malfunctions of the brain's neurological mechanisms. However, emphasizing autism as a defect, a problem, and something that needs to be rid of creates a stigma that keeps people with autism from community involvement. A different angle to understanding autism is to explore how biology and culture intersect to produce the concept of autism. Thinkers adopting this angle to understand autism are branded together as the field of critical autism studies. Theorists from this new field of study offer counter-narratives that value experience, skills, and agency of people with autism. They challenge the power dynamics that privilege dominant cultures and marginalize people with autism.

---

23. Prince, "An Exceptional Path," 65.
24. Bonker and Breen, *I Am in Here*, 72.
25. Broady, "Carers' Lived Experience," 224–33.
26. Mak and Kwok, "Internalization of Stigma," 2045–51.

This new academic field includes thinkers from groups such as the neurodiversity movement, the rethinking autism network, and others who advocate for a bio-social understanding of autism. These different approaches open up new spaces for us to rethink autism. They also point to a need for us to formulate a Christian perspective on autism.

Autism as a Social Construction

As mentioned above, within the autism spectrum are people with a wide range of human experiences. The vast heterogeneity invites the doubts that autism should indeed be considered a diagnostic category or a natural kind. For example, Richard Hassall argues that since the medical category of autism cannot offer a single unified account of the condition, then "there is really no such 'thing' as autism."[27]

Agreeing that autism should not be considered as a natural entity or a medical category, Berend Verhoeff, a Dutch psychiatrist, and philosopher, asserts that autism is regarded as a disorder only because of the social-cultural demands for normal behaviors and control of deviant behaviors. And what is normal is defined by the cultural norm of a person being social, empathic, and engaged.[28] By studying the historical and social development of the concept of autism, Verhoeff encourages us to consider how dominant social values and implicit social norms may have contributed to the definition of autism as a disorder. His idea points to a need for deeper reflection on how society has ignored the fact that diversity is, in fact, a norm, more so than any defined social norms. If we look at any social circles we belong to; we have to admit that people are all different. We must ask: How different does a difference have to be before it is considered an abnormality? Why is such a definition necessary?

As mentioned previously, the medical community recognizes the importance of early identification for achieving desirable therapeutic and educational results. The identification may also help parents and teachers understand the cause of the children's behaviors. However, there are many reasons why the autism label may not be beneficial. It is especially so when autism is associated with the aforementioned stereotypical images that may label the person with autism as "deviant." The possible exclusion from participation in society that may result from labeling needs to be balanced with the probable benefits.

---

27. Hassall, "Everybody with an Autism," 49.
28. Verhoeff, "What Is This Thing," 428–29.

Recognizing the significant adverse effects of labeling, thinkers such as Nick Hodge feel strongly that labels are used more for segregation and marginalization.[29] As an educator, Hodge demonstrates that he does not need diagnostic labels to provide an appropriate education for his students. He uses a three-step enabling strategy in the classroom: think about the student with his or her name first, personalities second, and abilities and challenges last. Put differently, Hodge sees each of his students first and foremost as a person; each of them has his or her unique personality and profile of abilities and limitations.

By now, we have seen enough stigmatizing effects of the autism label to be sympathetic to what Hodge is advocating. To accept persons with autism as one of us, we should not allow the autism label to blanket the person, blinding us from seeing him or her as someone who should be accepted, respected, and valued.

In sum, the social construction model demonstrates how the dominant discourse of normality constructs the idea of abnormality in autism. They also help us understand how these socially constructed concepts can be wrapped up in a label that prevents us from seeing persons with autism as who they are—each with his or her unique strengths and limitations. The social construction model has illustrated how wrong perceptions of autism form barriers for people with autism to enjoy a shared life with others in society. This understanding implicates us, people in society (in which the church is a part), in how our responses to people with autism affect their lives.

However, the social construction model of autism is not without its critiques. Sociologist Janine Owen indicates that viewing autism as entirely socially constructed fails to take into account the lived experiences of people with autism.[30] Without listening to the voices of people with autism, her concern is that the proposed social changes will continue to be based on non-disabled people's thoughts. The rise of the disability rights movement and their motto—"Nothing About Us, Without Us" supports Owen's view. It also indicates a need to respect the priorities identified by autistic people in all advocacy efforts. As Ari Ne'eman of the Autistic Self-Advocacy Network says, "the object of autism advocacy should not be a world without autistic people."[31] We will not fully comprehend the issues experienced by people with autism without learning from their points of view.

---

29. Hodge, "School Without Labels," 185–203.
30. Owens, "Exploring the Critiques," 389.
31. Ne'eman, "Future (and Past)," para. 3.

Furthermore, if our goal is to belong together with people with autism in the same church, same society, we need to be able to know how to establish relationships with them. As with any relationships, mutual understanding is key. It is, therefore, time to turn to people with autism to consider their perspectives.

Autism as a Difference

Many autistic people have been active in voicing their opinions on autism-related issues on social media and through publications. This loosely structured group is called the neurodiversity movement. They argue for recognizing autism as a minority group, a human difference, and not a disorder to be cured. By identifying themselves as a minority group, people with autism are forming their own allies. However, in that process, they might also be alienating themselves from society.

Judy Singer is credited as the founder of the neurodiversity movement. For Singer, autism is "a new addition to the familiar political categories of class/gender/race."[32] In other words, this group of autistic people seeks to be recognized as humans with variations in brain functioning, rather than as people with a disorder that needs a cure. They embrace autism as a fundamental part of their identity instead of a problem that needs to be eliminated. People in the neurodiversity movement argue that the difference between people with and without autism is in the ways the brains are wired. They refer to those who consider themselves "normal" as neurotypical.

In a nutshell, by aligning themselves with other minority groups, the neurodiversity movement advocates for autism rights and demands recognition and acceptance on their terms.[33] However, this social agenda does not necessarily help people with and without autism to see each other properly as persons and live together as a community.

The possible alienating effect of the neurodiversity movement can be seen in Temple Grandin's thought about people like herself who is given the diagnosis of Asperger's Syndrome (a syndrome that is now grouped under the autism spectrum of disorder). To Grandin, people with Asperger's Syndrome are exiles from planet Aspergia and aliens on Earth.[34] Being aliens, Grandin feels that autistic people who have difficulties navigating life on a strange planet will never quite belong with the neurotypicals. Observing the sentiments of alienation towards the neurotypicals, philosopher Ian

---

32. Singer and French, "Why Can't You Be Normal," 64.
33. Jaarsma and Welin, "Autism as a Natural Human," 20–30.
34. Sacks, *Anthropologist on Mars*, 295.

Hacking says, "The trope of the alien, then, is symmetric: autistic people are aliens, or neurotypicals are aliens for autistic people."[35] Hacking further comments,

> Our instinct has always been to exclude aliens. What distinguishes us from aliens (as we depict our contraries) is notoriously not rationality, but our emotional lives. We are fellow humans in that we grasp each other's intentions, feelings, and wants . . . They are the bedrock of our humanity.[36]

Hacking's remarks are helpful. While we should undoubtedly respect how people with autism see themselves, we cannot ignore the alienating effects of separating people into different groups and insisting that people cannot belong together as one human race with all these differences.

Understandably, protecting ourselves often involves erecting walls around us, but we need to be cognizant that these walls also prevent us from reaching out to others. Autism is evidently socially constructed, especially when *we*, people in society, think about *them* as different from *us* because *they* don't act or think the same way as *we* do. Still, the solution offered by the neurodiversity movement, in effect, proposes a different separating wall—the *us* as neurodiverse versus *them*, the neurotypical. To break down these divisive walls, as Hacking suggests, we need to acknowledge that we are fellow humans despite our differences. Instead of building walls and alienating each other, we should strive to understand and accept each other.[37]

Helping the non-autistic society understand the experiences of autism is where the neurodiversity movement is most helpful. Their approach demonstrates that if we want to remove the social barriers and integrate people with autism as full members of society, we need to understand autism from the perspectives and experiences of people living with that identification. Only then will we appreciate how the neurobiological effects of autism affect their social relationships. This knowledge will also help us learn to interact with persons with autism in ways that facilitate mutual understanding.

Autism as a Bio-Sociological Phenomenon

In addition to voicing their rights as a minority group, people with autism have also been writing about their own experience with autism. The biographies and autobiographies published by and with people with autism

---

35. Hacking, "Humans, Aliens & Autism," 51.
36. Hacking, "Humans, Aliens & Autism," 57.
37. Hacking, "Humans, Aliens & Autism," 56.

included some who have profound autism. These voices of autism provide a window for us to look into their lived experience. When we attempt to understand the "deficits" of autism from the perspectives of people living with the condition, we begin to understand better the autistic behaviors and how these behaviors affect their lives. We will also learn that autistic behaviors have meanings. Learning to understand these behaviors and appreciate the difficulties people with autism have in controlling their bodies for communication and social interactions is a necessary first step towards removing the wall and building relationships with them.

Sensory-Motor Difficulties

Although the exact neurological mechanism of autism remains unknown, what is now made known to us through the publications of people with profound autism is the neurological effects of autism on sensory-motor control. Christie Welch and a team of occupational therapy researchers analyzed three books published by individuals with severe and non-verbal forms of autism. Their goal was to understand autism through their lived experiences. The central theme derived from the analysis, "My inside and outside do not match," indicates a mismatch between these individuals' desires for social relationships and the perception that they are not interested or capable of social interactions.[38] The mismatch is caused by the lack of understanding of the sensory-motor difficulties that have made communication difficult for them.

Carly Fleischman writes: "We see different than everyone else. We take pictures in our heads like a camera. It's like filling a camera with too many pictures; it gets overwhelming."[39] On the motoric side, all three persons in this study describe difficulties in starting and stopping their movements freely and especially when asked to respond to a request to do certain things. Naoki Higashida explains, "There are times when I can't act, even though I really badly want to. This is when my body is beyond my control . . . it's as if my whole body . . . belongs to somebody else and I have zero control over it."[40] The sensory-motor difficulties affected how these three individuals with profound autism interacted with people in ways that society expected of them. They express frustration with their inabilities to move their body parts "on demand" to interact with people

---

38. Welch et al., "Autism Inside Out," 2314.
39. Welch et al., "Autism Inside Out," 2312.
40. Welch et al., "Autism Inside Out," 2311.

appropriately.[41] What is clear in these three accounts is that contrary to the common understanding that people with autism want to live in a world of their own, these three individuals want to interact with others. Although they are well aware of the expected etiquettes for social communication, they are frustrated that they cannot participate in social interactions in ways that society expects of them.

More than helping us understand their sensory-motor control difficulties, these three individuals' experiences make apparent our share of responsibilities in establishing social relationships. If we hold tightly to how communication should be expressed without considering the difficulties that are beyond our autistic communication partners' control, we, the non-autistic, are the ones who are refusing to have relationships with them.

Effective communication has to be established mutually. In this regard, we also need to note that the repetitive behaviors in autism could result from the individual's attempt to control the sensory stimuli in unfamiliar environments.[42] Further, these behaviors could also be intentional communicative acts. Communication breaks down when people cannot interpret the observable behaviors of people with profound autism. In some cases, designating the autistic behaviors as defects and attempting to control them might hinder these individuals' development of communication skills.[43]

Being overwhelmed by sensory input and having difficulties controlling their movements on demand are often compounded by the amount of time required for individuals with autism to process sensory information. They need time to sort through the sensory information gathered from different sensory modalities, assemble the data in a way that makes sense to them, and finally direct their body to make a response.[44] The sensory processing difficulties create delayed responses and behavioral expressions that affect their abilities to communicate and participate in social interactions effectively. Often, people with autism are either misunderstood or ignored by their conversation partners while struggling to express their thoughts.

For decades, health care and social science professionals have accepted autism as a social disorder. They consider people with autism to have no intention of social interactions, no ability to make sense of social cues, and no communication capabilities.[45] As will become clear in the following two sections, the knowledge of sensory-motor difficulties of autism is crucial in

41. Welch et al., "Autism Inside Out," 2313.
42. Boyd et al. "Sensory Features," 85.
43. Donnellan et al., "Rethinking Autism," 124.
44. Bogdashina, *Sensory Perceptual Issues*, 79–80.
45. Hollin and Pilnick, "Infancy, Autism," 279–86.

challenging the concept of autism as a social disorder. This understanding also illuminates how the responses of people in society contribute to the social-relational breakdown and what we should do differently.

Language and Communication

Many people with autism do not use speech as their primary method of communication. Even when they can speak a limited number of words, their speech, to an unfamiliar listener, may not be easy to understand. With the sensory-motor difficulties, their non-verbal communication can also be different from what we commonly consider as non-verbal communication, such as facial expressions and gestures. Importantly, having difficulties with speech and language does not necessarily mean people with autism do not want to communicate. The three individuals with severe autism in the study of Welch et al. mentioned above make this point very clear. They do want to communicate, but their sensory-motor difficulties make it impossible for them to express their thoughts verbally.

Bernice Olivas is a professor in the English language and a mother of two sons with severe autism. Her wish, as she sent her sons to school, is worth quoting in full.

> I want them to surround themselves with people who get that sometimes hello can only be said with a gentle headbutt, and those people will headbutt back because they understand that their first language isn't really talking. It's fluttering hands, or spinning, or just silence. These people will have taken the time to become semi conversational in Gareth-ese (the language of her older boy). Conversations between my sons and their closest friends will be a beautiful mix of speech and flapping. This is what I want for my sons. Because it burdens them with an identity that was built by folks who only speak for them, not with them. In order to change that dynamic, we, the neurotypical, the parents, the medical field, the educators, and especially the advocates, must stop seeing ourselves as the driving force of the autism community and instead become allies; we must begin by learning second languages and being willing to hear and see Autistics.[46]

In this passage, we can see a beautiful, idealized scenario in which these two young persons can communicate and have friends if people can

---

46. Olivas, "What I Mean," 53.

learn to interact with them in ways that may be considered unusual but nonetheless full of joy and meaning.

Olivas also makes an excellent point. Communication is a mutual act. No communication can happen unless both communication partners make efforts to understand each other. If we genuinely want to communicate with persons with autism, we need to be willing to hear and see them as who they are and learn to communicate in a way that facilitates mutual understanding. If we impose our communication method on them without considering their neuro-biological limitations, we, not people with autism, are causing the communication breakdown.

Mindblindness

Mindblindness is a prevailing theory that was developed to explain the social-communication difficulties of autism.[47] According to this theory, people with autism cannot understand their own or other people's emotions and intentions and respond accordingly. As a result, people with autism are considered to be lacking in empathy and uninterested in social relationships. Scholars from different fields have contested the validity of the mindblindness theory.[48]

However, people with autism and their parents provided the most persuasive arguments in the biographies and autobiographies of their lived experience. These publications demonstrate that people with autism, including those who are identified to have profound autism, are highly aware of themselves, including their difficulties, emotions, and desires about their lives. In their writing, it is also evident that these writers with profound autism are deeply concerned about their loved ones.[49] Listening to these

---

47. Duffy and Dorner, "The Pathos of Mindblindness," 201–15.

48. The critiques against the concept of mindblindness or lack of theory of mind thesis in autism surround how the theory was formulated, the assessment of it, and lack of evidence of mindblindness in people with autism. First of all, the theory of mind is a theory that does not have an established biological mechanism in the brain, like concepts of emotion and intelligence. Secondly, the tests for the theory of mind commonly consist of abstract concepts that do not take into account the difficulties of people with autism in this area. Thirdly, there is no documented evidence of the lack of theory of mind or empathy from Kanner's early description of autism to the current voices of autism. On the contrary, the consciousness of self and others' emotions are evident in the publication by people with various severity of autism. See: Stubblefield, "Knowing Other Minds," 143–66; and McDonaugh, "Autism and Age of Empathy," 31–51.

49. See, for example, Bonker and Green, *I Am in Here*, 38, 72; Higashida, *Fall Down 7 Times*, 3; Mukhopadhyay, *I'm not a Poet*, 35.

voices of autism make some of the proponents of mindblindness, like Uta Frith, concede that they do have extensive self-knowledge.[50]

Looking at the question of mindblindness critically, Janette Dinishak and Nameera Akhtar of the University of California asked a penetrating question: "When a non-autistic individual misinterprets an autistic's behavior, who is mindblind?"[51] Just as we expect people with autism to understand our emotions and intentions in the process of communication, we also need to understand theirs. Communication breaks down when we expect people with autism to think and act in our familiar ways, instead of accepting their unique ways of expressing their thoughts while acknowledging their sensory-motor control difficulties. Perhaps Dinishak and Akhtar are right—it is we who are mindblind when we fail to recognize that people with autism are communicating and expressing their empathy and friendship to us, albeit in their unique ways.

Embracing Differences

At this point, it would be helpful to sum up the preceding discussion. The medical model, coming from the focus of medicine on the cure of diseases, naturally promotes the need for treatment to remove what is considered to be defective. However, when the social behaviors of people with autism, instead of the gifts and strengths of individual persons, were the representations of autism, the defective view of autism caused stigmatization. In response, thinkers from different academic disciplines and people with autism who have the necessary language skills to express their opinions challenged the defect-model of autism. They help us see how autism is socially constructed because the definition of deviant behaviors is based on social norms. People with autism are rejected and excluded by society because their behaviors do not conform to the social norms of the majority in society.

Proponents of social construction theories advocate for socio-political changes to protect the legal rights of people with autism to be included and given equal rights as other members of society. Adding the experiences of people with autism to the social construction model, the biosocial view of autism directs our attention to the neurobiological effects of autism, as explained by people with autism themselves. These voices of autism challenged the predominant view that people with autism do not want social relations and lack empathy. People living with autism made it very clear that they want to engage in social relationships and that they can

50. Frith, *Autism: Explaining the Enigma*, 211.
51. Dinishak and Akhtar, "Critical Examination," 110–14.

understand their own and others' emotions. What hinders their expression of ideas and feelings are sensory-motor difficulties. The challenge for all of us in society is to recognize their desires and respond to them in ways that facilitate mutual communication and relationships.

All these counter-narratives to the dominant medical view are essential. They opened a space for us to rethink autism with the hope that these reframing efforts could help society see people with autisms as persons and not a disorder or a problem to be rid of. However, recognizing autism as a different human experience is not enough. We need to consider how to embrace people with autism as members of society.

Changing social environments and implementing laws to protect human rights are vital strategies for promoting the inclusion of people with autism. Still, as the story of Michael in the Introduction chapter has illustrated, the best we can do with these strategies is for them to be allowed into the building and be "tolerated." Hans Reinders has made an astute observation: "Disabled people are rarely chosen as friends, except by other disabled people."[52] As we will see in the experiences of two persons with profound autism in the following chapters, Reinders's comment is accurate. While some individuals with autism can attend church services, they stay very much in the margins of the church.

From my experience working with different church communities, I have no doubt that many churches want to welcome people with disabilities (autism included). The difficulties of belonging for people with autism are not because of a lack of love and compassion but because of some deeply rooted church traditions and misconceptions about autism. For instance, when we are attending a church service, the common expectation is that people would sit still and remain quiet. The rationale for this unspoken rule is seldom explored or challenged. It is merely an accepted behavior etiquette that has been taken for granted as a social norm. Individuals with profound autism who, out of the need for sensory regulation, make noises, or wander around during the service, are deemed disruptive. Parents, being well-conditioned by this unspoken expectation, feel embarrassed and helpless for their children's behaviors. When these behaviors invite harsh judgments and unfriendly stares, parents feel judged. They either leave the church altogether or be on a search for a more accepting one.[53]

Earlier I mentioned Prince's experience of the public's response to her and her son, that the stereotypical images of persons with autism could lead society to consider them "violent, unreachable people in worlds entirely of

---

52. Reinders, *Receiving the Gift*, 4.
53. Altiere and von Kluge, "Searching for Acceptance," 146.

their own making."[54] These distorted images induce unfounded fear and cause people to avoid or reject persons with autism unfairly. Although not specifically addressing the fear of autism, Jean Vanier observes from his many years of experience in living and working with people with intellectual disabilities that fear is often at the basis of prejudice and exclusion.[55]

Fear and discomfort may arise simply because people with autism look different from most people in the church. Church members may be afraid because they do not know what to do or say. The sense of uncertainty, the unwillingness to change, and the need to protect the status quo mean that the threats to our certainty need to be pushed away. "So, we build walls around our group and cultivate our certitudes," says Vanier.[56] These walls, however, are relational in nature. They keep people from approaching individuals with autism and barring those affected by autism from entering into the fabric of church life. The challenge for us is to break down these relational walls, embrace people with autism, and bring them into the community.

In his missional work, Paul worked tirelessly to bring people from different backgrounds into the church. He urged the early church to look beyond social, ethnic, and gender lines that might have divided the church and focus on the truth that they were all children of God (Gal 3: 26–9). Similarly, we ought to see the differences introduced by autism in the same light. In order for this to happen, we need to dig deeper into what is going on at the church and identify why it is difficult for the church to embody the biblical concept of oneness in Christ with different members (1 Cor 12:12).

---

54. Prince, "Exceptional Path," 58.
55. Vanier, *Becoming Human*, 73–81.
56. Vanier, *Becoming Human*, 73–81.

2

Problems with Inclusion

Strangers in God's Household

> My brothers and sisters, believers in our glorious Lord Jesus Christ must not show favoritism.—Jas 2:1

IN THE LAST CHAPTER, we began to see how the stereotype of people with autism as persons living in their own worlds was formed. This way of understanding autism separated people living with autism from society. To understand how the defective view of autism affects congregational life, I am taking the readers into two congregations: Red Hill and The Cross. The purpose of engaging these two communities is to help readers see the issues of belonging in the church through the lens of autism. These two churches' experiences will help us reflect on changes that are necessary to bring people with profound autism into belonging as members of Christ's body.

As we follow two young persons with profound autism, Dylan and Ellen, into their respective community, we will see that they both experienced alienation in their community Their experiences clearly demonstrate the pervasive influence of the stereotypical view of autism. We will also see that many factors, including but not limited to family dynamics and church cultures, affect how Ellen and Dylan can belong to the church. A Circle of Friends was formed in each of these two churches to facilitate Dylan and Ellen's integration into the community. With their Circle friends' help, Dylan and Ellen moved at different rates into the life of their community.

Chapter 4 will bring together Dylan and Ellen's experiences to look for common patterns and issues that warrant further examination. Before we can do that, we need to know what happened in these two communities. I will introduce Red Hill in the following chapter. This chapter will focus on the situation at The Cross. Here we see examples of what Aaron Earls said in the Introduction chapter about inclusion being accepted by church leaders and attendees as the right thing to do. Yet, not many people are doing anything actively to make sure that it happens. In describing the situations at The Cross, I am inviting readers to see the complexity of life with autism and how each person (at home and in the church) has a role in shaping Dylan's belonging.

Cultural Bias

Dylan is a quiet but cheerful young man. He lives with his parents, Vanessa and Simon, and his brother, Mark, in Somewhere, a suburban town in Canada. Vanessa and Simon came from China for their undergraduate studies. Mark and Dylan were both born in Canada. Venessa and Simon were members of a house church in China. With studying and subsequently working in different parts of Canada, they moved around and attended different churches. When Mark was six and Dylan was four, the couple settled in Somewhere. Soon after they arrived at Somewhere, a neighbor introduced them to The Cross, a local church. Simon and Mark began to attend the Sunday services there. Vanessa used to stay home on Sundays with Dylan, but she participated in the women's bible study group on Fridays during the day, when Dylan was at school. Mark started attending the Awana program offered by The Cross very soon after the family moved to Somewhere.

The identification of a dual diagnosis of profound autism and seizure disorder was given before Dylan turned three. When I visited with the family, Dylan was in the second year of his high school education. On my first visit to the family's house, I arrived before Dylan came home from school to learn about the family and how to communicate with him. When Dylan returned and saw me, he went into the kitchen to grab some snacks then went straight upstairs without acknowledging my presence. Fear of strangers is well documented in autism studies.[1] It is, therefore, not surprising that Dylan avoided contact with me initially. As he began to recognize me as a regular visitor at the house, Dylan warmed up to me and greeted me with a big smile and a high five when I arrived. He would also happily invite me to join him to play with his toys.

Mark, Dylan's older brother, had a very close relationship with him. According to Vanessa, Mark was the one who best understood Dylan and who communicated with him most effectively, with or without the use of the

---

1. In describing the stranger fear of children with autism, Jessica F. Scherr et al. explain that these children may avoid contact with strangers because of fear of being rejected or humiliated in some way ("Stranger Fear," 3743).

communication device. When Mark was home, he would always spend some time with Dylan, doing things Dylan liked, such as video games.

Dylan did not use speech for much of his communication. The only word I have heard him say aloud was "mom" when he wanted his mother's attention. Dylan used an iPad with Proloquo2Go application as his primary communication device, using a mix of picture symbols and words to construct short sentences. Dylan was also able to spell simple words such as "happy" and "sunny" without using any communication template. Vanessa wanted Dylan to communicate with his device, but during most of my visits with Dylan, he used the iPad for just a little while to respond to simple questions, then pushed the device away and used gestures instead. Reportedly, Dylan was quite fluent in sign language and signed to communicate with his teachers at school. However, Vanessa and the rest of the family did not learn to sign, and when they could not understand his signing, frustration ensued. The family believed that Dylan was reading at elementary grade two or three level. Vanessa shared that at school, Dylan could follow a recipe book with pictures and words to cook a simple meal with supervision. Dylan could manage some self-care tasks independently with direction but required assistance to complete many self-care activities.

Vanessa had not been working for many years since Dylan's care demanded much of her time. Simon worked at the management level with a school board in the city. He did not want his friends and colleagues to know about Dylan's condition. Besides traveling outside of the town on a family trip, Simon would not take Dylan outside of the house with him. For many years, he also forbade Vanessa from leaving the house with Dylan. Being at home, Dylan spent many hours in the basement, playing with toys or watching Disney movies.

While no one outside the family has witnessed Dylan's aggressive behaviors, Vanessa was very concerned about staying on his side to help him control his behaviors. She says, "He is like a young child. He doesn't know what to do with problems . . . Dylan can become aggressive when he loses control. Not that he will attack people, but he might grasp people very tightly. He doesn't know how to handle his temper." Vanessa suspected that evil spirits were behind Dylan's epilepsy and behaviors. Therefore, she did not believe in epileptic medications. Vanessa felt that Dylan's tantrums have increased since he started on the drug for seizure control. Her husband, Simon, disagreed. He considered the medication as having nothing to do with Dylan's behaviors and that they were "just his autism." For Simon, the best course of action was to avoid social contacts.

According to Peiling Farajallah, in the Chinese culture, associating epileptic seizures with possession by the evil spirit is common.[2] This background may well be why Vanessa's believed that Dylan was possessed by the evil spirit. Furthermore, Chinese traditions view children's behaviors as a reflection of their family upbringing. Having a child who exhibits "improper" behaviors in public brings a significant sense of shame and guilt to the parents. These behavioral issues can result in "loss of face and may negatively affect the perceived prestige of the entire family."[3] Many parents, like Dylan's father, would hide the child from the public.[4] This ingrained cultural attitude is likely why Vanessa felt the need to be present with Dylan at all times to help him control his behaviors.

Two years ago, seeing that Dylan was growing up, Vanessa felt that Dylan had to learn more skills. Therefore, she enrolled him in many programs: swimming, baseball, soccer, drawing, skiing, boating, and horseback riding. Out of all these activities, the one Dylan enjoyed most was swimming. According to Vanessa, Dylan indicated his choice of activities by his willingness to get ready for the event. If he did not like to do something, "parent pushing" would not work more than once or twice. Vanessa's decision to have Dylan more regularly involved in outside activities caused tremendous tension between the couple. Vanessa noted that their arguments significantly affected Dylan's emotions. When Simon raised his voice, it often made Dylan more prone to throwing a temper tantrum.

With the belief that evil spirits caused Dylan to become upset and lose control of his behavior, Vanessa wanted Dylan to have faith in Jesus so that the Holy Spirit would be in him. Vanessa asked a pastor from their previous church to cast out the evil spirits from Dylan, but the pastor refused. Vanessa believed that for Dylan to receive the Holy Spirit and "be well," he must accept Jesus as his Lord. Recognizing that Dylan was living in darkness, bringing him to the light of Jesus motivate Vanessa to enroll Dylan with Awana.

A few years ago, the family learned about a program offered by a megachurch in a neighboring town for individuals with disabilities. The family started attending this church on Sundays because they could leave Dylan in the specialized program. Other than Sundays, the family continued to participate in different groups organized by The Cross. For Vanessa, attending the megachurch was an opportunity to attend worship services and be involved in church activities on Sundays. However, with a strictly segregated

---

2. Farajallah, "Coping Styles," 783–95.
3. Wang et al., "Stress and Coping," 792.
4. Wang et al., "Stress and Coping," 792.

programming, Dylan could only have friends with other attendees and the volunteers of the disability program at the megachurch.

Talking about what she wanted for Dylan, Vanessa indicated that she was looking for a church where he could find belonging. She felt that it was important for Dylan to "be with others to worship and receive a blessing." While Vanessa enjoyed the opportunity to worship at the megachurch with others, she also wanted the same for Dylan. It was not enough for Dylan to be cared for in a segregated program. Vanessa would like him to belong to a community and join his fellow Christians in worship.

Additionally, Vanessa spoke of how Pastor George of The Cross often reminded the congregation of Christians' need to be in community. Her take on George's advice was that Christians need to have friends in a Christian community and not with people outside of the church. Vanessa said, "Our pastor says you cannot be individual because outside it is not just lonely. Lonely is one thing, but there are all the temptations. Better at the church that you have more friends." Therefore, she felt that the church is a safe place for Dylan to have his own friends.

Over the years, Vanessa had brought Dylan with her when she picked up Mark from The Cross's Awana program. On those occasions, she found George and his wife, Martha, to be loving and accepting towards Dylan. Therefore, Vanessa asked and received George's warm welcome for Dylan to start attending the Awana program at The Cross. Before we follow Dylan into The Cross, it will be helpful to learn about this church community.

Church as a School Community

The Cross Baptist Church had an unusual structure. A group of about twenty people who met on Sundays using a meeting room in a local library. According to Pastor George, different people attended on different Sundays. Two worship communities were formed in two homes for seniors. A women's bible group, led by George's wife, Martha, operated from their house. This group had an attendance of about ten. Many women in this group did not attend Sunday worship services at The Cross. Also, an Awana Club offered opportunities for children and adolescents to gather for worship and bible studies. About twenty young people were on the registry for Awana, but their weekly attendance was not steady.

The Cross has existed in Somewhere for well over ten years (The Awana Club operated at the same school for almost fifteen years). George described the various groups at The Cross as different ministries, each with their members. Amazingly, all these different ministries were organized by a small core group of about ten people, including the pastor and his wife. They had the support of volunteers who were residents of the town but attending different churches and some other long-term volunteers who used to participate in the church but have since moved to other towns. Age-wise, the core group, including the pastor and his wife, were older adults. The volunteers from various churches and the attendees, other than those in the senior homes, covered a wide age range. Among them were a good number of young adults. Although situated in a predominantly Caucasian neighborhood, people attending the various groups at The Cross came from diverse ethnic backgrounds. On the whole, The Cross projected itself as an inclusive community that welcomed people from different backgrounds in terms of age and ethnicity.

The tagline on The Cross' website is "holding forth the word of life." Their mission statement further elaborates on what that means: "Our mission is to worship God, who knows each one; to work at encouraging and teaching those who do know God; and, to witness to those who do not know God." A clear indication in this statement is the church's focus on evangelism. What is not expressed explicitly is George's commitment to discipleship.

In my first meeting with George, he talked about how he has been intentional in growing church youths to become leaders. The criteria for transitioning into leading roles seemed to be their abilities to recite Bible verses, share their testimonies with others, and willingness to be involved in different tasks. These potential leaders did not come regularly to Awana. Out of love and respect for George and Martha, many young people returned year after year to volunteer at the Vacation Bible Camp.

Other than the young adults who grew up at the Awana program, some young adults who lived in the neighborhood also volunteered at Awana. The key leaders for bible teaching were volunteers who previously lived in the region and attended The Cross. Although they have moved to other areas, these leaders continued to come back to share the teaching load because they have learned the importance of bible teaching from George. The occasional help from these volunteers was why a small core group of people could offer many programs at The Cross.

Interestingly, with people at The Cross coming from various churches, they refer to The Cross as their home or family. For Vanessa, it was George and Martha's love that made The Cross felt like a family. The volunteers who returned to serve at the Awana occasionally and at the Vacation Bible Camp also mentioned that being with George and Martha gave them a sense of homecoming.

However, with bible teaching and evangelism being the main foci of the church, the ethos of belonging presented at The Cross was more like a community of learning with very weak connections between its members. As a church of small groups, the sense of togetherness as one church did not seem to be an emphasis in George's teaching. His sermons were generally expositions of the biblical books. George described the core group at his church as a close-knit community because they have known each other for many years. They have also served together in many ministries. However, even this core group has less a sense of belonging than the women's bible group. The willingness of the women's group members to spend time together outside the study, to George, indicated their closeness in relationships. The implication is that members of all these other groups only met on Sundays or for ministry events. The Awana group, according to George, was the least cohesive. The reason was that the children came from different schools. Not all of them went to church, and for those who did, they attended different churches. As far as George knew, there was no interaction among the children outside Awana time.

A scattered church structure combined with the advanced age of George, Martha, and the core group also meant that caring for members was limited. The Cross's membership covenant states, "we will care for each another: remembering each other in prayer, aiding each other in sickness and distress by showing true Christian compassion, brotherly love, and comfort." According to Vanessa, the women group at The Cross had an active prayer ministry. They prayed for people with needs, which included Dylan. However, with the diverse groupings and a core group of people advanced in age, visitations and practical help were not possible. George and Martha would see people for counseling in their house, but they, too, were limited in what they could do in terms of practical tasks of caring.

If we look at how people at The Cross interact with each other at the Awana group and the Vacation Bible School, we will see how the church resembles a school. People came to learn the Bible, not necessarily for fellowship and mentorship, as the Awana was designed to be.[5] The program at The Cross included a time of worship, Bible learning, and group games. As people arrived for Awana, they gathered at the main room where the worship took place. Young people who entered would stand in small clusters of

---

5. Awana International indicates that the Awana program is designed to be an integrated evangelism and discipleship programs for children and adolescents between two to eighteen years of age. The goal is to provide a place for young people to build relationships and journey with one another as they learn about the Christian faith. Adult leaders act as mentors to the young people and to intentionally build loving, caring, trusting relationships with them and their families (Bell, *Annual Report 2017*, 2).

two or three boys or girls and talk among themselves. Some parents would stay for worship, but they typically stood at the back. There was very little interaction between the small clusters of people with other people in the room, sometimes not even exchanging greetings.

There was a core group of youths in Dylan's group on any given day, but there were also some people who attended irregularly. Even the volunteer leaders, other than two to three organizers who took attendance at the door, did not participate regularly. At one of the Awana meetings, George was the only person running all the activities, including worship, teaching in the classrooms, and supervising game time.

When I asked the attendees at The Cross what the church meant for them, the idea repeated by many was that it was a place to learn the Bible and to know Jesus. Even for people in Awana, fellowship and journeying with each other, which were fundamental concepts of Awana, did not appear to be their understanding of what Awana was about. To them, Awana was where they came together to study the Bible.

The other unique feature of The Cross is that it was a service outlet for many people who attended other churches on Sundays. George commented, "We have a lot a lot of help and encouragement from those in other churches so that—of our Awana leaders there are—oh maybe half of them attend other churches, but it is the way that they are able to serve." A significant number of volunteers only came to The Cross to serve in various programs, such as the residential homes for the seniors or the Awana. These people did not regard attending different churches or seeing each other occasionally as an issue.

With the desire to bring Dylan to Christ, Vanessa approached George and Martha about enrolling him in the Awana program. They readily agreed. A Circle of Friends program was organized to assist Dylan's attendance at Awana. George accepted Vanessa's invitation to be a member of the Circle. Among the young people who attended Awana, Vanessa found Anna and her mother, Lydia, their previous family friends, as suitable Circle friends for Dylan. Anna's father was a colleague of Dylan's father. When Anna and Dylan were young, they visited each other and played together frequently. At that time, Anna was not aware of Dylan's condition. Her parents have since divorced, and she had not seen Dylan for a few years. According to Vanessa, when they met again at Awana, Anna approached Dylan naturally and was very willing to help Dylan participate in the Awana activities. Therefore, Vanessa invited Anna to be one of Dylan's Circle friends. Lydia joined as a volunteer shortly after Dylan began to attend Awana. She explained her motivation to be Dylan's Circle friends, saying: "When I could, I want to try my best to interact with him. That is what I am thinking. I also want to see Dylan having more friends."

Experience and Openness to Disability

A common quality of Dylan's Circle of Friends was their comfort in being around people with autism. For George and Martha, the acceptance for people with disabilities came from their personal experience of having a son with a disability. Although their son's condition was very different from Dylan's, George felt that he could understand Dylan better than most people because of that "similar experience." According to George, accepting and welcoming youth with disabilities should not be a problem for the church: "If there was any problem, it was mainly because of us who were lacking familiarity with the child and his needs." George had received inquiries from other families with children with disabilities to join Awana over the years. He always extended a welcome to these families, but none of them attended regularly. Some came for a visit and never returned.

Anna had met other students with disabilities at school. She explained that the book *Wonder*, authored by R. J. Palacio, helped her understand disability. *Wonder* is a story about Auggie, a child with a severe facial difference. This book taught Anna that every person is different, and people need to learn to work with each other's differences. She said, "Kids like Auggie can be like us. They are smart, too, just that they are not talking. They still learn, and they can talk in some other ways." It could be true that the book was a tremendous help to Anna, but Anna seemed to be able to communicate with Dylan intuitively using high fives, gestures, and words typed on the communication device. More importantly, however, was how Anna saw Dylan. She said, "I treat him like a normal person that doesn't want to talk that much." 'Her determination to interact with Dylan as a whole and autonomous person enabled her to befriend Dylan in the same way she did with any other individuals.

Lydia was aware of Dylan's condition because of her friendship with Vanessa. Other than Dylan, she did not know anyone with a disability. However, like Anna, she also seemed to understand Dylan's emotions intuitively. With the Circle of Friends in place, Dylan started attending Awana. Vanessa stayed with him the whole time with the intent to help him control his behaviors. As a result, four people supported Dylan's entry to The Cross, but with three different approaches.

Three Approaches to Belonging

The school where the Awana program was held was not an unfamiliar place for Dylan. In addition to George and Martha, the volunteers, who helped them organize Awana, had known Dylan since he was young because he used to accompany his mother to drop off and pick up his older brother to and from Awana. Dylan also attended some activities at George's house. Unfortunately for Dylan, familiarity with the setting and some church members did not make the belonging process easy.

In the beginning, people at The Cross, other than George and Martha, very much ignored Dylan's presence. For instance, at the end of each evening, it was the job of a young man to pass around cookies made by Martha to his fellow students. This young man always passed over Dylan without offering him a cookie. In another instance, during a game session, Dylan stood on the side of the gymnasium, accompanied by Vanessa, to watch the goings-on. The organizer did not invite Dylan to participate in the games.

While Dylan seemed invisible to many people at Awana, some young men's attitudes were particularly despicable. Vanessa described the arrogances of several boys in the group: "They think they know better, and they will mock him, reject him, and make him feel bad." Anna confirmed that this particular group of boys was not friendly. She said that one of the boys had said something "real bad" to Dylan.

Before we look at how Vanessa and the Circle friends worked together to break the wall that separated him from the group at Awana, Dylan's response to the situation is worth noting. As Vanessa had indicated, Dylan had to be happy to attend an activity; otherwise, he would not be cooperative in leaving the house. Regardless of the negative responses of people at Awana, Dylan was amazingly happy to continue to attend. Vanessa fully credited George and Martha and their love for Dylan as the main reason. However, if Dylan's smile was an indicator, it was probably Anna's friendship that kept Dylan at Awana. Whenever Anna entered the room, she usually went straight to Dylan and gave him a high five, and the big smile on his face as he returned the high five was an unmistakable indication of his feelings.

With the group's initial response at Awana, Vanessa took an approach of relative invisibility with Dylan, meaning that she would keep Dylan away from people by sitting with him at a separate table. Vanessa explained her seating preference saying, "I want to respect people." This comment came from a need to "respect" people's discomfort around Dylan. Dylan had a habit of tapping on the table repeatedly but gently. Not being on the same table was Vanessa's way to ensure that "people won't be scared" by Dylan's tapping movements. Sometimes the Awana group sat in a circle for discussion, and what Vanessa would do was grabbing two chairs and sitting outside of the circle with Dylan.

In the face of the dominant culture that discriminates against people with profound autism and their families, Vanessa's idea of respecting and accepting people's discomfort to be around Dylan is common. Brian Watermeyer and Tristan Görgens call this kind of reaction internalized oppression.[6] When people with disabilities and their family members have been victims of discrimination because of stereotypical ideas for some time, they turn the experience inward and begin to feel that these stereotypes that society held were right. As a result, the oppressed persons would hold themselves back and isolate themselves from people in society. Having stood with Dylan on many occasions when he was rejected and mocked, Vanessa was well aware of people's discomfort to be around Dylan. She might have internalized society's consistent and dominant views that devalue and dehumanize people with profound autism and unconsciously accepted the oppression as an expected pattern that deserves respect.

However, separating Dylan from others in the Awana group does not help him to be integrated into Awana. It only further leads to the division of *us* (Vanessa and Dylan) and *them* (people in Awana). This statement is not a judgment against Vanessa. Adopting a position of relative invisibility is an understandable and often used protective mechanism in the face of oppression. As reported in the studies of many people who have internalized oppression (e.g., other disability groups, race, and sex), the unfortunate result of doing so is that the oppressed would devalue themselves and accept the messages of the inferiority of their group membership. The sense of inferiority prevents oppressed persons from connecting with the dominant group members, leading to intragroup fragmentation.[7] The awareness of this phenomenon should cause us to consider how we, as a church, should address the issue.

Meanwhile, George was fully aware of the group's attitude toward Dylan. He called it a "negative acceptance" meaning that they "don't let him . . . disturb them . . . what they have been trying to do is to ignore him." However, George did not attempt to intervene in the situation. George retired from ministry for many years and was eighty-five years old when Dylan began to attend Awana. George volunteered at The Cross because they lived nearby, and the church had difficulty recruiting a pastor. George explained that he did not have much time or energy to become too involved with Dylan because he was only a volunteer pastor. However, George indicated a willingness to

---

6. Watermeyer and Görgens, "Disability and Internalized Oppression," 253–58.
7. David and Derthick, "Internalized Oppression," 9.

do what he could to support Dylan. Therefore, from time to time, he would attempt to direct a question at Dylan during his teaching or invite a young person, in Anna's absence, to help Dylan with group games.

To George's defense, he often had to run the Awana program and attend to many students' needs simultaneously without the necessary help. With limited energies and much to attend to, George's approach was one of non-intervention. He trusted Vanessa as the one who knew Dylan the best, which was undoubtedly a correct assumption. However, when George did not address the discrimination against Dylan, he might have unintentionally conveyed an acceptance, even permission.

With Vanessa putting a protective shield over Dylan and George not intervening, the group ignored his presence. Thankfully, Anna and Lydia took a different approach. They intentionally engaged with him and invited others to do the same. The interactions between Anna and Dylan were particularly delightful to observe. As a teenager without much exposure to persons with disabilities, especially those who were non-speaking, Anna's ability to interact with him was exceptional. With or without using the communication devices, the two friends talked, played, laughed, and gave each other high-fives. Lydia also had an intuitive sense of Dylan's feelings. On one occasion, Lydia noted that when Dylan was left on his own while the other young people were playing a group game, he appeared agitated. When Lydia engaged him in a basketball game, he became happy and participated well. Anna's decision to approach and interact with Dylan is worth taking note of. As she said, what it took was for her to recognize that Dylan was like every other person except that he did not want to talk that much. In other words, Anna's desire to befriend Dylan came from seeing Dylan beyond the autism label and recognizing him as a person first and foremost.

Although Anna was reasonably new to Awana, her outgoing personality helped her establish a friendship with the other children in the programs quite quickly. She tried to invite her friends to greet Dylan with high fives, but unfortunately, her friends found Dylan "weird" and were unwilling to do so. However, as we will see later in the chapter, Anna's effort did have some effects on her friends. Her friendship with Dylan did not go unnoticed. Slowly, some people in the group began to see Dylan differently. Anna and Lydia's friendship has given Dylan a voice to express his desires for social relationships through actions.

A Learning Journey

Contrary to the young people with disabilities who came and visited the Awana but did not continue to attend, Dylan stayed. When I asked Vanessa her understanding of Dylan's willingness to join The Cross, she credited it to George and Martha's love. She says, "I feel that the first thing is the pastor. This couple really makes you feel like a family—the intimacy of it. I feel that their teachings and their love for each other and stuff make me feel that it is a gift from heaven. I mean, it is just really warm." There is no question that pastoral acceptance was vital for Dylan to step into Awana. Without George's blessings, Dylan could not participate in the Awana program. George's experience with his son's disability may also play a role in his openness towards people with disabilities. However, as we have seen, George's non-intervening approach did not help Dylan to be accepted by other group members. Therefore, it is instructive to follow Dylan's journey and explore what might have been helpful. As we do that, we will see that his entering to Awana was a learning journey for all involved.

For Vanessa, the first lesson that she learned was forgiveness. It came from her observations of Dylan's gracious attitudes towards the boys who mocked him. Vanessa comments, "Dylan is very forgiving. He doesn't take anything to heart. He gets upset for a little while, and then he is okay again." Dylan has also learned to give his feelings to God in prayers. Whether he was upset by what happened at home, at school, or Awana, Vanessa found that Dylan would go to a quiet corner, close his eyes and pray. Learning from Dylan, Vanessa also realized that she needed to learn to forgive. She says, "I need to forgive others who are mocking Dylan. We need to love them and pray for them. I need to forgive Dylan even when he has lost it." The practice of forgiveness as an act of obedience allowed Vanessa and Dylan to enjoy their time at Awana and not be hindered by the negative attitudes and actions.

Without a mutual commitment to spend time together, there would be no opportunity for friendship to be established. Honoring this commitment was challenging for Vanessa, who needed to take Dylan to Awana against her husband's wish. Still, with the belief that faith in Jesus was the most essential for Dylan, Vanessa timed their exit from home well before Simon's return from work so that there would not be open conflict.

Attending regularly at Awana was difficult for Anna and Lydia for a different reason. Lydia was a single mother who needed to work long hours. She also decided to move so that Anna would be able to walk to school. With the move and Lydia's work schedule, they were not at Awana every week. However, Lydia and Anna found a different way to honor their commitments to friendship. They arranged to meet with Dylan outside of Awana so that they could spend time with him.

As an introvert, I understand how intimidating it is to walk into a room full of strangers and how finding a couple of friends in the room is reassuring. For Dylan, this fear is more intense because of the experiences of rejection and verbal abuse. Therefore, it was quite remarkable that he remained happy to go to Awana despite certain group member's unwelcome attitudes. What Dylan has told us through his perseverance is the power of love and companionship. In a world where people with autism are often not chosen as friends, having even a few people who genuinely care about him goes a long way to encourage Dylan to be involved in community life. By extending a welcome, Dylan's Circle friends acknowledged Dylan's desire for social relationships and set an example for the rest of the group.

Whenever Anna was in the gymnasium for the group games, she would not leave Dylan standing on the side and watch. Anna was amazingly committed to helping Dylan be recognized as part of the group. Even when the volunteer leader did not invite Dylan to participate in the games, she would bring Dylan along during her turns. Having been an attached partner with Anna, Dylan would stand at the starting point when it was Anna's turn and wait for her to take him with her. The joy of the two of them in the game did not go unnoticed. One of the leaders started following Anna's example and assigned Dylan a turn on his own.

Lydia also learned to observe Dylan's emotions. In one of the game sessions, when Anna went off playing with the other children, Lydia noticed that Dylan seemed a bit upset. She went over and engaged him in a game, which made him very happy. Lydia explained that she wanted to learn to be Jesus to Dylan and love him as Jesus did.

Gradually, the group was more conscious about including Dylan in activities. Whenever Anna was absent from Awana, one young man, in particular, was able to step in and offer assistance to Dylan. Towards the end of the school year, Vanessa supplied that people were more understanding and accepting. She said, "At least they don't tease him now. In the past, they teased him. Now they accepted him better . . . Maybe they are growing up and becoming more understanding too." In the classroom, cookies were now offered to Dylan as well.

The progress, however, took an unexpected turn in the summer. Without giving any explanation, Vanessa suddenly cut off Anna and Lydia's visits with Dylan. It was not until close to the end of the summer that we learned what had happened. When the group met later in the summer for the Vacation Bible Camp held in George's backyard, we noticed that Vanessa had kept Dylan away from all the other children. He sat by himself in a small courtyard. With some encouragement, Vanessa revealed that shortly after the school was out, she hired a personal support worker to take Dylan to his summer activities. That contract only lasted a day. The worker resigned at the end of the day and warned Vanessa that she would be legally responsible for any damages Dylan might cause to a personal helper or a passerby. This comment worried Vanessa tremendously. Out of fear, she did not contact Lydia and Anna to arrange for any meetings.

According to Vanessa, Dylan became very unsettled without the daily routine of school. She truly believed that the potential for Dylan acting aggressively to others was quite real. George volunteered that he had never seen any sign of aggression from Dylan at the Vacation Bible Camp or Awana. The Circle reassured Vanessa of their commitments to being Dylan's friends, but Vanessa seemed very uncertain and cautious about Dylan getting too close to anyone. In her distress, she said that she began to think about what her husband had always wanted to do: to buy a house somewhere remote with a few acres of land and live there in seclusion with Dylan. This way, Dylan and other people would be safe.

Inaction Encourages Injustice

Regrettably, families with children with autism often experience judgmental attitudes in society. Out of the fear and concerns about the consequences of their children's autistic manifestations, withdrawing from society after a child is identified with profound autism is not limited to Chinese families. Perhaps the degree of social withdrawal may vary, but social scientist Timothy Broady and his colleagues observe that Australian families with children with profound autism also withdraw from society.[8] Feelings of shame, guilt, resentment, and embarrassment, compounded by fear of being blamed for their children's behaviors, mean that even carers may choose to isolate themselves from society. Raising a child with profound autism is hugely challenging, and one can understand why parents would want to avoid public judgment. However, the isolation from society severely limits opportunities for the parents and their children with autism to interact with others positively. The question for us, as a church, is what we should do to support the family?

George's support to Vanessa and Dylan was expressed in his acceptance for Dylan to join the Awana Club. However, the way that injustice within the community was tolerated was not reassuring and indeed quite troubling. George indicated that he was aware of what was going on. The

---

8. Broady et al., "Understanding Carers," 226–27.

volunteers working with him would have observed some of the boys' actions, even if they could not hear what they said. In effect, by doing nothing, the staff and adult volunteers who acknowledged each other as brothers and sisters of God's family have left Dylan in the position of a stranger, ignored and neglected by the community.

Reflecting on how to live out God's compassion in the Christian life, Henri Nouwen and his co-authors says,

> We cannot suffer with the poor when we are unwilling to confront those persons and systems that cause poverty. We cannot set the captives free when we do not want to confront those who carry the keys. We cannot profess our solidarity with those who are oppressed when we are unwilling to confront the oppressor. Compassion without confrontation fades quickly into fruitless sentimental commiseration.[9]

Doing nothing against the wrong done to Dylan by people at The Cross was certainly not compassionate. What is potentially more alarming is that inaction could be taken as an endorsement for the mistaken attitudes and behaviors. Learning from Anna and Lydia, an effective way to confront these wrong behaviors is to model the correct actions that encourage the group's solidarity with Dylan.

Lydia and Anna showed us that welcoming Dylan begins with recognizing that he is a person like anyone else. Through their interactions with Dylan, Lydia and Anna learned that Dylan could "talk" through actions (playing basketball), emotions (upset for being left alone, happiness in joining the games as attached partners of Anna), and gestures (high fives and pointing). At times, Dylan used his communication device to talk with Anna. She remarked that it was an "incredible" experience. It showed Anna that Dylan was indeed able to express his thoughts. She insightfully commented that this was not obvious to people who did not try to communicate with Dylan. Lydia stated that although Dylan did not speak, his desires to be with people were easily observable to people who were willing to see. While not a planned advocacy action, Anna and Lydia's interactions with Dylan gave him a voice to indicate to the group that he enjoyed social relationships. The joy that Dylan and Anna shared in joining the group games together caught the group's attention. Those who were willing to follow Anna's example also learned that Dylan was a friendly, fun-loving person.

Dylan's experience with The Cross reinforces the idea that inclusion is not enough. Being included in Awana meant that Dylan was able to be present physically at The Cross. Still, he faced discrimination and rejection

---

9. Nouwen et al., *Compassion*, 122.

within the Christian community he wanted to be a part of. Although Dylan has found friendship with a small group of people, his acceptance by The Cross was slow and continued to be shaky because of the family dynamic and the lack of strong support from the leadership.

Belonging will not happen if Dylan continues to be separated from the group. Members of the group need to be encouraged to see Dylan as who he is, engage with him as a friend, and welcome him into the group. To see what might happen if the church leadership assumes a more active advocacy role to encourage interactions with a person with profound autism, we will turn to Red Hill and learn from their intentional approach.

3

Belonging and Becoming

Concerted Efforts of the Circle of Friends

As iron sharpens iron, so one person sharpens another.
—Prov 27:17

Having a friend who supports and encourages us, accepts us unconditionally, and appreciates what we bring to the relationship, is essential for us to grow and fully become who we are created to be. We also need to have people who will share our joys and sorrows and help us manage unexpected turns in life. Unfortunately, as Hans Reinders astutely observes, people with profound disabilities are rarely chosen as friends. We saw that at The Cross and will, unfortunately, also see it at Red Hill. Thankfully, at Red Hill, we will see how the story unfolded differently.

Although Ellen, same as Dylan, experienced rejection at the beginning of her journey into the community of Red Hill, what is different between her experience and Dylan's is her Circle friends' concerted efforts in bringing her into the community. Compared to the three different approaches the family and the Circle friends used with Dylan, the Circle friends at Red Hill worked closely with Lillian, Ellen's mother, to support Ellen. Together, they intentionally made Ellen, as they said, "front and center" in the congregation to be seen and heard by people in the community. Once people could see Ellen as Ellen and interact with her as a person, she gained a voice, and her life in the community began to flourish.

The presence of Ellen at Red Hill did not benefit Ellen alone. In Red Hill's experience, we see most vividly what Jean Vanier means when he describes belonging as a journey and a discovery process for all traveling partners on this excursion. Vanier says, "We do not discover who we are, we do not reach true humanness, in a solitary state; we discover it through mutual dependency, in weakness, in learning through belonging."[1] As we engage with each other in a relationship of belonging, we will experience mutual discovery and growth. In and through the bond of belonging, we learn about the people we belong with; we also discover more about ourselves. As a result, we learn to see each other more clearly as the human persons God has created each of us to be and grow in our love for one another. The involvement with Ellen in a relationship of belonging, as Ellen's Circle friends would tell us, was "eye-opening." As Ellen was gaining affirmation from people at Red Hill, they too discovered something about Ellen and themselves. The Circle friends found the process to be transformative. To benefit from what the Red Hill community has learned, I will begin by introducing Ellen and her family.

Hit the Ground Running

Ellen is an energetic young woman with a long list of diagnoses, including profound autism, neurofibromatosis, Hypermobile Ehlers-Danlos syndrome, anxiety disorder, and legal blindness. Despite living with very complex needs, Ellen led a very active life. She enrolled in a soccer team and took up kayak paddling and horse-riding programs. She loved swimming and water play, enjoyed simple board games, went to the zoo, fairs, movie theaters, shopping malls, or took a train ride into the city. Ellen was also a member of a group for girls with disabilities. With reminders and supervision, Ellen was able to manage most of her self-care.

When I met Ellen, she was in her last year of high school. Ellen could not read or write. She spoke by articulating some simple words like "fun," "happy," "chips," and "cookies." At times, I needed her mother, Lillian's help to clarify what Ellen was saying. To help Ellen communicate, Lillian often used a fill-in-the-blank kind of approach. For example, she would say, "Cynthia asks you what you think about church. Church is . . . " Ellen had difficulties understanding changes in tenses, so sentences were always provided in the present tense. By phrasing the question in this particular way, Ellen was clear about the context in which she was asked to give a response.

On my first visit with the family, Lillian gave me the family photo album to use for my conversation with Ellen. The photos immediately made evident that Ellen was involved in a wide range of social activities. Lillian commented that Ellen liked being with people and would get agitated if she did not participate socially for more than two days. Her Circle friends used

1. Vanier, *Becoming Human*, 41.

the word "outgoing" to describe Ellen, which is a very unusual descriptor considering the prevailing impression that persons with profound autism want to stay in their own world.

Ellen's parents, Lillian and Bob, moved to Someplace, a suburban town when they got married. Initially, Lillian continued to attend a United Church in the nearby city, and Ellen was baptized there. When Ellen became a toddler, Lillian found the commute too demanding and switched to the more local Red Hill. On the other hand, Bob grew up in a Catholic church. He attended mass occasionally until his mother's untimely death. According to Lillian, Bob's mother's passing affected his faith profoundly, and he completely stopped associating with the church. Conversely, faith was a vital source of strength for Lillian. When Ellen was diagnosed with autism, Lillian said, "I went home and cried, and then I looked deep inside. I prayed for strength. Faith has always provided me with strength. Most of my life, it has been where I turned when things were tough, or when I was feeling lost."

Sustained by faith, Lillian said she did not mourn the news of Ellen's autism for too long. She knew if she wanted Ellen to flourish in life, she had to act quickly. Therefore, Lillian promptly started to gather information and make connections with community agencies so that Ellen could be enrolled in therapy programs. Even then, life was not easy for Lillian and her husband, Bob. With the determination to give Ellen as full a life experience as possible, Lillian brought Ellen with her when she had to run errands for the family. She also attended many community events with Ellen. In the process, Lillian said she learned "to develop a thick skin" and ignored the unfriendly stares and comments. Her outspoken personality and matter-of-fact approach also put her in a better position to be a parent advocate for Ellen's needs.

When Ellen was five, Lillian stopped working at her day job to support Ellen's attendance at a full-time therapy program. Subsequently, she trained as a behavior therapist and opened a small day program for two to three children at home. Lillian also volunteered with two disability-related organizations on boards of governance and ran a parent support group.

When Lillian started attending Red Hill, she brought Ellen with her but found that she often needed to be with Ellen at Sunday school and consequently missed her own worship time. Fortunately, there was one year when a young woman from Red Hill offered to take care of Ellen once a month to give Lillian a chance to attend Sunday services. But when this young woman was no longer able to assist, and the Sunday school staff did not know how to handle Ellen's behaviors, Lillian stopped going to church for a few years. Since then, Lillian has taken Ellen to occasional church events such as the annual bazaar or Christmas dinner. Ellen did not seem very eager about going to church at this point. Lillian described those outings as her "dragging" Ellen to these events.

As Lillian and Bob negotiated their life with Ellen's increasing needs that arose from additional medical concerns on top of autism, Bob needed to make a career change. He sold the family business and took on a salaried job with benefits to ensure income stability. To offset a limited, single source of income, Bob often worked overtime shifts in evenings and weekends. The extended hours of work did not aid the couple's already strained relationship, with Lillian spending most of her energy and attention on Ellen. In a bid to save their marriage, Lillian asked Pastor Tom, the pastor at Red Hill at the time, to provide counseling for them. Tom visited once and quickly launched a respite service at church for Lillian, Bob, and other families in the local community. However, Tom never returned to provide any marriage counseling, nor did he encourage church members to visit Lillian, Bob, and Ellen.

Lillian and Bob eventually agreed that staying together was the best option for all of them, but they ended up living very separate lives. Bob focused on work, and Lillian focused on Ellen. Their approaches to Ellen's autism were also very different. According to Lillian, Bob preferred not to deal with Ellen's personal care. He tried to work as many shifts as possible and was not at home very much. Meanwhile, Lillian became a friend of Ellen, not just her mother. Lillian frequently took Ellen to a variety of places and tried new and different activities with her.

The most crucial reason for Lillian to bring Ellen back to Red Hill was her belief that faith is a source of strength in difficult times. This belief came from Lillian's experience in managing the difficulties of raising a child with profound autism. As Ellen was transitioning into adulthood, Lillian wanted her to have faith in God, thus able to find the strength necessary for dealing with difficulties in life. Lillian remarked, "I am hoping that somehow she learns that there is this person you can turn to there." Lillian added that although she had no way of knowing what God might have revealed to Ellen during the Sunday school years, she believed that God's hand had guided them back to the church through various social connections that they made over the past years.

As Ellen was growing up, Lillian had to think about what Ellen's adult life would be like and what could happen when she could no longer support Ellen. Ellen would be out of school in a year, so Lillian started to look for friendly, accepting, and vibrant places with activities appealing to Ellen. With the church being the center of activities for most of Lillian's life, she considered Red Hill potentially one such place.

While Lillian wanted to bring Ellen back to church, she was also very clear that for all the activities that she introduced to Ellen, including the return to Red Hill, would have to be Ellen's choice. This approach was in line with Lillian's commitment to fostering Ellen's independence in decision making. While acting as strong support, Lillian always encouraged Ellen to decide where she wanted to go and whom she wanted to be with. Helping Ellen to make her own decision, however, requires a certain amount of time and persistence, Lillian says,

> She has autism. You can't take her and introduce her to something new once and know whether she likes it or not. The first few times she is going is not the case if she likes it; it is just the case of her learning the expectations, learning the environment. Then after she's got that little piece down, what the expectation is, what the environment is, then it's when she starts forming some opinions, then you know does she enjoy doing this or not.

Applying the same philosophy that had prepared Ellen for an active life, Lillian brought her back to Red Hill.

Church as a Community Center

Red Hill United Church described itself as "a small-town church where everyone knows everyone else." Many members are older and have been with the church for more than forty years. Some of them attend Red Hill with their children and grandchildren. There are about five to six young families in the church, but teenagers and young adults are mostly missing. Carol, a church leader, comments that, like many other churches in Canada, their membership "has dwindled." On those Sundays when I visited Red Hill, about a hundred people were in attendance. Pastor John reported that there were 165 people on the church's registry. Some came to church only occasionally and especially for events such as the Christmas dinner.

As a church, Red Hill has a long history. In 2015, they celebrated their 180th anniversary. Before joining the United Church of Canada, Red Hill was a member of the Presbyterian Church in Canada. Their building is located in a residential area slightly off the main road of the town. Red Hill maintains a traditional style of worship. According to Lillian, the expectation was that the communal worship time should be respected as a "religious moment." Loud noises or photography are not tolerated. As with the church's long history, many members of Red Hill also have long histories with each other. Red

Hill is the place where they married, where their children were baptized, and where families and children grew together.

Many members of Red Hill considered the church a family because they have known each other for many years. According to Carol, being a family means that church members are "being there for each other." She gave the following example: "When my late husband was ill, my church family just stepped up, and I didn't ask them to do anything. They were just there, automatically there."

Perhaps things have changed over the years. When I was at Red Hill, Pastor John often preached and encouraged the congregation to be hospitable to newcomers and care for each other. In one sermon, John reminded the congregation about how all Christians were called to be shepherds for each other. He said, "So often the work of pastoral care is left to me as minister solely. However, this is the work of the entire congregation." The indication was that very few, if any, members of the congregation were involved with the church's caring efforts.

Like many churches, Red Hill had a prayer ministry. People were invited to submit their prayer requests in person on Sundays or online at any time. A group of people in the ministry would include these requests in their prayer time with God. A prayer shawl ministry complemented this prayer ministry. Several knitters and crocheters from the congregation and friends of the members made the prayer shawls. These shawls were distributed to people who were sick or had specific needs. The shawls were passed around the congregation on Sunday mornings for people to add their prayer to the shawls. However, according to John, he was the only person involved in these visitations to bring the congregation's prayers and extend their caring thoughts.

Another indicator for Red Hill's functioning as a caring family, to Katie, a church leader, was to see each other on Sundays. Katie says, as a family, Sunday was the time to "engage with each other saying hello and, you know, being there for each other." Looking at how people at Red Hill interacted on Sundays, it would appear that their interactions did not go much deeper than greeting each other. Although refreshment tables were laid out in the narthex for the congregation to fellowship with each other before and after worship, I rarely saw people mingle there. Most people went directly into the chapel without socializing. About twenty to thirty people stayed for coffee briefly after worship, but the church was often clear of people within twenty minutes after the service.

When I explored the idea of belonging as a family with the Red Hill leadership, I understood that while every person might be connecting differently and at their own pace, "belonging means, they have a role to play;

they can make contributions." This idea is perhaps why many people were involved in the various activities taking place at the church. Out of a small active congregation of approximately a hundred people, about twenty-five took on a formal leadership role, serving on the governing boards, Session, or personnel/ministry committees. On top of that were many involved in the ad-hoc committees to organize various activities offered by the church.

It was precisely because Red Hill was such a busy church with many community activities that Lillian thought it might be a good place for Ellen to get involved. Ellen's entry to the church was greatly supported and assisted by the leadership of the church. Pastor John, Carol, and Katie that I mentioned in introducing the community of Red Hill were the people who formed the Circle of Friends for Ellen. In addition to being leaders at Red Hill, they also had extensive experience living or working with people with disabilities.

Experience and Openness to Disability

Pastor John came to Red Hill in 2011. With experience working at a residential facility for people with developmental disabilities, he understood the serious effects of constant rejection experienced by people with disabilities. Once John took his friends with developmental disabilities to attend Sunday service at a nearby church. At the end of the service, the church leadership asked John not to bring his friends to church again, even though the group sat quietly throughout the service. While serving as a minister at Red Hill, John continued growing friendships with people with developmental disabilities and staff at the residential facility. Interacting with people with developmental disabilities was second nature to him.

Carol started attending Red Hill when she was seventeen because her boyfriend, who became her husband, was a member. Carol served on the Session and began her second term at the time of my visit. When John encouraged Lillian to post an invitation for people to join Ellen's Circle of Friends on the church's Facebook page, Carol responded and offered her help.

Carol has a daughter with Attention Deficit and Hyperactivity Disorder. Although the type of disability is very different between Ellen and her daughter, Carol felt that she could understand Lillian's difficulties in negotiating for therapy and education for Ellen. She also understood rejection from her daughter's experience with her "snotty" fellow students. Carol stated that her daughter has never been invited to any classmates' birthday parties.

Katie is a third-generation member of a Red Hill family. Both of her parents were key leaders of the church. Like Carol, Katie also served on the Session. She mentioned that she "grew up with disabilities." As a teenager, Kaite began volunteering at a swimming program offered at a church member's house. (This member has since passed, and the swimming program stopped many years ago.) Her role was to help people in wheelchairs to move about in this program. As volunteers of the swimming program, Katie also brought some of the children to church from time to time. It was at this very swimming program that Katie first met Ellen, who was a small child at the time. Katie now worked in a group home for children who were medically fragile and developmentally delayed. With this job, she became well versed in interactions with people with communicational difficulties.

As Katie has indicated, the Red Hill congregation had had some experiences with having people with disabilities from the swimming group visited with the church. Like what Ellen and Lillian used to do, these people sometimes attended the church's seasonal events. John was aware of these families and their struggles. He mentioned that some of these young people could not participate in church because their behaviors might be beyond what the congregation could handle.

Being someone with extensive experience and passion for people with disabilities, John intentionally exposed the Red Hill community to people with disabilities. He invited the Spirit Movers dance group to perform as part of a worship service.[2] John also asked his friends from the residential facility to visit Red Hill so that the congregation could learn to receive people with developmental disabilities as friends.

Additionally, some congregation members had a certain level of familiarity and comfort working with people with disabilities. Several women used to volunteer at the church's respite program for families with children with disabilities. A retired teacher had many years' experience working with students with disabilities, and another retiree used to work in a social service organization for people with disabilities. The congregation's introductions to people with disabilities over the years contributed to the current openness in welcoming people with disabilities to church. Their familiarity with disabilities was probably why all the Circle members mentioned that any unexpected behaviors made by individuals with disabilities would "upset nobody."

Lillian reported two incidents that supported this claim of openness. The first happened when Ellen was much younger. One Sunday, a young woman in the congregation took care of Ellen to give Lillian personal time

---

2. Spirit Movers is a dance group of committed performance dancers with all abilities. Their mission is to celebrate the sacred through dance.

to focus on worship. Ellen "got out of the pew, got all excited, went right down the main aisle of the church, right past the minister, up to the choir loft, running through the choir before Carolyn could catch her." Yet, no one made any complaint to Lillian or the pastor. The second incident happened one Sunday when the choir was singing the song *Lord of the Dance*. Ellen got up and danced in the middle of the aisle. Lillian tried desperately to get her to sit down, but the people around them stopped Lillian and encouraged Ellen to continue and dance.

Commitment to Inclusion

In addition to having some exposures to people with disabilities, the Red Hill community has made inclusion a part of their missions. They demonstrated their commitment to inclusion by adopting the Affirming Ministries model of the United Church of Canada. Affirming Ministries began with the church's desire to welcome people with different sexuality and gender orientations. However, the United Church of Canada states that their commitment to justice is far broader than sexual and gender differences. It includes "challenging bias and discrimination based on appearance, culture, class, or age; working to end racism; promoting economic justice; increasing accessibility; or caring for the planet."[3]

The process of becoming an affirming congregation involved a majority of the congregation participating in monthly training and discernment sessions for one year. In 2015, over 85% of the Red Hill congregation voted in favor of becoming an affirming congregation. Being a "safe place" was a phrase that Red Hill members used to describe what they wanted to achieve with their affirming initiatives. Katie says, "It [The affirming ministry] is we are a safe space for anybody is essentially what it is . . . It is accepting everybody for who they are."

Being inclusive towards people in the LGBTQ community was a very explicit intent for Red Hill. It was often mentioned in sermons and church documents, such as the monthly newsletters and annual reports. The congregation also took part in the local Pride parade to support the LGBTQ community. Their affirmation extended to the environment and animals, with an annual Blessing of the Animals Sunday in September.

Remarkably, although the Affirming Ministries included people with disabilities in its inclusive mandate, disability issues were rarely discussed at Red Hill. The subject was only brought up one Sunday when Lillian and Ellen gave a presentation to the congregation on their experience in living

3. Huntly, "*Open Hearts*," 1.

with autism. John arranged this presentation as part of the Circle's effort in putting Ellen "front and center for her to interact with people and they with her."

An Enabling Approach

A unified and intentional approach of the Circle, as we will see, brought about significant changes. In Lillian's opinion and from what I observed, a key element in Red Hill's effort was that John was "110% on board." He was enthusiastic and active right from the moment Lillian approached him about bringing Ellen back to Red Hill. He orchestrated the formation of the Circle by encouraging Lillian to post on the church's Facebook page on the need for Circle friends for Ellen. John also recommended Katie to Lillian to be part of the Circle.

Other than John, Carol and Katie's commitments were also vital to Ellen's re-entry to Red Hill. Carol's motivation to be a friend to Ellen came initially from a desire to help Lillian due to the similarity of experiences as mothers tending to daughters with disabilities. As her friendship with Ellen developed over time, Carol realized Ellen's participation at Red Hill brought about changes in the community, which kept her motivated and committed to working with the Circle. For Katie, she was very excited about being a part of the Circle because she was happy to learn about Ellen's recent interest in church and wanted to help Ellen become an accepted member of the congregation. Katie also wanted to be Ellen's friend in the most real sense of the word, beyond doing things together at church. Katie was open to going out with Ellen to do "friend things" when she was ready.

For her part, Lillian understood that if she wanted Ellen to develop relationships with people at Red Hill, she needed to be a committed member at Red Hill. Therefore, she offered herself for various church activities such as baking for the Christmas events and counting offerings on Sundays. Lillian said, "I think my involvement with my daughter; my involvement with the church also plays a factor in the success of this. I think a quieter or more shy or less involved parent might not get the same kind of responses I am getting." Once she got involved and interacted with more people, Lillian found that people became more understanding and helpful to her and Ellen. To be at church regularly and punctually required a shift of priorities. Sundays had been the only days Lillian could leave Ellen at home with Bob and indulge in an hour of running. As Lillian and Ellen got more involved at church, Lillian gave up her running routine.

A key phrase that can be used to describe the team's effort in bringing Ellen into the fabric of the community at Red Hill is "supported exposure." Lillian worked closely with the Circle to try many different church activities to purposely expose Ellen to various groups of people and church functions. This approach was beneficial to Ellen, but it was also an eye-opening journey for those who accompanied her into Red Hill.

Eye-Opening Experience

With Red Hill's commitment to be an inclusive church, the initial experience of returning to church with Ellen was a surprise to Lillian. When Ellen attended Red Hill's events occasionally in the past, Lillian did not pay much attention to how the congregation members received her. After obtaining permission from Pastor John, Lillian posted a message on the church's Facebook page to invite people to be Ellen's Circle friends. She asked interested members to talk with her and Ellen at the coffee time on the following Sunday. Lillian was disappointed when they stood in the narthex for the entire coffee time, and nobody approached and greeted them.

Unfortunately, even after the Circle was in place, only a few church members would greet Lillian and Ellen at church. According to Lillian, these were the people who used to volunteer at the church's respite program and already knew Ellen from those days. Many people in Red Hill would avoid interacting with Ellen or ignore her altogether. Some people would talk with Lillian but would not greet Ellen even when Lillian prompted Ellen to say "hello" to them. Ellen also experienced occasions of explicit rejections at church. For example, Lillian reported that one Sunday during the rite of peace, "one gentleman came across the aisle to shake my hand, and I got Ellen to extend her hand to him, but the gentleman didn't take it." A particularly painful incident for Lillian happened at a luncheon at church. After finishing her lunch, Lillian made sure that Ellen was safely sitting at a table to finish hers. She then got up and went to talk to someone while keeping an eye on Ellen. Lillian noticed that nobody approached Ellen or even acknowledged her presence. At clean-up time, a woman came to the table where Ellen was sitting, lifted Ellen's plate, and pulled the tablecloth from under it without saying one word to Ellen.

The unwelcoming experiences Lillian and Ellen encountered at this stage was certainly not reassuring. Amazingly, despite the unwelcoming situation they encountered at Red Hill at this stage, Lillian found that Ellen remained keen and willing to go to church on Sundays, which Lillian took as a sign that Ellen enjoyed being with her Circle friends.

The support of the Circle friends was significant for Ellen. Once they were on board, they wanted to see Ellen integrated into the congregation. One Sunday, when John was preaching, he invited the congregation to respond to a question. Ellen said something out loud, but what she said seemed irrelevant to John's question, and the congregation burst out laughing. At the end of the service, John spoke sternly to the congregation and pointed out their wrong.

Based on the experiences in the initial stage, the Circle friends, John, in particular, encouraged Lillian to increase Ellen's visibility at the church. The plan involved arranging for Ellen to light the Christ candle at the beginning of the service and serving as a greeter. John also invited Lillian and Ellen to the "Church at the Pub" night. At this stage, Carol or Katie would take turns to be on the same serving team with Ellen and Lillian to practice how to assist Ellen. These efforts slowly bore fruit. Roughly one month after Ellen started serving as a greeter, a woman at the other side of the door, without prompting from anyone in the Circle, reminded each person coming through the door to shake hands with Ellen. Gradually, Lillian noted, "You now got more people that Ellen is comfortable with and that more people are comfortable with Ellen, so you've got double the number of people that they know."

Perhaps what was most encouraging to Lillian was Ellen's responses in worship. Ellen usually conducted a fair bit of self-talk and sometimes rather loudly. Surprisingly, during the worship service, she was able to sit mostly quietly and remained still instead of getting up and walking around. Ellen was also often able to follow the group to stand and sit at intervals throughout service.

Ellen's friends noted that Ellen was actively engaging with people at the church. Katie provided an example from one of the pub events, saying, "She sat right beside the minister, and I swear she spent half of the time trying to engage him." Once Ellen began to feel comfortable with a group of people, she became more active in interacting with people. These occasions were what gave the Circle the impression of Ellen as an out-going young woman.

A major breakthrough in relationship building came from John's invitation for Lillian and Ellen to share their experiences with autism during service one Sunday. Immediately following the presentation, a good number of church members approached Lillian and Ellen and expressed how effective the presentation was in helping them understand their situation. Some offered information to Lillian for finding additional support in the community. Others offered their support. After that day, Lillian reported that more and more people approached them each week. Some spoke with Ellen directly and commended her for serving the church.

As Ellen began to spend more time with the Circle friends without Lillian's company, she also had growing interactions with church members who were not a part of the Circle. By now, it was clear that Ellen felt very comfortable with the church. As soon as their car was parked in the parking lot, Ellen would run up the church steps, enter the sanctuary, and sit down with random people without waiting for Lillian.

One day after the Sunday service, I asked Ellen how she felt about the church. Her answer that "church was fun" surprised people listening to us, including Lillian. Their surprise came from the fact that Ellen typically required prompting to give even one-word answers to most questions. Spontaneously saying a short sentence like this was very unusual. When I tried to ask more about how church was fun, the answers were harder to decipher. Like many people with autism, Ellen also focuses on objects. "Fun" included music, piano, guitar, and cookies. Lillian observed that Ellen seemed to be particularly engaged with the singing parts of worship. When the choir sang her favorite songs, the Circle friends noticed that Ellen was "bumping up and down" in her seat in apparent enthusiasm. Ellen also talked about her experience as a greeter with phrases such as "shake hand," "happy to see you," while grabbing my hand with a big smile on her face. A clear indication of Ellen's happiness with the church, as Lillian reported, was that she started talking about going to church during the week.

On another occasion, when I visited Ellen in her house, we went through pictures of her outings with different support workers and her activities at the family events and the church. I asked Ellen if the people in the photos were her friends. Ellen did not think her support workers were friends. Her Circle friends fell into this category of non-friends as well. Lillian was also not a friend, but Ellen indicated their intimacy by playfully falling into Lillian's lap. In the end, what surprised Lillian and me the most was a clear yes to the question of whether Jesus was a friend.

Despite all the progress made up to this point, there was still a lingering sense of ambivalence in Lillian's mind. Towards the end of the year, the Circle friends discussed the possibility of Lillian resuming her running routine on Sunday mornings. They offered to stay with Ellen if Bob would drop her off until Lillian finished running and join her at the church. Lillian was unsure if she should accept their offer. When I was alone with her, Lillian said, "They are okay when I am there," indicating that the Circle friends were comfortable being with Ellen alone only when Lillian was available and nearby in the same building. Lillian was not sure if the friends would feel as comfortable with Ellen if she was not in the building.

Nevertheless, there were clear indicators that Ellen was being accepted as part of the community. Other than the Circle friends, different church members began to take a more active role in spending time with Ellen. Some invited Lillian and Ellen to sit with them during service and events. Others invited them for coffee in the narthex or luncheon at the church. Several women invited Ellen to join them at the mid-week activities after finishing high school. A good indication for expanding friendships was an invitation by some church members for Lillian and Ellen to join them for events outside of the church. An example was an invitation to join the group on a trip to an Indigenous community's Powwow.

Ellen's growing independence with her friends at church was another sign that Red Hill was becoming her community. She continued to be involved in different church activities but without Lillian on her side. Carol and Katie have served as greeters and spent time in the kitchen with Ellen without Lillian needing to supervise or keep watch. The Circle friends also engaged Ellen independently on Sundays to give Lillian some personal or social time. When Ellen began to engage with her Circle friends and some congregation members independently, she started to understand what it meant to be a part of a congregation. One day after the church luncheon, when some people began to put away the chairs and tables while Lillian was talking with a friend, Ellen got up and, without prompting, joined other people to fold the chairs and put them away.

The Red Hill congregation also began to understand and respect Ellen's specific needs. For example, during coffee time on a Sunday, Ellen started to spin around and appeared self-absorbed. Instead of trying to stop her, people gave her the space and time she needed to regain control. Another time, Ellen stopped at the preschool room on the way to the church kitchen. She started pulling out some of the toys and played with them. Katie and Carol allowed her some time to play before guiding her to leave. They later learned that the toys she pulled out to play with had been her favorites when she had participated in the preschool room as a small child.

Further, Ellen's interactions with people at the Church at the Pub are good examples of the growing friendships. John recalls that at one of the meetings, Ellen kept poking at a man's glass on the table, and they ended up having a game of "pushing the glass" between them. Katie remembers a funny occasion when Ellen tried to engage John in talking about basketball for "half of the night." Lillian often needed to be present to interpret and provide the context for Ellen's expressions. Still, people showed that they were learning to interact with Ellen in ways that she felt included.

An interesting comment expressed by different Circle members was that Ellen's presence at the church "opened their eyes and the eyes of the congregation." By actively involving Ellen at church, everyone learned more about her. The group also noticed a new or renewed sense of synergy within the congregation. They felt that it might be related to a feeling of shared purpose around Ellen, which reportedly increased the sense of community in the congregation.

Mutually Enriching Journey

As positive an experience Ellen has had at Red Hill, we must not forget that Ellen experienced explicit rejection at the beginning of her re-entry to the church. The key to changing the congregational responses to Ellen was a committed leadership that intentionally supported her re-integration. Lillian's commitment to work in a concerted manner with the church leaders, who were also Ellen's Circle friends, was also essential to moving her along the path of belonging. On the whole, several learning points from Ellen's experience are worth highlighting.

First of all, Red Hill, as a community, was probably readier than many in their inclusive missions. The denominational leadership in this direction should be noted. Although the Affirming Ministry originated from the intent to welcome people from the LGBTQ community, the United Church of Canada has established several policies and directives on ministries with persons with disabilities to demonstrate their commitments to include people with disabilities in the church. They have also published a theology of disability to guide the church's practices in 2015. However, the disability focus has not been emphasized at Red Hill other than John's exposures of the congregations to his friends with intellectual disabilities.

A study conducted by Eric Pridmore, a denominational leader of the Christian Reformed Church, helps us appreciate the complexity of belonging with people with disabilities in a local church.[4] Pridmore's study explored the non-conformity of a local church with their denominational guidance on the inclusion of people with disabilities. He identified that the local context, the congregational makeup and culture, the decision-making process, and the church's theologies regarding disabilities could all affect the congregation's welcome for people with disabilities. Importantly, Pridmore demonstrated that denominational influence has its limit. What ultimately determines a church community's welcome to people with disabilities are congregational culture and the decision and modeling of the church's leadership, which is clearly exhibited in Red Hill.

The "front and center" approach devised by the Circle that consisted of three church leaders created many opportunities for intentional engagements between Ellen and the church members. Pastoral influence from the

4. Pridmore, "The Christian Reformed Church," 93–107.

pulpit and John's stern correction of the church's wrong responses set the tone for the church's welcome for Ellen. As mentioned earlier, John's commitment throughout the whole period was instrumental to Ellen's belonging to Red Hill. Additionally, Katie and Carol's friendship with Ellen no doubt modeled for the community how they should interact with her.

If we look at Red Hill and The Cross together, we can see the values of the Circle of Friends program. The Circle of Friends is an approach developed at the time of deinstitutionalization to support people with disabilities reintegrate into their local communities. In recent years, the Circle of Friends program was used most extensively in education settings to help students with developmental disabilities build community connections and foster a sense of belonging to the school community.[5] The Circles of Friends at The Cross and Red Hill served a similar purpose: to support Dylan and Ellen's integration into the church community. Their mandate was to be available to listen, to give loving advice, and to provide support when it is needed.[6]

The experiences in both churches, especially Red Hill, parallel what has been reported in the Circle of Friends program in the educational settings.[7] The intentional exposure of Ellen to church members helped them see beyond the surface effects of autism and become more accepting. Through the Circle's acceptance and support, Ellen gained more confidence in social situations, as evidenced by increased communication. Many church members became more aware of how they could support Ellen's belonging to Red Hill.

A remarkable point to note in the composition of the Circles at The Cross and Red Hill is that they were primarily people with personal or professional experience with disabilities. This composition was not intentional as previous experience with people with a disability was not stated as a recruitment criterion for the Circle friends. The indication could be that people with some backgrounds with disabilities are likely more comfortable to offer themselves to be a Circle friend. However, it does not mean that someone with a personal experience with a disabled person will necessarily approach a person with profound autism and offer friendship. Take Carol as an example. She had noticed Lillian and Ellen at church events in the past, as Carol was often operating the cashier desk. However, she never attempted to interact with Ellen before joining the Circle. Carol did not communicate with Lillian either beyond polite greetings or small talks at events. Her experience with her daughter's disability was perhaps helpful in eliminating some fear

---

5. James and Leyden, "Putting the Circle Back," 52–63.

6. Falvey et al., *All My Life's a Circle*, 5.

7. See Frederickson and Turner, "Classroom Peer Group," 234–45; and Schlieder et al., "Circle of Friends," 27–40.

in approaching Ellen. Still, the change in Carol's willingness to interact with Ellen began with Lillian's invitation and John's encouragement.

Although most people in the two Circles had previous experiences with people with disabilities, their interactions with Dylan and Ellen were described as a learning journey or an eye-opening experience. This comment was particularly surprising to me, given that people like John and Katie, who mentioned that interacting with someone with profound autism, was their second nature. In conversations with them, I discovered that their learning was in their change of perspectives. In a carer-receiver relationship, there is a power deferential embedded in giving and receiving. In some instances, the caring actions could come out of a sense of pity or charity. When that relationship is changed to friendship, there is an equalizing effect. As friends, Anna found Dylan to be an incredible teacher, who had shown her the capabilities of people with autism that she didn't know before. With Ellen, Katie and John learned that she could engage others as a fun young woman and participate in the community as a contributing team member. In both settings, people began to see how the relationship of belonging could be mutually enriching. In the following chapter, I will further unpack this intriguing phenomenon and illustrate how the lens of profound autism will help us better understand the concept of belonging in the church.

4

From Rejection to Belonging

> The head cannot say to the feet, "I don't need you!" On the contrary, those parts of the body that seem to be weaker are indispensable. —1 Cor 12:21–22

IN THE INTRODUCTION CHAPTER, I explained that entering through the door of a church is not the same as belonging to the congregation. The experiences of Ellen and Dylan confirmed this assertion. They were both included by their church in terms of being able to attend church activities. However, being included, as we have seen, did not necessarily mean they were readily received into the community.

If we recall, Vanessa and Lillian's primary motivation to bring Dylan and Ellen back to church was for their faith to be nurtured by a Christian community. Although the two mothers wanted their children to have friends at church, they yearned for them to have more than a social relationship with other Christians. Vanessa and Lillian hoped that Dylan and Ellen would accept Christ as their Lord so that faith would give them the strength they need to navigate the complicated life with autism. In other words, Lillian and Vanessa desired for Ellen and Dylan to become Christians and belong to a Christian community. That being the case, we need to ask if Red Hill and The Cross had been the Christian community that nurtured Dylan and Ellen's faith?

To answer this question, we need to be clear on what it means for us to be called Christians and the differences between a Christian and a non-Christian community. When we confess ourselves as Christians, we are testifying that Jesus Christ defines our identity and belonging. We belong to the church, the body of Christ, because we belong first and foremost to Christ, serving Jesus as our Lord (Col 3:24). As a community that belongs together to follow Christ, we share a common vocation as servants of Christ. Spelling out what is involved in the Christian vocation, John Swinton says, we, as a Christian community, should "learn to love God, and in coming to love God, learn what it means to love and to receive love from all of its members." As servants of God who is love (I John 4:16), what holds us together is God's love. We serve God in the way of life that is characterized by our love for one another. However, as Swinton rightly indicates, we do not right away become a loving Christian when we confess our faith in Christ. We need to learn to love God and others. As a Christian community, we need to help each other to become disciples of Christ and follow Jesus's commandments of love.

From his experience in living with people with intellectual disabilities in the Christian community of L'Arche, Jean Vanier illuminates how we can learn to love. He suggests that to be human is to be on a journey of belonging with each other.[1] On the journey of belonging, we discover each other as persons uniquely created by God. Knowing that we are all loved by God, we recognize that every person has been given the necessary capacity to love God and others. As such, we learn to discover and empower each other's gifts as we journey together so that we can grow together in the measure of the fullness of Christ (Eph 4:13).

Vanier's idea of mutual discoveries in the belonging process is evident in the experiences of The Cross and Red Hill. In the previous chapters, we have seen how the two groups of Circle friends describe their journeys with Dylan and Ellen as a learning or an eye-opening experience. The task of this chapter is to further unpack their experiences. I want to note the discoveries that people involved in the two church communities have made in their journeys of belonging with Dylan and Ellen. Following that, I will examine the implications their experiences may have on our practices of belonging with people with profound autism.

Journey of Belonging

As we have seen, Ellen and Dylan came from very different family backgrounds. Red Hill and The Cross were also two distinctively different communities in terms of traditions and ethos of belonging. However, through their mothers and the Circle friends' efforts, Dylan and Ellen both gained better acceptance. They progressed towards belonging on a similar trajectory, but at differing rates and fashions. In Figure 1, I put Dylan and Ellen's experiences together to demonstrate the similarity and the differences in their movements towards belonging. The diagrammatic depiction shows

---

1. Vanier, *Becoming Human*, 5.

the changes in Dylan and Ellen's relationships with the church and where their mother stood in those relationships. The texts that follow will explain the significance of these relational changes. For depiction purposes, I describe Ellen and Dylan's journeys of belonging in four observable stages. These stages, which I call invisible stranger, growing comfort, expanding friendship, and community, do not divide neatly into equal time components during the year. Instead, the stages are defined by what characterized the mutual relationships at various stages.

FROM REJECTION TO BELONGING 65

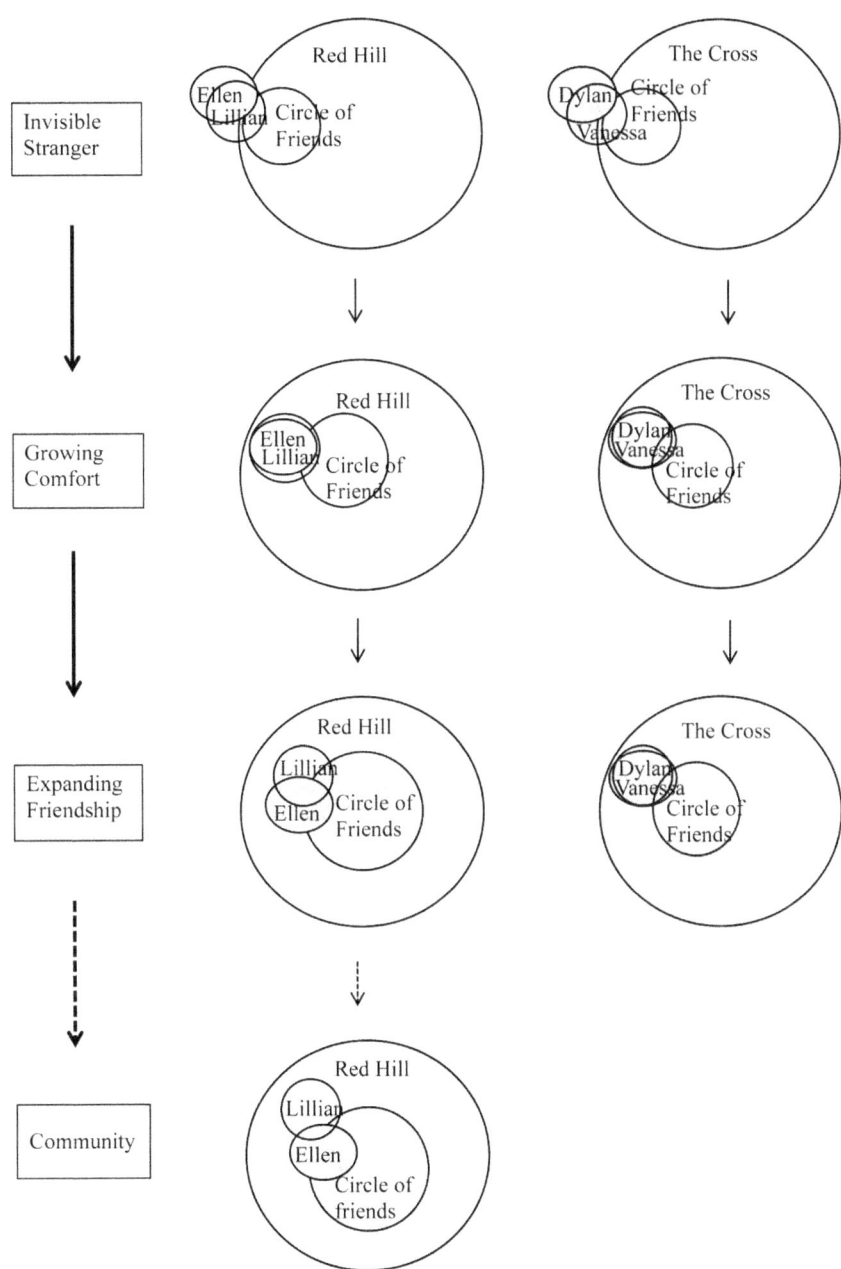

Progression of Belonging in Red Hill and The Cross

Invisible Strangers

In Figure 1, we see that both families were initially standing on the church's margins, with the two mothers making connections with the Circles of Friends. At this stage, the Circle friends began to learn to interact with Ellen and Dylan, with Lillian and Vanessa's assistance. If we recall, this is also when Dylan and Ellen occupied a social space of relative invisibility in the church. Some church members ignored their presence and refused to greet them with a handshake or a high-five.

From Lillian's perspective, people at Red Hill were avoiding interaction with Ellen because "despite what people say, we are still very judgmental of people's physical appearance and behaviors . . . there are lots of preconceived ideas about dealing with someone with autism." Lillian's comment echoed the experience of Dawn Eddings Prince mentioned in chapter 1. In that chapter, I also pointed out how we understand autism determines how we interact with people with autism. If we see persons with autism as "defective," we disregard the complexity of their lives and reduce them to a "disorder." If we see them as people with "deviant" behaviors, we avoid and reject them as people that do not belong with "us," the "normal." Therefore, it is possible that people at The Cross and Red Hill identified Dylan and Ellen with the defective view of autism and avoided them instead of welcoming them into their midst.

The negative reception that Ellen and Dylan experienced was regrettably common among families with children with autism who want to attend a church.[2] When families met with unwelcoming attitudes, they either kept switching churches until they could find an accepting church or leave the church altogether.[3] The reason why Dylan and Ellen continued to stay with The Cross and Red Hill was the active engagement of a small group of Circle friends. From what the families have described, Ellen and Dylan had negative experiences with people in their neighborhood and the community activities that they have attended. As with many other individuals with severe disabilities, their social circles were limited to family members and support workers. Having people who wanted to be their friends was a refreshing and encouraging experience.

As Dylan and Ellen's relationships with their friends progressed, both groups of Circle friends acknowledged that they liked being with people and participating in community activities. The Circle friends' discoveries were consistent with what was mentioned in chapter 1 by other people

---

2. Altiere and von Kluge, "Searching for Acceptance," 142–52.
3. Ault et al., "Factors," 187.

with profound autism. This recognition is vital because if Dylan and Ellen had no interest in social relationships, they would not be interested in having a Circle of Friends, not to mention entering a relationship of belonging with a church community.

Conversely, if we accept that people with profound autism, like Dylan and Ellen, want to belong to a church community, we need to seriously consider how to respond in a way that respects their desires and values their belonging to the church. Unless the experience of attending a church is positive, it is possible that Dylan, Ellen, and their families would leave the community.

Growing Comfort

Having met some unfavorable responses from the community, it is not surprising that both Lillian and Vanessa had a sense of ambivalence about Ellen and Dylan's re-entry to the church. For them, the decision to stay the course was their belief that having faith in Jesus was what Dylan and Ellen needed to navigate their lives with profound autism. Additionally, Ellen and Dylan were both teenagers, having their own friendship circle, and growing into supported independence with their friends' assistance was essential.

With the ambivalent feelings, what we see in Figure 1 is how Vanessa and Lillian have stayed very close to Dylan and Ellen as they entered into The Cross and Red Hill. Although Vanessa had much more concerns about Dylan's behaviors than Lillian had for Ellen, both were very anxious about their child's ability to conform to the church's requirements, especially about not making noises and following the liturgy or the program routine. Therefore, Lillian and Vanessa felt the need to be present to help Ellen and Dylan control their behaviors. Their anxieties about Ellen and Dylan's ability to conform to the unspoken behavioral norms implied that should Ellen and Dylan had difficulties meeting these norms, they would not be staying. In this regard, the acceptance of the Red Hill community for occasions when Ellen acted differently, such as dancing in the aisle, was reassuring to Lillian.

For Vanessa, it was difficult to let her guard down totally. Her approach was to be present at all times to facilitate the communication between Dylan and his Circle friends and take Dylan away if and when she felt that he was losing control. Understandably, Vanessa was also very nervous about the few boys who teased Dylan. A sense of growing comfort eventually arose from Vanessa's and Dylan's willingness to forgive these young people. Being able to leave the negative feelings behind allowed her to work with Anna and Lydia to slowly establish relationships with the young persons and volunteers at Awana.

On the other hand, Lillian took an active role to ensure a smooth transition of her support role to the Circle friends. With John and Katie having extensive experience working with people with profound disabilities, Lillian did not have to do more than giving them Ellen's *All About Me* booklet to explain Ellen's specific needs.[4] With Carol, Lillian spent time with her to demonstrate how to communicate with Ellen and support her care needs. Worthwhile to note again is how the Circle worked seamlessly with Lillian to help Ellen get to know them, and through them, acquaint with more people at the church. The teamwork and commitment of all involved were keys to Ellen's progress in belonging to the community.

Supported by their mother and Circle friends, Ellen and Dylan moved slightly into the community and began participating in congregational activities. Ellen and Dylan engaged very well with people who approached them and participated in the activities they were invited to join in. Their willing participation spoke loudly to their abilities to establish social relationships and their eagerness to be part of their respective community. Their increasing involvement with community activities also allowed people to get to know them beyond their autism label.

Expanding Friendship

At this stage, we begin to see the differences between Ellen and Dylan's progress in belonging to their respective community. Figure 1 shows that both families stepped away from the margin and moved into the community, but Ellen's circle of friends had expanded further than that of Dylan. She also began to engage in some church activities without the constant companion of Lillian.

With the growing trust in the Circle friends' caring friendship with Ellen, Lillian began to step aside, allowing Ellen to spend time with Katie, Carol, and John independently. John's arrangement for Lillian and Ellen to speak to the congregation achieved the purpose of helping church members understand Ellen and the family's situation. With these efforts, Ellen's social circle at church began to expand to include people she served with and others who wanted to be friends. Through the process of assisting Ellen, the Circle friends noted that there was an increasing sense of community commitment.

---

4. All About Me is an interactive picture book that provides background on the person and the family, what he or she likes and dislikes, some precautionary notes, and suggested activities that the person with autism might enjoy.

More than offering to love and help Ellen's life flourish, church members became increasingly involved in serving the church.

Progress at the Cross was slower. The unfortunate setback mentioned in chapter 2 and the church leadership's lack of intervention accounted for the difference. The concerns for Dylan's behaviors meant that Vanessa continued to stay close by Dylan's side. Anna and Lydia's inconsistent attendance also reduced the possibility of serving the function as bridges for Dylan's relationship with the group. However, Dylan's friendship circle did expand slowly, with specific people such as David, who helped him during activities, and others who began to acknowledge his presence at The Cross and invited him to join the group's activities.

As the Circle friends developed deeper relationships with Ellen and Dylan, both groups found the experience to be eye-opening and transformative. The indication is that when people began to get to know Dylan and Ellen, the autistic label began to fade into the background. People who engaged in relationships with them began to see their unique personalities, individual gifts, and specific needs. The fun that was shared between Ellen and the church member at the pub was one such example.

The transformational experiences of these two churches are not unique. Thinkers of different disciplines have reported similar experiences. William Gaventa noted, from his role in supporting churches and organizations to welcome people with disabilities, that the experience of community transformation is quite common. The most evident change is the move from fear or pity to love.[5] Similarly, Stephen Post suggests that for those who are willing to interact with people with cognitive disabilities, the encounters allow both sides in the relationship to experience the power of love.[6] Without speech, Ellen and Dylan are giving and receiving love. The power of mutual affection is transformational for them and the church members who engaged them in relationships.

Community

I use a dotted arrow in Figure 1 to indicate that Ellen was in the process of making Red Hill her community. For Dylan, the unfortunate setback meant that he remained at the stage of expanding friendship. However, as we look closely at what happened in both communities, we will have to question whether Red Hill and The Cross had been the community that fostered Ellen and Dylan's faith, as Lillian and Vanessa hoped for.

5. Gaventa, "Learning from People," 104.
6. Post, "Drawing Closer," 30.

On the part of Ellen, we saw clear signs that she understood what it meant to be a member of the community. Her involvement in cleaning up after luncheon was a good example. This kind of incidences indicated that Ellen has learned the etiquette and commitment to be a member at Red Hill. However, no discussion has been initiated by the family or the church regarding Ellen's need for discipleship.

Ellen was baptized as an infant. However, John did not have a specific plan to help Ellen develop her relationship with Jesus and become eligible to receive confirmation. When I brought up the topic with John, he mentioned that the curriculum he planned for the next confirmation class would include visits to different organizations such as the local L'Arche community and doing something together at the food bank. John indicated that if Ellen was interested in participating, he felt confident that Ellen would be able to join these classes with the Circle's support. But until John can put a clear discipleship plan in place for Ellen, Red Hill remains a social community for her.

With The Cross being a Bible school, Dylan had no lack of opportunities to study the Bible and be a part of the learning community. The questions are whether Bible learning alone constitutes discipleship, and how can Dylan be accepted as a member at The Cross? When I asked George these questions, George shared how he discipled the selective youths at Awana. For George, a rising leader knows the Bible well and can share his or her testimonies to encourage others to become disciples of Christ. These young leaders also need to be baptized into an evangelical church (As indicated previously, young leaders at The Cross attend different churches). To the question of baptism for Dylan, George used the seniors in the retirement homes who had "somewhat limited intellectual capacities" as examples to explain his openness to this matter. He clarified that he was not expecting Dylan to recite the whole catechism, but Dylan would need to study the Bible and demonstrate his understanding of the simple truth that Jesus is his savior and Lord. Dylan would also need to memorize some Bible verses and profess his faith publicly. Unfortunately, even with these "simplified" requirements, it is hard to see how Dylan would qualify as a member of The Cross with his current speech and cognitive abilities.

When the issue of faith was not addressed, it is unclear what position Ellen and Dylan occupy within the church. They are certainly loved by their pastors, the Circle friends, and some church members, but we need to ask if they could gain the identity of a Christian? Without an intentional discipleship pathway, how can they be admitted to Christ's body and be regarded as indispensable members of the church?

Issues of Belonging

At the beginning of the book, I mentioned that using the perspective of people with profound autism as a magnifying glass would give us a clearer picture of the belonging issues existing in the church. Now that we have followed Dylan and Ellen into The Cross and Red Hill for one full year, it is time to reflect on what we have seen. Just as the Circle friends describe their journeys with Ellen and Dylan as an eye-opening experience, their collective experiences opened our eyes to three issues: 1) societal value influencing how church members recognize Ellen and Dylan's personhood; 2) the social and superficial nature of the relationships among members of Red Hill and The Cross; 3) lack of spiritual care and discipleship pathways for Ellen and Dylan to belong to Christ's body and participate in the church as contributory members.

Seeing the Person Properly

As Lillian rightly pointed out, many preconceived ideas about autism affect how people in society (the church included) perceive people with autism. Initially, people at Red Hill and The Cross ignored Dylan and Ellen's presence. Without attempting to interact with Ellen and Dylan, people assumed they did not want to communicate with others. According to Carol and Katie, the behaviors that gave Ellen and Dylan the identification of profound autism "bothered nobody," or in George's words, "passively accepted." The congregations might not be "bothered" by their behaviors, but it did not mean that they accepted Dylan and Ellen as a young person worthy of love and respect. The rejection, and in Dylan's case, teasing and mocking, communicated a disregard of their dignity as human persons.

Discussing how we should learn to see every person's dignity and sacredness, Paul Wadell says,

> We have a sacredness and dignity that must be respected and can never be taken away . . . It is not a functional dignity that is determined by social standards and achievements, but an inherent, inviolable dignity that is imprinted in our being by God . . . Our responsibility is to recognize and respect the dignity that is already and always there.[7]

While not addressing the issue of personhood of people with disabilities specifically, Wadell's comment helps us understand that, every

---

7. Wadell, *Happiness*, 123.

person, autistic or not, is created by God and possesses a divine-given dignity. However, Christian traditions do not have a uniform understanding of what constitutes the image of God. When autism is added to the consideration, it further complicates an already complex concept. Therefore, the discussion has to be deferred to the next chapter. What needs to be emphasized here is that people with and without autism should be afforded the same moral status as human persons. The danger of not being recognized as a human person goes deeper than not being welcomed and integrated into a church community. If people with profound autism are not properly regarded as human persons, their lives will not be valued, making them vulnerable to oppression and abuse.

Conversely, loving and respecting people like Ellen and Dylan would help us recognize, as Vanier said earlier, that we are all God's creatures, loved into being by the Divine. To be able to recognize Ellen and Dylan's as persons with their unique personalities, as we have seen at Red Hill and The Cross, was not possible until the Circle friends engaged with them intentionally. These intentional engagements brought about the essential changes in perspectives that opened further opportunities for us to see the issues in our understanding of Christian relationships.

Examining Christian Relationship

By saying that Ellen and Dylan were on a journey to belonging, I have indicated that the model adopted by both Red Hill and The Cross was, at least at the initial stage, one of inclusion. Red Hill's slogan: Everyone is welcome to come in and sit down expresses that sentiment. While every person can come in and be a pew friend, it does not mean that the group, as a whole, functions as a family that they claim it to be. As mentioned previously, Red Hill operates like a community center where people are welcomed to participate in their chosen activities. Certainly, Red Hill expects its people to attend Sunday service. However, beyond greeting each other and extending well wishes, church members did not seem to be aware of what was going on in each other's lives to provide care and support. The situation in which Lillian and Ellen left the church substantiated this conclusion. If Red Hill was a family to Ellen and her parents, why would Ellen not be welcomed at the Sunday school? When Pastor Tom brought the attention of the family's care needs to the church, why would no one visit and offer support? As well, why would the absence of Lillian and Ellen be unnoticed and missed?

Moreover, although Red Hill encouraged its members to organize various events and activities, their participation was not considered as involvement in the family's businesses. Instead, they were recognized as volunteers. This idea was evident in how Lillian referred to Carol and Katie as volunteers, and never in terms such as sisters or aunts, and not even friends.

Putting these observations together, it is evident that the relationships among Red Hill people were mostly social. The ethos of Red Hill as a community of social acquaintances is not uncommon in Canada. In a cross-Canada study titled *Hemorrhaging Faith*, researchers explored why many young adults are leaving the church. In this report, some young people mentioned that they could not find the authentic community they were looking for. They were also disappointed with the hypocrisy of the "superficial people" who do not live out what they believe.[8] One young woman, Anna, was quoted as saying, "I guess one of the things I really struggle with is how people can have a firm belief in God, but they can treat people so horribly at the same time."[9] The rejection of Ellen by some church members reflects the troubling difference between the welcoming community that Red Hill said they were and how they lived it out.

The situation at The Cross indicates a different issue of belonging. Serving on various ministries of The Cross are people who attend multiple churches, a phenomenon not unique to The Cross. David Gay and John Lynxwiler made a cross-sectional comparison of different generational cohorts' spirituality and religiosity. They found that young adults are the cohorts most likely to be "church shopping" and "church hopping."[10] These young people flit around different churches and participate only in activities of immediate interest to them without committing to membership of any specific church. In effect, they belong to no particular church community.

Vanessa commented on these volunteers at the Cross, "They are all outsiders. They didn't need to get in very much and know very much about us." The Cross, in its Awana ministry, functioned almost like a school but without any expectation for regular attendance. Many volunteers and some children came sporadically. The relationship between the volunteers and the children was comparable to an occasional instructor and random students. There was very little friendship between them, not to mention any significant caring for each other's well-being. When most people belong to multiple churches and ministries, the relationship of belonging cannot exist.

How these two congregations practiced their belonging raises the question of the relationship within the church. If the church is the family that is often cited by people in Red Hill and The Cross, how should we relate

---

8. Penner et al., *Hemorrahaging Faith*, 59.
9. Penner et al., *Hemorrahaging Faith*, 59.
10. Gay and Lynxwiler, "Cohort, Spirituality, and Religiosity," 3.

to each other in ways that embody the idea of a family? The question of relationship is a pressing one because until our understanding of the Christian relationship can be reshaped, we will not belong as a family of God. If we belong only superficially with each other, the best that we can offer to Ellen and Dylan is fitting them into the weak models of belonging. Belonging as a social community is not enough for us to fulfill our vocation as Christ's servants that love God and one another. We also would not be able to journey together on a shared path of discipleship.

Belonging to Christ as Members of His Body

The last but arguably most important thing that we need to open our eyes to see is how we value each other's contributions to the body of Christ. Jean Vanier says, "People who are the weakest and least presentable are indispensable to the church. I have never seen this as the first line of a book on ecclesiology. Who really believes it? But it is the heart of faith, of what it means to be the church."[11] Using the human body as a metaphor to help us understand the reality of the church as the body of Christ, Paul says we cannot make the foot feel that he doesn't belong because he is not the hand. We also cannot allow the eye to tell the hand that she is not needed (1 Cor 12:15,21). Therefore, how we can recognize the indispensability of people with profound autism, like Dylan and Ellen, is a question that we need to address.

As Dylan's and Ellen's social circles in the two church communities expanded, what became noticeable was the lack of discussion on their need for discipleship and membership of the church. The church is commissioned by Jesus to make disciples (Matt 28:19). Yet, Red Hill is a social community for Ellen, and The Cross is a school with no monitoring for Dylan's progress nor goals set for his learning. As a church, The Cross encouraged all young people to consider baptism, and Red Hill expected them to seek confirmation. However, these opportunities were never discussed with Ellen and Dylan or their families.

The question of baptism or confirmation is a challenging one for Dylan and Ellen. As we will see in chapter 6, for Dylan to receive baptism and Ellen to receive confirmation, making an intellectual assent to faith publicly is necessary. This requirement raises several questions: How can they receive instructions in ways that fit their unique learning style? Can they be baptized or confirmed when they are not able to communicate their faith? Fundamentally, what needs to be considered is the relationship between faith and cognitive abilities. We must ask if faith in Christ necessarily entails

---

11. Hauerwas and Vanier, *Living Gently*, 74.

skills such as rote knowledge of the Bible, understanding the doctrines, and professing one's faith publicly that are often required to be baptized or confirmed as a member of the church.

Additionally, we also need to explore how to address the indispensability of Ellen and Dylan's membership to the church. Being involved in the church's ministries is a core value in both Red Hill and The Cross. With support, Ellen could serve as an usher and do work in the kitchen. Various members of the church commended her contributions. For Dylan, Vanessa felt that he would not be able to make any contribution to the church because he is dependent on others for his care. Is she right? If not, how are we to understand his contributions to the church and recognize him as a valuable member?

A Way Forward in the Belonging Discussion

As much as The Cross and Red Hill's experiences allowed us to see the issues of belonging with Dylan and Ellen, they also showed us what is essential in bringing about changes. As depicted in Figure 2, the key to change is the intentional engagement church members had with Ellen and Dylan.

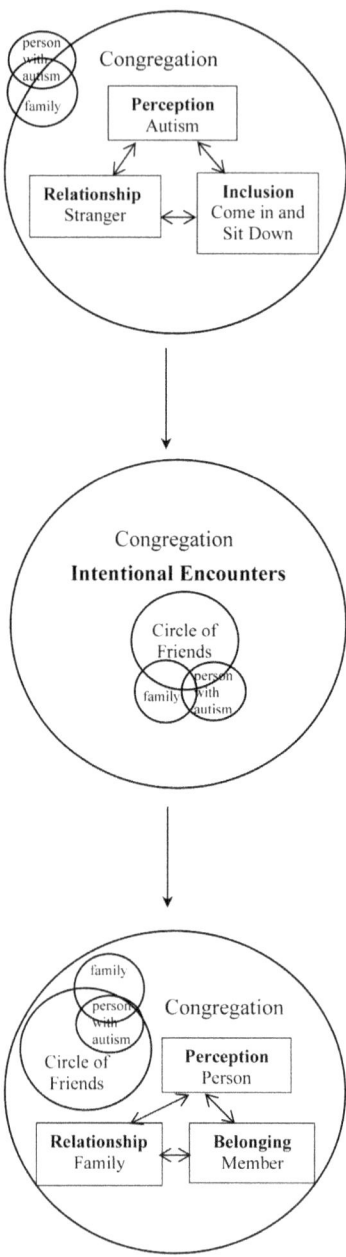

Changes in Perspectives Resulting from Intentional Engagements

When Dylan and Ellen stepped into The Cross and Red Hill, people saw the label of autism and viewed them as strangers. People avoided contact with them. As such, Ellen and Dylan were present physically but invisible to many church members. Before entering into a relationship with Ellen, even people like Carol, who had experience raising a child with a disability, did not try to know much about Ellen. Without approaching Ellen, Carol only knew her as a person with autism and thought she might not want to have relationships with others.

Changes occurred when the Circle friends intentionally engaged with Dylan and Ellen. These encounters helped them recognize the friendly, fun-loving character of these two young persons. Knowing who Dylan and Ellen were beyond the autistic label changed the relationships. Keeping with Carol as an example, her knowledge of Ellen altered dramatically after she approached Ellen and established a relationship with her. Instead of desiring to offer help to Lillian, she began to see Ellen as a friend. Knowing that Ellen wanted to be a part of the community also motivated Carol to create opportunities for Ellen to engage with other church members and be involved with church activities. The expansion of the relationship network and Ellen's participation in church activities further enabled those who intentionally engaged with Ellen to know her personality, skills, and needs.

However, as mentioned earlier, these changes did not go far enough to bring Dylan and Ellen into belonging as disciples of Christ and indispensable members of Christ's body. Even though Ellen and Dylan have begun to move towards belonging, they cannot belong to Christ as members of his body unless their discipleship needs are addressed. The failure to create spaces for Dylan and Ellen, as John Swinton says, "to experience, participate in, and have the opportunity to share the love of God, is a failure of theology and discipleship."[12] Too often, people with limited language and communication skills are assumed to have difficulties understanding the fundamental concepts of the Christian faith. Sadly, this assumption means that people like Ellen and Dylan will be denied the opportunity of discipleship. Without recognizing their potential contributions to the church community, Dylan and Ellen will remain as care receivers and not equal and indispensable members of the body of Christ.

To chart a way forward, we need to consider how the inter-related concepts of personhood, relationship, and membership work in the concept of belonging to the church. A careful look in Figure 2 will show that all three concepts are conceived in the congregational context. With people coming from different churches and getting involved with The Cross as their service

---

12. Swinton, *Becoming Friends of Time*, 93.

outlet, their sense of belonging to The Cross was very week. As Vanessa said, these people did not bother to get to know her or Dylan when they stepped into Awana. The only people who cared about her and Dylan were the pastor and his wife. Most church members treated Dylan as an invisible being, some even mocked him. The indication is that how we function as a church impacts how we acknowledge each other as a person worthy of love and respect. It also determines how we relate with each other and how we practice as disciples of Christ. Therefore, changing how we practice in these three areas requires that we go back to the basics and reconsider what it means to be the church of Christ.

The church is instituted by Christ and powered by the Holy Spirit. It is not an organization established by human will and power. As such, our belonging is first and foremost to Christ, and through him to each other. Acknowledging Christ's headship should remind us that Jesus's commands should govern our community life, not societal standards. In Christ, as members of his body, we engage with each other with the love of Christ, allowing the Spirit to shape our recognition for one another as God's precious creation. This view will enable us to engage with one another in relationships, regardless of our neurological status. We are disciples of Christ and pilgrims on a shared journey of belonging, learning to live out God's holiness requirements in our community life.

With this in mind, I submit that we need to examine the three issues brought up in the above discussion with a "we" approach, with "we" being the church, the body of Christ. In the following chapter, I begin by showing how we should understand humanity and personhood from this collective perspective. Looking at personhood communally does not mean that we ignore the unique person each is created to be. Instead, it allows us to value every person's unique contributions to the corporate whole. The knowledge of "who and whose we are" shifts the focus to Christ, thus enabling us to acknowledge that we, autistic or not, are all indispensable members of Christ's body, existing to be with and for each other.

5

Created in Love to Be with and for Others

> Know that the Lord is God. It is he who made us, and we are his; we are his people, the sheep of his pasture.—Psalm 100:3

BEING A HUMAN PERSON ourselves, we may consider the concept of humanity as a relatively straight forward one. Surely, to be human, one just has to born of a human. This is true in terms of the fundamental nature of human beings. However, when we ask what makes a human being a person, our discussion will become more complicated because personhood is a status given according to certain criteria. A common definition is the one provided by John Locke: "An individual is a person when that individual is a thinking intelligent being, that has reason and reflection, and can consider itself as itself, the same thinking thing, in different times and places."[1] According to this description, a person is an individual who is autonomous and rational. As such, people with profound autism who have cognitive difficulties are humans because of their human descent, but not persons!

Philosopher Peter Singer is a notorious example in this regard. He has long maintained a view that individuals who lack cognitive abilities are non-person.[2] To Singer, human beings who do not have a superior cognitive capacity disqualify them from having a higher moral status than animals. Moral standing, in Singer's definition, is based on the utilitarian value of different beings. Any being that does not please him is not a person. Therefore, an individual with profound autism who cannot communicate with Singer, thus causing displeasure, is less a person than an animal that offers him small pleasure! When the moral status of people with profound autism is slighted, potential danger to their lives arises. The reported cases of murder of children with autism by their parents are stark examples. Anne McGuire of the

---

1. Cited in Vukov, "Personhood," 262.
2. Singer, "Twenty Questions," 72.

University of Toronto describes how the courts considered two murder cases involving young people with autism as forgivable because "it is understandable and condonable."[3] The court's judgments sadly communicated society's lack of regard for the lives of people with autism.

Although the topic of eugenic will not be addressed in this book, the awareness of the danger of misconstruing the personhood of people with profound autism is essential. As Christians, we must speak up for the rights of the voiceless (Prov 31:8). In and through how we value people with profound autism, we can offer an alternative view of personhood to the world, demonstrating that all human lives are valuable. It is also a vital way to testify to God's impartial love for all peoples. That said, we should return to Ellen and Dylan's situations and consider what a Christian concept of personhood that values their lives and contributions would look like.

In 1 Corinthians 12:22–23, Paul says, "the parts of the body that seem to be weaker are indispensable, and on those parts of the body that we think less honorable we bestow the greater honor." The phrases "seem to be weaker" and "we think less honorable" are significant. The indication is that those parts of the body that view themselves as strong are mistaken in how they see themselves and the seemingly weaker parts of the body. Like Ellen and Dylan, some parts of the body are deemed dispensable because they *seem to be* weak in the sight of those who consider themselves wrongly as the body's stronger and vital parts. The question is, how can we see them more appropriately as indispensable members and persons worthy of our love and respect?

Answering this question will require a deeper reflection of how we should behave as the body of Christ. Paul says, "I appeal to you, brothers and sisters, in the name of our Lord Jesus Christ, that all of you agree with one another in what you say and that there be no divisions among you, but that you be perfectly united in mind and thought" (1 Cor 1:10). Disunity happens as soon as we begin to see some people in the community as *them*, who are different from who *we* are. When *we* see ourselves as seemingly strong, we don't think *they*, the seemingly weak, belong. With the strong language of "appeal," Paul impresses upon us that we are brothers and sisters to each other and that we should be perfectly united in our thinking. He draws our attention back to Jesus and reminds us that our common identity is found in Christ. Seeing each other from this common perspective is how we can see that division along the social, economic, or ability line betrays our identity as a united body in Christ.

---

3. McGuire, *War on Autism*, 218.

Therefore, to value the life of people with profound autism, like Ellen and Dylan, we need to change the way we conceive the idea of personhood. If we keep looking for how *they*, people with profound autism, are different and how *we* should receive them, then the dividing line remains. As this chapter progresses, I demonstrate that we need to acknowledge every individual as persons created in God's love to be with and for each other. Focusing on the common identity of all human persons helps us understand that all of us are created for the same purpose—God's creative purpose towards the world. This way of conceiving personhood does not remove the unique characteristics that each of us is given. On the contrary, looking at differences from a collective perspective helps us see each other as parts of the whole and a precious gift.

To demonstrate why a corporate concept of humanity is needed for valuing the belonging of people with profound autism to the church, I begin by guiding readers through the issues in the Christian traditions that use the doctrine of the image of God to define human value. I then offer critiques on several theologians' concepts of the humanity of people with profound disabilities. The goal is to illustrate why these individual concepts of humanness and personhood are essential but insufficient for people with profound disabilities to be regarded as valuable and indispensable members of the body in Christ. These critiques lay the groundwork for presenting a concept of personhood that values each human person as a needed component for the relational network God has created for human flourishing. Applying Bonhoeffer's theology, I submit that autistic or not, all human persons are created in God's love to be with and for others.

Image of God

The creation account in Gen 1:26–27 tells us clearly that God made humankind in his image and likeness. However, comprehending the divine image in humanity is an intricate task. The Bible provides scant information to aid our understanding of the image. The entry of sin (Gen 3) further complicates the issue. To discern God's image as it was given to humanity at creation, theologians have to grapple with the impact of sin on the image and the effects of Christ's redemptive work on the restoration of the divine image in human beings. Although the original image may be considered to be lost or damaged, theologians commonly recognize that it is being restored and moved towards perfection in the eschaton.[4]

---

4. Grudem, *Bible Doctrine*, 190.

Among the many interpretations of God's image on humanity, there are three prominent views: substantive, functional, and relational.[5] Proponents of the substantive view find God's image in human nature (e.g., holiness and rationality) that reflects the divine being in some way.[6] The functional view focuses on God's assignment for human beings to have dominion over the creation. In this view, God's image is what human persons do to represent God's sovereign rule to the world.[7] The relational view confesses God as a relational being based on the plural pronouns, us (God) and them (humanity), in Gen 1:26–27, and the male and female that were created in a relationship. Therefore, theologians holding to the relational view consider relationality as the image of God in humanity.[8]

In what follows, I will explore how theologians holding to different views conceive their ideas on the image of God and how these views might impact the lives of people with profound autism. I will begin with the substantive and functional views of the image of God. I am grouping these two views because of their shared emphasis on human capacities as the substance of the image of God or the ability to represent God's rule over the created world.

Substantive and Functional Views

Among the proponents of the substantive view, rationality is commonly regarded as the nature of humanity that reflects a rational and wise God. As such, humanity is classified as *Homo Sapiens*, the thinking being.[9] In the functional view, God's image is found in what humans do and not in what humans are. However, to be human in this view still necessitates a high level of cognitive abilities. This is because the functional view considers human beings as divine representatives with responsibilities of shepherding and exercising dominion over creation.[10] To be able to fulfill this role, a certain level of cognitive abilities is required. In the following illustration, we will see how the emphasis on rationality will cast doubt on the humanity of people with profound autism.

Augustine of Hippo is a prime example of patristic theologians who assert that the image of the triune God in humanity is found in the rational

---

5. Erickson, *Christian Theology*, 168.
6. Cortez, *Theological Anthropology*, 18.
7. Cortez, *Theological Anthropology*, 21.
8. Erickson, *Christian Theology*, 523–27.
9. Erickson, *Christian Theology*, 523–27.
10. Erickson, *Christian Theology*, 529.

mind, which is also where the knowledge of God exists.[11] The human mind reflects the image of the Trinity with a triad of capabilities: intellect, memory, and will.[12] The original image of God created in the first humans was "defaced" by sin and needed reformation.[13] Faith in Jesus Christ is how people can "get those qualities back again when he [humanity] is reformed and renovated."[14] The reformation process is continuous until humanity regains the image that is "according to the likeness" of Christ.[15] The growth of divine likeness, according to Augustine, depends on a gradual deepening of knowledge and love of God in their minds.[16]

In Augustine's example, we can clearly see the issues of identifying rationality as the image of God. When Augustine defines the rational mind as the locus of God's image in humans, it denies the humanity of people with profound autism and intellectual disabilities who lack rational abilities. Furthermore, if being a part of Christ's new creation requires gaining the knowledge of God in the rational mind, then people with profound disabilities who may not be able to develop this knowledge cannot be included in Christ's new creation. The implication is serious because, with this definition, Augustine has cast doubts on the humanity of people with profound autism and the prospect of them ever becoming humans.

As the example of Augustine has illustrated, using rationality to define humanity is problematic. Whether rationality is considered the nature of human beings as in the substantive view, or human ability to exercise God's dominion in the world as in the functional view, it renders people with profound autism sub-human or non-human. In his comments on Augustine's idea of the image of God, theologian Brian Brock points out that Augustine did not write with an intent to undermine the value of people with reduced intellectual capacity.[17] However, Brock observes from the example of the Holocaust that the emphasis on rationality as the indicator for humanity has an undesirable effect on the moral status of people with limited intellectual capacity.[18] When people with limited intellectual capabilities are considered sub-human or non-human, it makes them vulnerable to exclusion, oppression, and even abuse.

11. Augustine, *Trinity*, 329.
12. Augustine, *Trinity*, 286–303.
13. Augustine, *Trinity*, 387–88.
14. Augustine, *Trinity*, 387–88.
15. Augustine, *Trinity*, 391.
16. Augustine, *Trinity*, 279–80.
17. Brock, "Augustine's Hierarchies" 71.
18. Brock, "Augustine's Hierarchies" 71.

Relational View

More recently, some theologians have moved away from identifying God's image in human capacities and offered a relational understanding of the image. In this view, the divine image refers to the relationship that Adam and Eve had with the Creator.[19] God's image in humanity was lost in the Fall but restored by Christ. Theologians holding the relational view uses God's triune nature to assert that God is a relational being. Therefore, the image of God in humanity should be found in relationality, not rationality.

Karl Barth is a strong proponent of the relational view. He argues that we can only learn about human nature from the revelation found in the humanity of Jesus.[20] Therefore, Barth is critical of any correspondence and similarity between humans and God, as suggested by proponents of the substantive and functional views. He declares that "the being of God cannot be compared to that of man."[21] The image of God, to Barth, "is a question of the relationship within the being of God [as triune] on the one side and between the being of God and that of man [sic] on the other."[22] The correspondence is "an *analogia relationis*," that is, an analogy of relations.[23] What Barth refers to as the corresponding relationship is the I–Thou relationship. He says, "Man [sic] created as a Thou that can be addressed by God but also an I responsible to God; in the relationship of man and woman in which man is a Thou to his fellow and therefore himself an I in responding to this claim."[24] To Barth, the image of God is the human relationality that reflects the loving I–Thou relationship within the Trinity.

Barth's approach of the image of God is persuasive in that rationality, and any other human qualities simply cannot be compared to God, who is far greater than what we could possibly know. The triune nature of God indicates that God is a relational being. Therefore, it is reasonable to suggest that the image of God is found in human relationships. Refuting any human capacity as a corresponding capacity of God, Barth seems to have avoided the issues posted by the substantive and functional views on the humanity of people with disabilities. However, as Barth has pointed out, being in a relationship with God requires that we respond to God and be responsible in the relationship, which implies a need for certain capacities.

---

19. Cortez, *Theological Anthropology*, 24.
20. Barth, *Church Dogmatics* III, 222.
21. Barth, *Church Dogmatics* III, 220.
22. Barth, *Church Dogmatics* III, 220.
23. Barth, *Church Dogmatics* III, 220.
24. Barth, *Church Dogmatics* III, 198.

Therefore, theologian George Hammond is unconvinced that Barth's relational view would not exclude people with "certain severe forms of intellectual disability."[25]

The issues of response-ability and responsibility entailed in the relational model can be seen quite explicitly in Kathryn Tanner's relational view of the image of God. Tanner proposes that being created in the image of God indicates a particular relational vocation. It is a vocation because being the image of God demands that "Human beings reflect God by adopting God's own project of universal well-being. Like the shepherd kings of antiquity, they mediate God's blessings, as best they are able, to both their own kind and the rest of creation."[26] The idea of relational vocation means that people need to act as the shepherd kings to deliver God's blessings. As such, Tanner's relational interpretation of the image of God takes us back to a functional view that would again make personhood inaccessible to people with profound autism.

The trouble in using the doctrine of the Image of God in defining the value of human beings, as Bruce McCormack indicates, is that we have asked the wrong question.[27] Over the centuries, theologians attempted to understand the image of God as a way to justify how humanity is more significant than animals, which is why they looked for capacities that set humanity apart from the animals. McCormack alleges that this approach is wrongly headed. Since humans are created to bear God's image, we should look to God and seek to understand how humanity is like God. When we look to God, we will quickly see that the holy God cannot possibly be described in any humanly conceived property, such as intellect or response-ability. For McCormack, the image of God can only be described Christologically in how Jesus exemplified holiness with his self-giving love.

Humanity from the Lens of Disability

Looking to God, instead of human characteristics, for an answer to the question of the image of God in humanity is an approach supported by several theologians who reflect on the humanity of people with profound disabilities. These theologians identify the values of life with profound disabilities from different perspectives. Some focus on Christ's redemptive work or God's gracious gift of friendship. Others argue for the intrinsic value of life as given by God in the creation of human life. We will see that while the

25. Hammond, *Not Yet Appeared*, 53.
26. Tanner, "Trinity," 65.
27. McCormack, "Misuse of Imago Dei," para.2.

deliberations of these theologians help enhance our understanding of the humanness and personhood of individuals with profound disabilities, they do not go far enough to affirm people with profound disabilities as valuable individuals for the human communities (the church included).

Gift of Friendship

With the belief that "people with profound intellectual disabilities are people just like other people," Hans Reinders, ethicist and theologian, offers a theological consideration of personhood that is dependent on God's grace and not on human capacities.[28] To make his case, Reinders bases his arguments on the observations of Kelly's life. Kelly is a young woman living with a micro-encephalic condition. Although the caregivers talked about Kelly's emotions, Reinders felt that these descriptions were metaphors used to support her humanity. He refutes the idea that Kelly can communicate her feelings because, in Reinders's understanding, Kelly is what the moral culture would call a "vegetable."[29]

To explore how the humanity of Kelly and other people with profound intellectual disabilities should be affirmed, Reinders aptly demonstrates what is true to every person in that God's all-embracing and self-giving love defines our humanity. The value of human life is determined by God's gracious gift of friendship and not on any human capacity or humanly defined worth. Reinders is careful to make sure that reciprocity of love is not a requirement because his understanding of people like Kelly is that they cannot reciprocate love. He argues that friendship, as the gift of God, does not depend on our capabilities to reciprocate the divine love. The truth is that none of us can return God's love in the same way God has loved us.[30]

For those who are able to express love, Reinders alleges that offering friendship to others is our vocation. The idea is that to be friends with people with profound intellectual disabilities is a calling that demands obedience.[31] Reinders find in the example of the L'Arche communities and Vanier's writing that befriending people with intellectual disabilities means seeking to be with them without considering what we may be able to do for them.[32] Through being with people with profound intellectual disabilities, we receive the gift of friendship from God. The process is transformative

---

28. Reinders, *Receiving the Gift*, 1.
29. Reinders, *Receiving the Gift*, 21.
30. Reinders, *Receiving the Gift*, 307–8.
31. Reinders, *Receiving the Gift*, 365–66.
32. Reinders, *Receiving the Gift*, 336.

because the Spirit is at work in our relationship with people with profound intellectual disabilities.

Reinders has brought significant theological insights to the discussion of the humanity of people with profound autism. Instructively, he helped us locate human value in God's gracious gift of friendship. The primary concern I have is Reinders's total disregard of Kelly's potential for communicating her emotions. Indeed, we would not know exactly what Kelly was thinking or feeling, but how do we know that she has no feelings and emotions towards others? Disallowing the possibility that people like Kelly can express their emotions and wishes is an issue because it can be seen as a patronizing gesture. It also eliminates the potential of the relationship to be a mutual one.

Conversely, looking at the experiences of those who have spent a significant amount of time with people with profound intellectual disabilities, we see ample support for people experiencing the love of those with profound intellectual disabilities. The relationship between Henri Nouwen, a priest, and Adam, a person with severe intellectual disabilities, that Reinders referred to in his book, is an example.[33] Although Reinders would not admit that Adam could understand his relationship with Nouwen, by engaging with Adam, Nouwen clearly indicates his experience of Adam's love.[34]

Sociologist David Goode spent extensive time with two individuals who were "deaf-blind and profoundly mentally retarded [sic]."[35] He found that they "had a tremendous repertoire of communication acts."[36] These communication acts were understood by people who knew them intimately like their parents and in Goode's case, by spending extended time with one of the participants.

Acknowledging the possibility that people with profound autism are communicating in their unique ways is crucial. We have seen with Dylan and Ellen that although the two of them use very different communication methods, their Circle friends and others in the community who intentionally spent time with them were able to understand what they liked and disliked without speech. If we interact with people with profound autism without believing that they are competent in communicating in their unique ways, we prevent them from expressing their views and emotions. More importantly, it is an indication of disrespect—thus undermining their humanity.

---

33. Reinders, *Receiving the Gift*, 369–71.
34. Nouwen, *Adam*, 49.
35. Goode, *World without Words*, 7.
36. Goode, *World without Words*, 42.

Moreover, with the belief that people with profound intellectual disabilities can only be passive receivers of friendship, Reinders has not considered the possibility of friendship as their vocation. When friendship is only a vocation of those who can express God's love in ways defined by society, Kelly and others with profound disabilities will remain passive receivers, not participants, and indispensable members of the community.

Intrinsic Worth

In his book *In God's Image,* Archbishop Peter Comensoli articulates a Catholic understanding of the image of God in people with profound disabilities. This book is largely a defense against Reinders's assessments of the Catholic Church's substantive view of the image of God. Comensoli advocates for the intrinsic worth of life with a disability and questions the need and justification of Reinders's extrinsic approach of defining humanity with God's friendship. To counter Reinder's idea, Comensoli stresses the importance of valuing lives with profound disabilities substantively in their bodily existence. He explains that in the Catholic view of humanity, "person" is a dignifying name (*nomen dignitatis*). Being human is "being someone of humankind, living a human life—is simply 'being a person.'"[37] Like every other person, the humanity of people with profound disabilities was conferred at the time of conception. Therefore, their rights and values as human beings should not be put in doubt.[38]

While Comensoli finds the values of lives with a profound disability in the origin of their lives, he is also certain about the telos of their lives.[39] He alleges that people with profound disabilities have the advantage of not knowing how to choose to move away from God. As such, they fare better in moving towards Christ-likeness.[40] What Comensoli implies is that people with profound disabilities are already closer to being like Christ, if not already like Christ, because they are unlikely to do wrong. However, educator Douglas Biklen points out that regarding people with disabilities as holy innocents, not able to do anything wrong, are false. People with intellectual disabilities, Biklen says, "are capable of a broad range of behaviors, and possess individual and complex personalities."[41] Furthermore, Comensoli's proposal is not consistent with Paul's teaching that "all have sinned and fall short of

---

37. Comensoli, *God's Image*, 4.
38. Comensoli, *God's Image*, 24.
39. Comensoli, *God's Image*, 184–88.
40. Comensoli, *God's Image*, 181.
41. Cited in Baglieri, *Disability Studies*, 34.

the glory of God" (Rom 3:23). The danger of considering people with profound disabilities as already or close to being Christ-like, as Biklen astutely observes, is that they may not receive proper guidance. The risk is that their needs for discipleship could be neglected.

To illustrate the value of life with disabilities, Comensoli quotes Pope John Paull II to explain that people with profound disabilities are "living icons of the crucified Son" and "exemplars of how God's salvific plan is meant to unfold for all human beings."[42] This is because the suffering of people with profound disabilities (understood broadly to include physical suffering and marginalization) reflects the human suffering experienced by Jesus.[43] What Comensoli wants to demonstrate with these measures is that the disabling condition is a crucial feature of the humanity of people with profound disabilities. Their values as human beings with disabilities are found in how they can help all of us move towards Christ-likeness. As Stanley Hauerwas points out, the trouble of idolizing the suffering of people with disabilities instead of addressing the social issues that cause their suffering has the effect of accepting avoidable suffering as God's will.[44] Instead of taking the suffering of people with disabilities as a virtue, the church should consider what and how we could advocate on their behalf and work against societal factors that cause their suffering.

Comensoli has successfully made a point throughout his book that people with profound disabilities are humans by virtue of being born as humans. Affirming the essence of the humanity of people with disabilities is undoubtedly essential. However, his arguments do not necessarily help with the issue of marginalization. Even though Ellen and Dylan are human beings and have the rights to be treated as such, sadly, we have seen how people in society and the church have disregarded their humanity and ignored their presence. As Reinders rightly points out, the arguments for human rights will not fundamentally change the marginalizing attitudes against people with profound disabilities.[45] Therefore, our reflection cannot stop at affirming the essence of Ellen and Dylan as human beings. To recognize their personhood, we need to acknowledge the value of their friendship and intentionally choose them as friends. Like people in Red Hill and The Cross have learned, the willingness to engage Dylan and Ellen in relationships opened their eyes to see them more accurately.

---

42. Comensoli, *God's Image*, 200–201.
43. Comensoli, *God's Image*, 201.
44. Hauerwas, "Suffering the Retarded," 104.
45. Reinders, *Receiving the Gift*, 42–3.

Hope in Resurrection

So far, we have read Reinders, an academic, and Comensoli, who contributes academically with an ecclesial perspective. The next thinker I want to engage in this conversation is George Hammond, who wrote his doctoral dissertation from a father's perspective. Hammond's work, *It Has Not Yet Appeared What We Shall Be*, was a reflection on the humanity of his daughter, Rebecca, who has significant cognitive disabilities from birth.[46] As a parent, Hammond advises the church to realize that disability is not just a difference, but that "something is *wrong*."[47] Recognizing Rebecca "as utterly and profoundly broken," Hammond seeks to understand how her broken life can be considered as being made in the image of God.[48]

Hammond argues that the image of God is "badly defaced" by sin. The effects of sin pervasively affect all of human life. Therefore, the world, according to Hammond, is "abnormal."[49] In terms of the existence of disability itself, Hammond reckons that it is the result of surd evil. "Disability is clearly an *abnormal* part of an abnormal world."[50] However, Hammond also stresses that the effects of the surd evil could not obliterate the image of God in people with severe cognitive disabilities. The image is defaced and damaged, but their physical existence as human beings means that they exist as God's image.

With a rather negative view of life with a severe cognitive disability, Hammond's hope for his daughter, Rebecca, is found in the hope for healing and redemption in Christ. With this in mind, Hammond discussed the need for people with profound disabilities to receive the sacraments of baptism and Eucharist. He acknowledged that the cognitive requirements for receiving baptism in a denomination, such as the Baptist, would make the sacraments beyond the reach of people with profound intellectual disabilities. However, Hammond is confident that without baptism, Christian churches such as the Baptist will consider people with profound intellectual disabilities as "redeemed by Christ and in some sense members of the church."[51] Hammond's confidence that people with profound intellectual disabilities as among the elect is essential for his conviction

---

46. Hammond, *Not Yet Appeared*, xxv.
47. Hammond, *Not Yet Appeared*, 218; emphasis original.
48. Hammond, *Not Yet Appeared*, xxvi.
49. Hammond, *Not Yet Appeared*, 121.
50. Hammond, *Not Yet Appeared*, 121; emphasis original.
51. Hammond, *Not Yet Appeared*, 205.

that Jesus remove cognitive disabilities in the eschaton and give Rebecca a transformed body that is without disabilities.[52]

I do sympathize with the difficulties that parents have in raising a child with severe disabilities. However, I have concerns about the significant effects of designating disability as something wrong. This perception would substantially impact the lives of people with profound disabilities and their belonging to the church and society. What we have seen in Dylan's case reflects my concern. In chapter 2, I discussed how his father saw autism as something shameful to have in a family. We have also seen how Vanessa considered evil spirits as being responsible for Dylan's epilepsy and behaviors. These ideas kept the family very much in fear of bringing Dylan out to the community. When the family viewed autism as an effect of evil and a source of shame—something "wrong," something that needs to be rid of, Dylan was kept hidden in the home and away from others.

The literature does not support Hammond's suggestion that Christian churches will accept people with severe cognitive disabilities as members without baptism. They may be included, but their status as members of the body of Christ is untenable without baptism and discipleship.[53] The idea that church communities generally accept and love people with severe cognitive disabilities is also incompatible with Ellen and Dylan's experiences. In The Cross and Red Hill we have seen that before we can even think about their membership with the church, their acceptance by the congregations as persons and not strangers is the first step. It again begs the question that if life with a severe intellectual disability is "wrong," how would the church learn to accept people with a "wrong" and "abnormal" life? How can this kind of life be viewed as valuable?

Although I have serious reservations about Hammond's concept of humanity of people with profound disabilities, he has highlighted the effects of sin on all people. People with profound autism are not holy innocents to be treated as icons. Like all of us, they are affected by sin and in need of Christ's redemption. Acknowledging the need for redemption, Hammond's setting of his hope on the work of Christ is a good reminder. Looking to Christ as the definition of the value of life with severe autism is also the emphasis of Jennifer Cox, the last theologian I will engage in this section.

---

52. Hammond, *Not Yet Appeared*, 231.

53. See, for example, Swinton, *Becoming Friends of Time,* 96–97; Whitt, "Baptism and Profound Intellectual Disability," 60–67.

Gospel-Based Approach

In her book, *Autism, Humanity, and Personhood*, Jennifer Cox seeks to articulate a theological anthropology inclusive of people with severe autism.[54] She uses a gospel-based approach that grounds the humanity of people with severe autism extrinsically on Christ. Cox's attempt is to view the humanity of autism with the lens of Christ instead of the lens of disability.[55]

Cox aligns her understanding of the image of God with the relational view.[56] However, from the way she articulates the issues of the humanity of people with severe autism, a substantive understanding of the image of God is in view. Cox identifies the features of autism as difficulties in "embracing newness, communication, and community participation."[57] With these difficulties, Cox posits that people with severe autism are not like God, who spoke and created the world. As such, they do not possess the image of God.[58] Cox further states that since the first humans who were created in God's image communicated well with God before sinning against God, people with severe autism are also not like Adam and Eve. These observations lead Cox to the similar position of Hammond that sin is the origin of autism, and the redemption of Christ is the solution.[59]

In Jesus, who is the only true human person and the perfect image of God, humanity can regain the image of God.[60] Cox believes that by the power of the Holy Spirit, "the low-functioning autist can have a genuinely reciprocal relationship with God through Christ."[61] However, even when joined to Christ, people with severe autism will not experience healing in this life. Their complete healing will have to wait until the time of resurrection.

Cox contributed to the thinking of humanness and personhood of people with severe autism by grounding them in the person and work of Christ. It provides a way for us to think about our common humanity, as found in Christ. I agree with her suggestion that recognizing the humanity of people with severe autism "provide[s] a sound basis for action in two arenas: The church and the wider society." However, I am not convinced that Cox's

---

54. Cox, *Autism, Humanity and Personhood*, 7.
55. Cox, *Autism, Humanity and Personhood*, 6.
56. Cox, *Autism, Humanity and Personhood*, 49.
57. Cox, *Autism, Humanity and Personhood*, 52.
58. Cox, *Autism, Humanity and Personhood*, 51–2.
59. Cox, *Autism, Humanity and Personhood*, 60–68.
60. Cox, *Autism, Humanity and Personhood*, 126.
61. Cox, *Autism, Humanity and Personhood*, 219.

description of the humanness of people with severe autism could influence the actions of the church and the wider society positively.

In the autism literature mentioned in chapter 1 and the experiences of the two church communities, we learned that how we understand autism determines how we relate with people with autism. We can see quite clearly in Cox's book that she sees people with severe autism with a defective view. The emphasis on their social-communicational difficulties and lack of creativity can be seen throughout her book. These difficulties are also evidence for the loss of the image of God in persons with autism, and why sin is the origin of autism.[62] With a defective view of autism, Cox focuses on finding healing for them; and she sees it in the eschatological healing of their bodies and minds. The implication is that in this life, people with severe autism remain "defective" beings who cannot have relationships with others and, therefore, unavoidably living in perpetual loneliness. As I have discussed at length in chapter 1, considering autism as a defect is fundamentally flawed. The focus of autism as a defect that needs to be fixed or be rid of would lead to marginalization, not inclusion, still less belonging.

If the goal of Cox's project is to influence the church's actions to be more inclusive to people with severe autism, I expect the church's roles to be discussed at some lengths. Yet, the actions of the church are completely missing in Cox's book. Cox's discussion of the loneliness of people with severe autism is one example. Cox alluded to the presence of Christ as their present help, which is true, but where is the church?[63] Being the body of Christ, how should and could the church be their friends and alleviate their loneliness? Cox only very briefly touched on the idea of union with Christ as necessary for people with severe autism to regain their humanity and personhood. The meaning of being united to Christ in his body, the church, is not elaborated. It is only in her conclusion that Cox addresses and encourages the church to receive the gifts of people with severe autism. However, when "defects" of autism are the only qualities discussed in the book, how is the church to discover their gifts?

Humanity: An Individual and Corporate Concept

At this point, it is helpful to summarize what has been discussed. The arguments presented above aim to show that using any human capacity, such as rationality or response-ability, to define personhood will inevitably undermine the values of people with profound autism. Reinders and Cox

62. Cox, *Autism, Humanity and Personhood*, 60–68.
63. Cox, *Autism, Humanity and Personhood*, 138.

share the same concern. They, therefore, look for the definition of humanity extrinsically to the human person. Reinders and Cox's approaches aim to demonstrate the significance of human existence as grounded on who God is and how God relates to human beings. While their strategies are helpful, the trouble is that both have denied the possibility for people with profound disabilities to associate with other human beings. That being the case, they have also prevented people with profound autism from being regarded as relational beings who could connect with others and participate in the community as valued members.

When looking to God for the understanding of humanity, Comensoli's work reminds us of the need to acknowledge the intrinsic values of human life. Each human person is created and gifted uniquely and should be respected as such. Hammond shares Comensoli's belief that the value of human life needs no further justification beyond being born of humans. While acknowledging the intrinsic values of human life is vital, this position has not considered the way human values are accorded in society. Confirming the essence of people with disabilities as human beings alone cannot counter the social factors contributing to marginalization. Hammond's comment about his daughter being an "useless eater" is a case in point. It clearly shows that being recognized as a human does not mean one is necessarily considered a human person with dignity and value.[64]

Hammond and Cox's discussion on sin and their focus on redemption are essential to keep in mind. Although I contest the idea of associating sin with autism, it is necessary to acknowledge that people with profound autism are the same as us—sinful beings who require Christ's redemption. Without losing sight of the hope for the final redemption, we need to understand that Christ's redemptive work should impact how we live as the body of Christ *today*. As Reinders says, the church has a vocation to bless each other and the world with the friendship of God. How we, the church, can live with each other in ways that value the friendship of people with profound disabilities is our testimony to the world that lives with disabilities are as valuable as all human lives.

What I hope is becoming evident in our engagements with the existing concepts on the humanity of people with profound disabilities is a bias of their lack of capacity to express their love and to engage in mutually enriching relationships. Designated as receivers of love and not givers of love, people with profound disabilities remain *them*, the receivers, not part of *us*, the givers. This way of looking at their personhood fails to regard them properly as bearers of God's image that is understood as relationality. It also

---

64. Hammond, *Not Yet Appeared*, xxvi.

disallows them to be engaged in the human relational network, which, as we have seen in Red Hill and The Cross, is vital for recognizing their personhood. When Ellen and Dylan were not recognized as people who desired relationships and able to express their emotions, they were ignored. It was only through intentional engagements that their personhood was revealed to the church members. What this suggests is that personhood must be understood in the relational network of a community.

Moving forward, I engage with the theology of Dietrich Bonhoeffer, whose anthropology is interwoven with ecclesiology and Christology.[65] In engaging his theology with Ellen and Dylan's experiences, we will see how Bonhoeffer's anthropological concept goes beyond illuminating value of individual life. His corporate understanding of personhood provides a framework for us to consider what it means to be "we," a collective being in Christ that live together relationally. Through encountering each other, we learn to become what God wants humanity to be, which is to live with and for each other.

Created in Love to Be with and for Other

Clifford Green describes Dietrich Bonhoeffer's theology as a theology of sociality.[66] In Bonhoeffer's own words, "The social intention of all the basic concepts, 'person,' 'primal state,' 'sin,' and 'revelation' can be fully comprehended only in reference to sociality."[67] The significance of sociality in Bonhoeffer's theology means that the concept of the image of God is also conceived relationally. Bonhoeffer's relational concept of the image of God is found in God's freedom that is for us. With freedom being the image of God, every person who is created uniquely by God is free to be who he or she is. This concept paves the way to consider how we can be a community that is a unity of diversity, in which all, including people with profound autism, are engaged in relationships that support and release each other's freedom.

Bonhoeffer's theology is also strongly Christo-centric. "In Jesus Christ, the reality of God has entered into the reality of the world . . . All concepts of reality that ignore Jesus Christ are abstractions."[68] His concept of humanity is no exception. With the emphasis on Christ, Bonhoeffer elaborates on the pervasiveness of sin and the effects of Christ's redemptive work on the

65. Green, *Bonhoeffer*, 13.
66. Green, *Bonhoeffer*, 2.
67. Bonhoeffer, *Sanctorum Communio*, 21.
68. Bonhoeffer, *Ethics*, 54.

restoration of human relationships with God and each other. The restored humanity is found in Christ, who exists as the church community. This complex Christo-centric and relational concept of humanity add the needed communal understanding of personhood to our discussion. With Christ-likeness as the human telos, Bonhoeffer introduces the idea of relational encounters as how we gain the knowledge of the person of God and the personhood of each other. With this concept, Bonhoeffer helps us see that personhood is not a static concept. Continual engagement with each other is essential for the appreciation of each other's personhood. As we engage with each other in relationships, we grow together and become the humanity God intended for us to be.

Created in Love

To illustrate Bonhoeffer's theology of human, I begin with his exposition on the doctrine of creation in *Creation and Fall*. Here, Bonhoeffer leads us to experience God's love with a moving account of God's creation of humankind with dust from the ground.

> To say that Yahweh fashions humankind with Yahweh's own hands expresses two complementary things. On the one hand, it expresses the physical nearness of the Creator to the creature—expresses that it is really the Creator who makes me, the human being, with the Creator's own hands; it expresses the trouble the Creator takes, the Creator's thinking about me, the Creator's intention with me and nearness to me. On the other hand, it expresses also the omnipotence, the utter supremacy, with which the Creator fashions and creates me and in terms of which I am the Creator's creature; it expresses the fatherliness with which the Creator creates me and in the context of which I worship the Creator.[69]

What Bonhoeffer describes very profoundly is the value of each person in the sight of God. Autistic or not, every person is loved by God and created with the same loving care. The divine love defines the values of all human beings. Each person, autistic or neurotypical, is valuable in the sight of God. While God gives each person unique characteristics, the innate worth of Ellen and Dylan's lives is not reduced because of autism. On the contrary, the differences we see in individual human persons are part of God's design for humanity.

69. Bonhoeffer, *Creation and Fall*, 76.

With a theology of sociality, Bonhoeffer's exposition of the doctrine of creation emphasizes how humans were created as a community. In His love for Adam, God observed that "it is not good that the man should be alone" (Gen 2:18), and He made for him a helper, thus forming a community of two. The two first humans were different yet bonded intimately in a union. "Adam knows that he is bound in a wholly new way to this Eve who is derived from him. This bond is best described in the expression: he now belongs to her, because she belongs to him."[70] In its primal state, the human community was characterized by how humans were created in love and for the love of each other. In this thought, to be human is to be loving beings. Each person is created differently, yet humans are designed to be united with each other in a loving relationship.

Freedom as the Image of God

In addition to creating human beings lovingly, the Bible tells us that God makes humans in the divine image. This image, in Bonhoeffer's theology, is freedom. He says, "To say that in humankind God creates God's own image on earth means that humankind is like the Creator in that it is free."[71] If God's image defines humanity, then what constitutes us as human beings are that we are free to be what God has created us to be. Some may have autism; others may have a superior cognitive capacity, but our cognitive ability does not define our humanity. A person with superior rational capacity is not more human than one with less intellectual capacity. As their friends and some church members have discovered, to see Ellen and Dylan properly is to perceive them as the persons they are. Ellen and Dylan have their unique characteristics. Ellen is outgoing, and Dylan is shy and reserved, but both are God's beloved and should be treasured as such. They should also be given the freedom and support to be what God desires for them to be. To make them conform to any humanly defined standards is to deprive them of their God-given freedom and human dignity.

Remarkably, the freedom that is understood as the image of God is not how we understand freedom in the Western world in that we are free to do whatever we want. Freedom, as an image of God, reflects God's freedom to relate with His creation. "God wills not to be free for God's self but for humankind. Because God in Christ is free for humankind, because God does not keep God's freedom to God's self, we can think of freedom only as

---

70. Bonhoeffer, *Creation and Fall*, 97.
71. Bonhoeffer, *Creation and Fall*, 64.

a "being free for."[72] This is part of the reasons why Bonhoeffer stresses that God's being is for us, but this "for us" concept is more profoundly seen in the giving of Christ, which will be discussed later.

To be created in God's image that is freedom; humanity is to be free for God and others. Towards God, human freedom is for the worship of the Creator. Towards others, "freedom is a relation between two persons. Being free means 'being-free-for-the-other' because I am bound to the other. Only by being in relation with the other am I free."[73] Simply put, freedom is a freedom of love, a love for God, and a love for others.

Bonhoeffer emphasizes that relational freedom does not require a capacity for relationships. "Freedom is not a quality a human being has; it is not an ability, a capacity, an attribute of being that may be deeply hidden in a person but can somehow be uncovered . . . instead, it is a relation and nothing else."[74] Our freedom, as an image of God, is a "created freedom," meaning it is not the same as God's freedom.[75] In divine freedom, God gives us the relationship that we have with God and each other. Our freedom is in reflecting and participating in God's freedom to be with and for others. This idea will again become clearer when we see how Bonhoeffer explains human nature as it is re-created in Christ.

Human's Limitedness and Fallenness

With God's image interpreted as freedom, which is not related to human quality, we may wonder if it is affected by the Fall. Bonhoeffer's Christology takes sin very seriously. To understand his concept of sin, we need to follow his thoughts on freedom and the limit that God has set for the freedom of the first humans.

After making Adam and Eve in the divine image, which is freedom, God sets a limit to their freedom by prohibiting them from eating the fruits of the tree of life and tree of knowledge. Bonhoeffer explains that this limit God sets for Adam and Eve defines the differences between the Creator and creatures. By pronouncing the prohibition, God "indicates to this human being (Adam) who is addressed as a free person his limit or boundedness."[76] What Bonhoeffer wants to point out to us is that human beings are creatures with limits. This limit was set between creatures and

---

72. Bonhoeffer, *Creation and Fall*, 63.
73. Bonhoeffer, *Creation and Fall*, 63.
74. Bonhoeffer, *Creation and Fall*, 63.
75. Bonhoeffer, *Creation and Fall*, 64.
76. Bonhoeffer, *Creation and Fall*, 85.

CREATED IN LOVE TO BE WITH AND FOR OTHERS

God, but also in the human relationship. Eve is "the limit given to Adam in bodily form . . . this very revelation of the limit in bodily form, in the love he has for the other person, would have brought Adam an ever-deeper knowledge of the grace of the Creator."[77] As Bonhoeffer's exposition of Genesis progresses, he explains how these limits were given out of God's loving care for humanity. To have the trees at the center of the garden as limit denotes God's command for humanity to regard him as the center of human existence.[78] When humanity moves away from having God as their center, that is when they face death.

Bonhoeffer's concept of sin reflects his concern for humanity's egocentrism and its social consequences. Sin, according to Bonhoeffer, is humanity's willful act in placing themselves at the center instead of respecting God as the center of our lives.[79] The consequences of that are the broken relationship between humanity and God and among themselves. "Whereas the previous spiritual form had grown up upon the basis of love, the Fall changed this to selfishness. This gives rise to the break in immediate communion with God, as it did to that in immediate communion with man [sic]."[80] The broken relationship can be seen from how Adam and Eve hid from God and covered themselves with leaves. The relational consequence of sin is far-reaching. It is expressed in "the fact that we no longer accept the other as God's gift but instead are consumed with an obsessive desire . . . a desire to get something from others."[81]

In Bonhoeffer's exposition, we can appreciate the pervasiveness of sin and how we are all implicated. However, it is worth noting that sin's effects are found in our broken relationships with God and each other. It is not related to the lack of capacity for relationships. Therefore, it is not only people with profound autism who need Christ. All of us need Christ's redemption to be restored to the relational freedom that we should have as human beings.

Re-Created in Love to Love

In introducing the concept of sin as an issue that affects human's freedom to relate with God and others, Bonhoeffer explains two important theological concepts: vicarious representation and collective person. The

---

77. Bonhoeffer, *Creation and Fall*, 122.
78. Bonhoeffer, *Creation and Fall*, 84–87.
79. Bonhoeffer, *Creation and Fall*, 87.
80. Bonhoeffer, *Sanctorum Communio*, 107.
81. Bonhoeffer, *Creation and Fall*, 124.

fallen Adam is a collective person who represents the humanity that is "extremely egocentric."[82] To reverse what Adam has done in his sinfulness, the God-man Jesus paid the wages of sin on the cross. The love of God in the giving of Jesus constituted a new humanity. As such, Jesus is the vicarious representative for the new humanity and the collective person who "exists as church community."[83]

Significantly, the new humanity regained relational freedom. In Christ, the new humanity is free to be with and for others. Emphasizing our freedom as one that is won by Christ and our continual need for Christ to be the mediator of our relationship, Bonhoeffer says,

> In their freedom from me, other persons want to be loved for who they are, as those for whom Christ became a human being, died, and rose again, as those for whom Christ won the forgiveness of sins and prepared eternal life. Because Christ has long since acted decisively for other Christians, before I could begin to act, I must allow them the freedom to be Christ's.[84]

Like all of us, Ellen and Dylan are members of the new humanity created through Christ's death and resurrection. With the Christ-given freedom, Ellen and Dylan are freed to be who they are. They should not be required to fit into any humanly created standards to be accepted into Christ's body, the church.

With the concept of the vicarious representative of Christ, Bonhoeffer shows us that having received our new humanity in Christ, we now stand in Christ, thus able to freely share in his relationship with God and love God and others as Christ loves us. Just as Christ's freedom is for us, the new humanity created in Christ is called to love God and each other freely. If freedom does not involve capacity, people with profound autism should be included in the new humanity and share in the freedom to love and be loved.

A question that needs to be raised with Bonhoeffer's definition of the new humanity in Christ is the personhood of people who do not profess the Christian faith. If we go to the Scriptures, we can find ample evidence (e.g., John 1:29; 3:16) supporting the effectiveness of Christ's death and resurrection for all people in the world. The possibility of their participation in Christ rests in God's grace and each person's obedience to God's call. Yet our love for all people with profound autism is the same because every one of them is whom Christ has died for.

---

82. Bonhoeffer, *Sanctorum Communio*, 146.
83. Bonhoeffer, *Sanctorum Communio*, 141.
84. Bonhoeffer, *Life Together*, 44.

Being Human, Becoming Human

For Bonhoeffer, although the new humanity has been constituted, humanity still needs the transforming Spirit of Christ to grow into Christlikeness.[85] In this sense, although we have received our new humanity, we need to continue to be molded and shaped to become fully human. This growth process only happens in the community by encountering God in each other and learning our limits.[86] Bonhoeffer describes this process as encounters in an I–Thou relationship. There is a sense that our encounter with each other is what we need to grow into full humanity collectively. Fundamentally, for an individual to exist, "others" must necessarily be there. The nature of the person, "I," arises through the ethical encounter with the other, the "Thou" as a limit, a boundary that "I" cannot cross. In so doing, "Thou" makes "I" responsible or calls him to be accountable for his ethical responsibilities. The divine "Thou" dwells in the human "Thou," therefore, in encountering the human "Thou," one encounters the divine "Thou." Through these encounters with the divine "Thou" in each other, the human person is continually being transformed.[87]

Bonhoeffer's idea of encountering each other as the transforming encounter with the divine "Thou" brings to mind what the Circle friends said about their eye-opening encounters with Ellen and Dylan. These friends reported changes that happened to themselves and the church community as a result of these encounters. John Swinton comments that changes from encountering people with profound developmental disabilities are quite common. He calls these changes a process of "transvaluation."[88] What Swinton sees is that those who encounter people with profound developmental disabilities in friendship, "their priorities are reshaped, and their vision of God and humanness are altered at their very core."[89] Swinton's observation reinforces a need to see people with profound autism properly and encounter and relate with them deeply through Christ, in his body, the church. As Bonhoeffer says, when we recognize each other as a person freed to be what God has created him or her to be and encounter him and her with the love of Christ, we will encounter the divine "Thou" who will transform us in the process.

---

85. Bonhoeffer, *Sanctorum Communio*, 157.
86. Bonhoeffer, *Sanctorum Communio*, 51.
87. Bonhoeffer, *Sanctorum Communio*, 51–55.
88. Swinton, "Body of Christ," 67.
89. Swinton, "Body of Christ," 67.

Personhood Recognized in Relationships

In Bonhoeffer's emphasis on sin's pervasive effects, we can see how we all bear the relational consequence of sin. God loves the world and gives Jesus Christ to die for our sins (John 3:16) and through him to restore our humanity, which is a renewed relationship with God and others. However, we remain dependent and limited beings who need God's grace to regain relational freedom. We also need to experience God's grace through encountering one another in the community to discover and grow in our humanness. The implication is that we cannot be who we are without God and each other. It also suggests that while we have been formed in Christ as the new creation, we still need to grow into the humanity that God intends for us to be. Encountering Christ in and through our relationships with each other is what will enable us to grow collectively in the measure of Christ-likeness.

As discussed in the last chapter, the key to recognizing Dylan and Ellen's personhood at The Cross and Red Hill is the intentional encounter that church members had with them. The indication is that it is our willingness to engage with them in a relationship and the quality of that relationship, instead of their cognitive capacities that are essential to our understanding of their personhood. That being the case, we can say that our personhood is acknowledged in and through the concrete relationships we have with each other.

If the church, as the body of Christ, is where we encounter Christ in our relationships with each other, an essential question to ask is, what happens if Dylan cannot be baptized into the body of Christ? This question is crucial because the church tradition that requires the profession of faith may limit Dylan's freedom to be who he is in Christ. Although Dylan is in the church and may have faith in Christ, his limited communication skills may mean that he will not be baptized, thus remain outside the body of Christ. We need to challenge this church tradition and acknowledge that faith is not something that we can produce no matter how cognitively capable we may be. As this is an issue that deserves a detailed examination, it will be deliberated in chapter 7.

With the communal understanding of humanity, Bonhoeffer's concept of relationality has an ethical emphasis. This ethical dimension of humanity is expressed in his concept of vicarious representation. Just as Christ, who is always with and for us, the new humanity created in Christ, assumes "vicarious representative actions" to live with and for others. Imitating Christ is indeed a biblical mandate for all Christians (1 Cor 11:1). The question is, how are we to understand people with profound autism's role as vicarious representatives? If the vicarious representative actions involve having certain capacities to act, Ellen and Dylan may also be excluded from Bonhoeffer's concept of relational beings.

What we should do is to explore a different way to conceptualize the relational freedom that focuses on who Ellen and Dylan are as persons and not what they can do in the relationship. If we believe that God is love and that "we love because He first loved us" (1 John 4:19), then the freedom to love is not from us but God. To affirm that Ellen and Dylan, like all people created by God, are created to love God and others, we need to expand Bonhoeffer's concept of vicarious representation and consider how Ellen and Dylan can be included in the ideas of "being with" and "being for" others.

To conclude, seeing Dylan and Ellen properly means that we should see them through God's lens. Same as every human person, they were created uniquely and lovingly by God to be with and for God and others. However, to recognize Ellen and Dylan's personhood properly, just as the Circle friends have learned, we need to encounter them in relationships. The question is: what is the nature of the relationships that would allow each person's personhood and value to be readily recognized and affirmed? This question is what I will take to the next chapter, where I will explore the nature of the Christian community and how the relationships in a Christian community could release Ellen and Dylan's God-given freedom to live with and for others.

6

Covenantal Kinship Community

> Yet to all who did receive him, to those who believed in his name, he gave the right to become children of God—children born not of natural descent, nor of human decision or a husband's will, but born of God.—John 1:12–13

IN THE LAST CHAPTER, I explained the connection between personhood and relationship. Although God's love defines Dylan and Ellen's personhood, the recognition of their personhood emerges from their relationship with the church members. What I want to do in this chapter is to explore the nature of this relationship. Agreeing with Bonhoeffer that Christ is always with and for us and that to be like Christ is to be with and for others, I want to explore how to understand our relationship with Dylan and Ellen in this framework.

As we have seen in chapter 4, a community's culture affects the nature of relationships amongst its members. With Red Hill functioning like a community center, the relationship between its members is social in nature. The community at The Cross is comparable to a loosely structured school with no requirement for regular attendance. The relationship among people is thus casual and superficial. As such, people in these two communities could not belong with each other at a deep enough level to be there with and for each other at times of need, much less being there with and for each other's spiritual growth.

In this chapter, I propose an ethos of Christian community that respects human differences and acknowledges all members' values. This proposal arises from engagement with Paul's theology of the Christian community. As the apostle for the gentiles, Paul had to bring people from different geographical, ethnic, and social backgrounds into the body of Christ with the Jews. His instructions on setting aside divisive issues and living a life for others are helpful to our understanding of Christian relationships.

In an attempt to understand Paul's concept of community and Christian relationships, it is necessary to appreciate how Jewish background and the Hebrew Scriptures had a profound influence on his theology. From that background, we will see that the covenant God established with Israel was the blueprint for Paul's thinking of the Christian community. With a theology that centers on Christ, Paul demonstrates that the Christian community formed in Christ restores and renews the covenantal relationship God established with Israel. All Christians, regardless of their backgrounds and social status, are joined to the Abrahamic lineage through Christ. Understanding Paul's theology this way, Christian relationship with God and each other can be described as covenantal in nature.

As covenantal partners of God, Christian relationships took on another dimension. Prominent in Paul's moral instructions to the churches is how Christians should live out their relationships with each other as adopted children of God. In these instructions, Paul points out how they have wrongly allowed social biases and traditional practices to divide the church. Reminding them that Christians are siblings in Christ, Paul urged them to relate to each other in ways appropriate to their identity.[1] Put differently, Christian relationship is one of kinship. United in Christ, Christians are connected in a new relational network as children in God's household, thus siblings to each other.

Having identified the Christian relationship as covenantal in nature and kinship in expression, this chapter examines how this relationship would help us recognize people with profound autism as valuable members of the church. I will pick up from where I left off in the discussion of Bonhoeffer's theology, I demonstrate how the covenantal kinship relationship helps us recognize Ellen and Dylan as beings-for-and -with-others. When we relate with each other as siblings in Christ, the Spirit helps us to live with and for each other in a way that respects differences in abilities and social status. Learning to love each other as siblings in Christ, as we will see, is a discipleship process that brings about transformation.

Paul's Covenant Community

Understanding Paul has to begin by acknowledging that he was a Jewish man with Pharisaic training but living within the Hellenistic culture. All of these backgrounds have some influences on his theology. However, as Victor

---

1. Thompson, *Moral Formation*, 62.

Furnish points out, Paul's theology is primarily guided by Jesus's teaching and the Old Testament.[2] With a belief in God's covenant faithfulness that is fulfilled in Jesus, Paul teaches that Christian identity essentially is "sharers in Israel's identity."[3] In and through Christ, gentiles are joined to God's covenantal promise to Israel and share in the covenant relationship of God with Israel. Together, Jews and gentiles are made into a renewed people of God in Christ. By defining the Christian community as God's renewed covenant community in Christ, Paul applies Israel's covenantal commitment as the holy people of God to the New Covenant church.[4]

The influence of covenant theology on Paul's thoughts, as N.T. Wright commented, is "usually neglected, for understanding Paul," but it is a growing conviction of several Pauline scholars.[5] It is worth noting at the outset that when we say Paul often appeals to the covenant concept in his writings, we are not referring to a central idea that Paul has expounded in any of his epistles. In his book, *Paul's Covenant Community*, David Kaylor explains that "Covenant is a conviction rather than as a concept occupying a persistent presence and a dominant reality in Paul's life, work, and thought."[6] This conviction is evident not by the frequency of the word "covenant" in the Pauline epistles. Rather, the covenant concept is found most prominently in Paul's instructions on the ethical living of the Christian community that "presupposes the thought-world of the Mosaic covenant."[7] With the concept of the covenant being an underlying conviction of Paul and not explicit teaching, before we examine Paul's idea of the church as a covenant community, it would be helpful to briefly describe the covenant concept in the Old Testament. This description will aid our understanding of the Pauline concept of the covenant community that will be elaborated later in this section.

The covenant relationship refers to the relationship that God established with Israel through several covenants (e.g., Abrahamic covenant, Gen 12–17; Mosaic covenant, Exod 19–24). The relationship begins with the divine election of Israel as God's people.[8] The Bible testifies that God, out of love, calls Israel to be God's own son: "When Israel was a child, I loved him, and out of Egypt I called my son" (Hos 11:1). God's

---

2. Furnish, *Theology and Ethics*, 28.

3. Dunn, *New Perspective on Paul*, 444.

4. Brower, *God's Holy People*, xii.

5. Wright, *Climax of the Covenant*, xi. Other scholars who recognize the covenant as the bedrock of Paul's theology are referenced in this section.

6. Kaylor, *Covenant Community*, 3.

7. Kaylor, *Covenant Community*, 10.

8. Chennattu, *Johannine Discipleship*, 59.

unconditional love for Israel in a parent-child relationship forms our understanding of the covenantal relationship between God and Israel, which continues into the New Testament church. However, God's love demands a response. Walter Brueggemann maintains that God's love is "never cheap and never mocked."[9] The covenantal relationship, therefore, carries a mutual obligation. To be chosen as the people of God, Israel is to be holy, as the God who calls them is holy (Lev 11:44). Mary Rekha Chennattu, a New Testament scholar, stresses that remaining loyal to the covenantal requirement of holiness is how Israel can maintain its unique status as God's chosen people.[10] Keeping this brief introduction to the covenant concept in mind, we can now examine how Paul uses the concept of a covenant community to instruct the church.

Biblical scholars who studied Paul's moral teaching identified Paul's concept of covenant community from his insistence on holy living as the embodiment of God's holiness and witness of God's covenantal faithfulness. For instance, New Testament scholar Kent Brower understands Paul as instructing Christians to adopt a holy way of life as their proper response to God's love.[11] According to Brower, Paul teaches that although Israel has failed to uphold their covenant commitment, God remains faithful. The giving of Jesus to the world demonstrates God's fidelity and commitment to the divine covenantal promise.[12] Through the faithfulness and obedience of Christ, God created a new people. The divine election of the new people has an eschatological objective of blessing the nations and all of creation.[13] God also gave the new people of God the Holy Spirit to lead them to live a life not as slaves but as children of God.[14] In Brower's understanding of Paul, living faithfully in a kinship relationship and loving God and each other is how Christian communities embody God's holiness as a witness to God's covenantal love to all peoples and nations.[15]

Thomas Deidun (2006) arrives at a similar conclusion by identifying Paul's moral imperatives from the key indicatives in Paul's instructions. From the ways that Paul addressed the Christians, Deidun points out the covenantal concept embedded in Paul's language.[16] The examples include the language

---

9. Brueggemann, *Unsettling God*, 39.
10. Chennattu, *Johannine Discipleship*, 59.
11. Brower, *God's Holy People*, vii.
12. Brower, *God's Holy People*, 6–13.
13. Brower, *God's Holy People*, xii.
14. Brower, *God's Holy People*, 42.
15. Brower, *God's Holy People*, 209.
16. Deidun, *New Covenant Morality*, 3–35.

of election such as "people loved by God and called to be saints" (1 Thess 1:7); the reference of the church as the assembly of God (e.g., 1 Cor 1:2); and Paul's call and supplication for the church to be the holy people living in a way that is fitting to their calling (e.g., Eph 4:24). With the covenant-infused language, Paul indicates to the church that they are now the new people of God. His imperatives for them are that they should live according to their calling and offer themselves as a holy sacrifice to God (Rom 12:1). The holy way of living, in Deidun's exegesis of Paul's instructions to the Thessalonians, is expressed in "brotherly [sic] love."[17]

Although Deidun and Brower approached Paul's theology from different perspectives, they both identified that Paul's teaching to the church builds upon their identity as God's covenant people. To be in a covenant relationship with God is to be faithfully living out God's calling for Christians to be holy. In Deidun and Brower's understanding of Paul's instructions, to live as God's holy people is to love God and each other with a kinship love. To examine if this understanding is correct, I will turn to the discussion on Paul's "in Christ" theology, another key area of study in Pauline scholarship. Being found in Christ is what links believers to God's covenantal promise. It is also what establishes Christians as children of God, thus siblings of one another. Putting Paul's theological concepts together, we will see that covenantal kinship is the ethos of belonging that describes the relationship that we should strive for as a church. It is also a relationship that will help us think about valuing the belonging of people with profound autism in the church.

Kinship in Christ

As we recognize the significance of covenantal concepts in Paul's writing, we also need to remember the firm conviction of Paul that Jesus is Israel's Messiah. With the establishment of the New Covenant through Jesus's death and resurrection, the church finds its belonging to God only in Christ. The idea of being "in Christ" via union with Christ is central to Paul's idea of what it means to be a Christian. As we will see later, we can only share the covenantal promise of God and the privilege of being children in God's family in and through Christ.

In his seminal work, *Union with Christ in the New Testament*, Grant Macaskill explains,

---

17. Deidun, *New Covenant Morality*, 101–3.

> The union between God and humans is covenantal, presented in terms of the formal union between God and Israel. The concept of the covenant underlies a theology of representation, by which the story of one man (Jesus) is understood to be the story of his people. Their identification with him, their participation in his narrative, is realised by the indwelling Spirit.[18]

Representing humanity, Jesus, the Son of God, fulfills the covenant conditions so that those who are united with Christ can be restored to God and enjoy a covenantal union with the Divine. The union with Christ happens by the power of the Holy Spirit through baptism. Joined to Christ, believers' identity is changed because of their participation in Christ's sonship to God. In Christ, by the leading of the Holy Spirit, Christians cry out to God as "Abba, Father" (Gal 4:6) and enter into a kinship relationship with God and with each other.[19]

Susan Eastman further elaborates on Paul's "in Christ" concept that emphasizes the work of the Spirit. She explains that in Paul's teaching, it is the Spirit who works with, between, and among Christians to join Christians together "in a relationship of shared inheritance with others."[20] This new relationship replaces the old relational web that Paul calls "the flesh" that is dominated by sin (Rom 8:4–9). The grace of God in Christ by the Spirit breaks down the fleshy relationship and "reshape the constitution of persons in Christ."[21] With the familial metaphors of "father," "son," "children," and "siblings," Paul intends to remove "the potentially divisive influence in his mixed congregation" and bring about a unity grounded in our shared identity as heirs of God and coheirs with Christ.[22]

In Macaskill and Eastman's deliberation of Paul's "in Christ" theology, we see Paul's strategic theological move to establish a new and shared identity of all believers. By joining all persons called to Christ into his body, Paul teaches that we have been taken from the world into a new mode of existence. In Christ, Christians now live by the Spirit as siblings in God's family.

The concept of the church as a family and the people of the church as kin permeates the entire Bible, particularly the New Testament.[23] But arguably, Paul is the one who uses kinship language most extensively. In Paul's letters to the various churches he planted; he often addressed his audience as

---

18. Macaskill, *Union with Christ*, 1.
19. Macaskill, *Union with Christ*, 221–3.
20. Eastman, "Oneself in another," 116.
21. Eastman, "Oneself in another," 117.
22. Eastman, "Oneself in Another," 117.
23. Mengestu, *God as Father*, xv.

brothers and sisters. Paul's intensive use of kinship language is widely considered to have significance in defining Christian relationships.[24]

With extensive use of the familial language, Paul impresses upon us that all persons, autistic or not, belong to Christ. When different members are incorporated into the body of Christ, the oneness in Christ establishes the cohesion and solidarity within the body. As a community defined by Christ, our identity is no longer defined by socially defined features such as ethnicity, social status, gender, and for that matter, ability (Gal 3:28).

To create the shared identity in Christ, as Caroline Johnson Hodge explains, Paul joins the gentile believers to the family lineage of Israel through Christ, who is "the seed of Abraham" (Gal 3:29). As such, gentiles who belong to Christ also belong to Abraham, the founding ancestor of Israel. "By means of this kinship-creation, gentiles are adopted sons [sic] of God and coheirs with Christ."[25] Abraham's faithfulness is what guarantees that the divine promise will come to all of God's descendants, both Jews and gentiles. "Christ's faithfulness implements this promise for the gentiles" and forms the new lineage.[26] Hodge uses both the rebirth and adoption metaphors to explain how gentiles are given a new identity in Christ. She sees baptism as the rite through which transformation takes place.[27] To Hodge, baptism is both an adoption rite which shows that the gentiles are accepted into the new family, and an occasion of rebirth. The transforming work of the Spirit in baptism causes the rebirth of gentiles as the sons and daughters of God.[28] With the exposition of the texts, Hodge suggests that being in Christ cuts across ethnic identities. However, she maintains that it does not abolish them.[29] What Paul emphasizes with the concept of common heritage is that Jewish and gentile believers are now brothers and sisters in Christ.

Instead of understanding Paul as establishing a common heritage for the gentiles, biblical scholar John Barclay contends that a common trust-relationship with God is Paul's strategy for joining the gentiles to the family of God. He points to Gal 3 to support his argument. Barclay holds that the promise was given because of Abraham's trust-relationship with God. The gentiles are given a new identity when they share the same trust in God's

---

24. See, for example, Birge, *Language of Belonging*, xxi; and Rhoads, "Children of Abraham," 284.

25. Hodge, *If Sons, then Heirs*, 5.

26. Hodge, *If Sons, then Heirs*, 91.

27. Hodge, *If Sons, then Heirs*, 75.

28. Hodge, *If Sons, then Heirs*, 115.

29. Hodge, *If Sons, then Heirs*, 135.

promise that is fulfilled in Christ.[30] Barclay further observes the difference between the children born according to flesh and those born through the promise in Gal 4. To support his argument, he uses Paul's teaching that children born through the promise are accepted as children of God. It is trust in God's promise and not the ancestral relationship with Abraham that is important. Those who trust in God's promise, be they Jews or gentiles, are children of God.[31] The identity of being in Christ is a new identity for both Jews and gentiles. Both need to be adopted and led by the Spirit to cry "Abba, Father."[32] The particularities of the believers—ethnicity, gender, social status, etc.—are not erased by their new identity in Christ. In fact, these differences are "of inestimable value."[33] In Christ, our primary identity is the child of God. However, according to Barclay, this new identity "takes its shape (not its origin) in a life of human reciprocity and mutual construction."[34] As we will see later in this chapter, it is in learning to negotiate differences in our life together that our kinship can be fully developed.

Approaching Paul's efforts in uniting the Jews with the gentiles differently, Hodge and Barclay arrive at the same crucial point. What is central to the Christian identity is that all are children of God and siblings to each other. With or without autism, each person is created uniquely by God; thus, differences are part of who we are as human beings. These differences do not change our identity as God's children. Commenting on the question of equality among all who have been adopted into the new family of God, John Elliot offers a useful metaphor:

> To put it in a musical idiom, the concern was to get as many persons as possible into the same choir and on the same page conceptually, religiously, and emotionally, not to make them all organists, directors, or one mass *Favoritchoir*.[35]

When people with and without profound autism are grafted into Christ, we all share the same identity as children of God that praise God with different voices and in various roles in the "choir." Differences that exist in harmony are what make the music beautiful to God's ears.

However, as indicated in the previous chapters, there are barriers for Dylan and Ellen to be accepted as members of Christ's body, thus sharing

---

30. Barclay, "An Identity Received," 357.
31. Barclay, "An Identity Received," 361.
32. Barclay, "An Identity Received," 363.
33. Barclay, "An Identity Received," 371.
34. Barclay, "An Identity Received," 371.
35. Elliott, "Jesus Movement," 105; italics original.

the same identity with us as children of God. If Ellen and Dylan are to be recognized as children of God, as Hodge and Barclay pointed out, they have to share in the faith of Abraham and be baptized into the body of Christ. If their baptism or confirmation is denied because of their difficulties in articulating their faith, the question is whether they can be counted as God's children and our siblings? When the question is framed this way, we can appreciate the serious implications attached to it. With the complexity involved in addressing the issue, the examination of it has to be deferred to the following chapter.

Thus far, we have discussed the importance of covenant in Paul's theology. We have also seen how in Paul's theology, regardless of backgrounds and abilities, all Christians are grafted into Christ and gained a shared identity in Christ. Joining in Christ's relationship with God, his father, believers, being found in Christ, are siblings to each other. In the following section, I will draw together the concepts of covenant and kinship in an attempt to get closer to the relationship between our identity as siblings and how we should relate in a way appropriate to our Christian identity.

Covenantal Kinship

Kinship as an expression of covenantal relationship is a concept that existed throughout biblical history.[36] In his influential work, *Kinship and Covenant in Ancient Israel*, Frank Moore Cross observes that the biblical covenants have many parallels with the ancient Near East's treaty culture. In this culture, kinship terms such as "love," "brotherhood," "fatherhood," and "sonship" are used to characterize the covenant relationships.[37] Scott Hafemann elucidates that the biblical concept of covenant establishes the God-people relationship in the following ways: (1) the essential character of God as King or Sovereign Ruler, (2) the election of a people under God's rule as the "adopted" children in the divine family, living in dependence upon him, and (3) the corresponding nature of God's bond with them as their "Sovereign Father."[38] Essential to this way of understanding God's covenant-giving grace is that the covenant is not a legal or economic treaty but an expression of God's steadfast love. Over biblical history, God pursues a people, calling them into a binding covenant expressed in a parent-children

---

36. See Hahn, *Kinship by Covenant* for extensive research on kinship as the divine-human covenantal relationship over biblical history.

37. Cross, "Kinship and Covenant," 5.

38. Haffmann, "Covenantal Relationship," 24.

relationship. God's faithfulness to the everlasting relationship with people reveals a purposefulness in God's covenantal acts.

The Covenanting God

Compellingly, Walter Brueggemann demonstrates to us the Bible's witness to God's fidelity to people that God has chosen to be divine possession.[39] Beginning with Abraham (Gen 15:7–12) and continuing through Noah (Gen 9:8–17) and Moses (Exod 19:1–Num 10:10), God had promised to be the God of Israel and claimed them as the people of God. Legitimately, when Israel failed to fulfill its covenantal obligations, God could terminate the covenantal relationship. However, in what Brueggemann calls God's pathos and passion, instead of ending the relationship, God "deepened and intensified" it.[40] Even when Jerusalem was being destroyed, and the Israelites were being sent into exile, God would not give up the beloved child.[41] God's enduring fidelity led to the pronouncement of the New Covenant in Jer 31:31–34 and Ezek 36:24–28 and the subsequent fulfillment of it in Jesus (Matt 26:26–29).

With a detailed exposition on the covenant formula, Rolf Rendtorff's (1998) echoes Brueggemann's assertion of God's unchanging commitment to Israel. The covenant formula refers to God's declaration to Israel: "I will be your God, you shall be my people" (Jer 7:23). Rendtorff observes that the formula is used in three various forms along with different formulaic elements: the term "choose," a transitional reflection ("in order to be"); the term "covenant" (*bérît*) itself, an exodus (or, deliverance) statement; a self-introductory formula ("I am the LORD"), and a recognition formula ("they will/you will know").[42] The use of these elements indicates a process by which Israel becomes God's faithful people. During this process, Israel was not always loyal; but God remains faithful to the "everlasting covenant" established with Abraham.[43] Through the prophets, God promises to give people a new heart and put a new spirit within them (Jer 36:26; Ezek 36:26) so that people will have God's law in their minds and hearts (Jer 31:33). Rendtorff's interpretation is that the prophets were proclaiming an "impending future of the

---

39. Brueggemann, *Theology of the Old Testament*, 296–313.
40. Brueggemann, *Theology of the Old Testament*, 299.
41. Brueggemann, *Theology of the Old Testament*, 301.
42. Rendtorff, *Covenant Formula*, 14, 39–49.
43. Rendtorff, *Covenant Formula*, 83.

final, untroubled relationship between God and Israel" that is to be found in the New Covenant—the final and everlasting covenant.[44]

This brief review of the covenant scholarship shows that no matter how we understand the covenants in the Bible, what is clear is, as Roger Beckwith says, the covenant has "controlling importance" in both Old and New Testaments.[45] Consistently, God demonstrates his love for the chosen people (Israel in the past, the New Testament church now). Through the covenants, God guides us to respond to the God-initiated gracious promises with obedience and faithfulness.[46]

Using Hos 11:1–4 as an example, Duane Andre Smith illustrates the covenantal kinship between God and Israel. In Hosea, we learn how Israel was claimed as God's son when the Israelites were still slaves in Egypt. With intimate language that describes God as father and mother to Israel, Hosea describes the kinship relationship that God desires to have with Israel. This relationship is covenantal because it involves mutual obligations. However, these obligations are not legal in nature. With the images of cords of kindness and the bands of love (v. 4), Hosea's idea is that God loves Israel like a parent attached to a child by the umbilical cord. The cord binds both sides intimately and mutually in a parent-child relationship of love. Therefore, Israel's rightful response is to love God and commit to being God's obedient children.[47]

Having established the significance of covenant kinship in biblical history, we can appreciate why Paul emphasizes the covenantal commitments of holy living and sibling love in his teaching. God's untiring covenanting efforts with the people of Israel, according to Rendtorff, moves humanity along the process of becoming "*one* people with *one* king in *one* kingdom."[48] Jesus Christ fulfilled this ultimate covenanting purpose of God, but the consummation of the oneness of the kingdom is to be realized in the eschaton. In the meantime, the church which lives under the New Covenant needs to consider what it means to be living faithfully as a covenant community of God in response to the divine love and to obediently love God and others.

---

44. Rendtorff, *Covenant Formula*, 90, 63.
45. Beckwith, "Unity and Diversity," 98.
46. Beckwith, "Unity and Diversity," 103.
47. Smith, "Kinship and Covenant," 41–53.
48. Rendtorff, *Covenant Formula*, 36; emphasis original.

Covenanted People

If we consider the covenant with God as a binding commitment, the key command of God for the people is that "You shall be to me a kingdom of priests and a holy nation" (Exod 19:6). The Ten Commandments given at Mount Sinai and the detailed prescriptions of community life in the Torah were given to direct people to holy living.[49] Elmer Martens, an Old Testament scholar, indicates that we often view the idea of commandments as something "legalistic and harsh."[50] What is often neglected is that the Ten Commandments were given after God self-identified as "I am the Lord your God" (Exod 20:2). In other words, the Ten Commandments are the required responses to God's offer to be our God. The indicative that "the Lord is our God" is what leads to the imperative of a "rightful response."[51]

With a deep appreciation of fidelity as the essence of God's covenantal relationship with Israel, Brueggemann brings an affective dimension to understanding Israel's response to God's covenantal love. He finds that at the core of Israel's obligation to God is the desire to please God and to be with God.[52] This way of responding to God's covenantal love will bring "the dimension of joy" instead of a sense of burden.[53] Brueggemann explains this kind of response as the obligation to listen and to do justice and the invitation to see and be holy.[54] To listen is to obey God and do justice. To do justice is to treat each other well and sustain each other as full members of the community. Justice as a response is to listen as God is listening. Just as God has "a preferential option for the poor and the marginalized," God's people need to be aware of the needs of the oppressed and marginalized.[55]

Paul Hanson brings a thought similar to that of Brueggemann in terms of the motivation behind acting justly towards each other, especially those who are oppressed and marginalized. In his book, *The People Called*, Hanson pieces together a set of characteristics of the people called by God. From the narratives in Gen 12:39 and Exod 11:5, he constructed what he calls "the Yahwistic notion of community" using three seemingly unrelated terms: worship, righteousness, and compassion.[56] Hanson explains that

---

49. Brueggemann, *Unsettling God*, 32.
50. Martens, *God's Design*, 69.
51. Martens, *God's Design*, 69.
52. Brueggemann, *Unsettling God*, 26.
53. Brueggemann, *Unsettling God*, 26.
54. Brueggemann, *Unsettling God*, 26–33.
55. Brueggemann, *Unsettling God*, 27.
56. Hanson, *The People Called*, 10.

worship is the primary defining feature of the initial community of God. This worshipful community praises Yahweh for His holiness. "The holy God Yahweh did not look on injustice with indifference, but with incisive action."[57] God's righteous judgment against oppressive practices, thus becomes the foundation of Israel's law and social structures. As a worshipful community, Israel remembers the fidelity of God in keeping the covenantal promise to them. Consequently, God's compassion (*ḥesed*) forms the norm of all relationships.[58] Righteousness and compassion should be evident in God's community because they emerge from the worship of the God of all compassion and righteousness. As such, God's people are called to be agents of God's compassion and righteousness with the "final goal of drawing all humans into the *shalom* intended by God."[59]

In a different way, Brueggemann and Hanson conveyed the same idea that the covenantal relationship is a relationship of love. It is not a coincidence that these two biblical scholars are both drawing our attention to God's special loving care for the marginalized. As Hanson rightly points out, out of a worshipful life should be faithful practices of justice and compassion. God takes the initiative to love us and binds us into a parent-children relationship. None of us deserves God's love. As we receive God's unconditional love, our proper response is to love God back and enjoy our relationship with the Divine as an act of worship. As God loves us and shows concern for our lives, our response to God is to love God and show love and concern for others' lives.

Implications for the New Covenant Church

We have come a full circle in following Paul's theology of community. Thus far, I have explored the theological underpinning of Paul's idea of the Christian community and examined the concepts of covenant and kinship. I also considered the relationship between these two concepts. Given that the covenantal kinship is the relationship God desires to have with the elect, we can conclude that the Christian relationship is covenantal in nature and kinship in expression. It is covenantal because our relationship with God is found on God's covenant with Israel but fulfilled in Christ. The New Covenant, established through the redemptive work of Christ, brings believers into the covenantal relationship with God. If each of us is in a covenantal relationship with God, our relationship with each other is also covenantal in nature.

---

57. Hanson, *The People Called*, 27.
58. Hanson, *The People Called*, 10–29.
59. Hanson, *The People Called*, 471.

Christian relationship is one of kinship because it is the relationship established by our covenant with God through Christ. In Christ, we are given the new identity as God's children and connected in a relational network of kinship. This identity unites all of God's children as one family in Christ. When the oneness in Christ defines who we are as a community, individual differences, such as those presented by autism, should be a non-issue for our love for each other. Striving to live harmoniously and lovingly with different siblings is what we should do to reflect God's love for all peoples. The relationship of kinship also means that the Christian relationship should be a nurturing one, not the superficial and social relationships we have seen at The Cross and Red Hill.

Additionally, since being a child of God is an identity given by God, our relationship with each other is both a given and a gift. It is a given because, as a child in the family, we cannot choose our siblings. It is a gift because each person is a bearer of God's gift for the common good of the community (1 Cor 12:7). Accordingly, the sibling community welcomes Ellen and Dylan because they are God's gifts given for the good of the community. We should receive them as such and love them as beloved siblings.

The covenantal nature of our kinship carries with it a commitment—a commitment to love God and each other. God's covenantal relationship with us modeled for us how we are to relate with each other. The divine covenanting act is unconditional. God takes the initiative and offers divine love to all peoples and nations. Therefore, our love for others cannot be conditioned on any socially defined standards. As a kinship community established by God's covenant with us, we are committed to loving every person: autistic or neurotypical, rich or poor, strong or weak, in the same way.

Loving our siblings with profound autism should also include a recognition of their love towards us. Ellen and Dylan express their love for people in ways that are unique to their communication styles. Their communication efforts should be respected and supported so that there can be a mutuality of love between siblings.

Looking at God's covenantal purpose, it is clear that the divine desires to have a people who belong to God, who love God, and who love one another. This community created in Christ includes people of differing backgrounds, status, and abilities. Paul's mandate then, and the church's continual mandate now, is to consider how to live out our community life in a way that pleases God and fulfills the Eternal God's purpose to and for the world. With this understanding, I will now explain what belonging with people with profound autism in a covenanted kinship community should look like.

Kinship Love

The relationship between Paul's extensive use of kinship language and his moral teaching has caught the interest of scholars from different disciplines.[60] Some thinkers consider that Paul is using the kinship language as a rhetorical device; others compare his instructions to the concept of family in the Greco-Roman world. However, regardless of one's approach to understanding Paul's teaching, when the contents of these instructions are inspected, there is an agreement that love is central to Paul's ethical teaching for the community.[61]

The love that Paul emphasizes in his teaching on Christian relationships, according to Scott Bartchy, is a sibling love that is counter-cultural.[62] Paul urges Christians to "not think of [themselves] more highly than [they] ought to think," but "love one another with brotherly [sic] affection. 'Outdo one another in showing honor' (Rom 12:3, 10)." This way of treating each other is different from the common practices in society, be it at Paul's or our time. Contrary to giving higher honor to people of certain social status (e.g., gender, ethnicity), Paul teaches Christians to live a life as a "living sacrifice" (Rom 12:1). As such, Christian siblings should seek to *give* themselves to others rather than to *take* from others.[63] Imitating Christ's self-giving love, the community of siblings should also be a community that is committed to living with and for each other. If Bartchy is correct in his interpretation of Paul's teaching, then there is a clear parallel between Paul's idea and Bonhoeffer's concept of Christian's responsibility to live with and for others. In my critique of Bonhoeffer, I indicated a need to explore further his idea of "being for others" to ensure that it does not entail certain capacities for doing things for others. In what follows, we will see how Paul's teaching helps to clarify what it means for us to live with and for each other in a way that respects differences in abilities and social status.

Nature of Kinship Love

Love is an easy word to say, but it is not easy to practice. James Thompson highlights that "love is not an emotional response, but the responsibility

---

60. See, for examples, Aasgaard, "Brotherhood," 166–82; and Birge, *Language of Belonging*.

61. Banks, *Paul's Idea of Community*, 52–54.

62. Bartchy, "Undermining Ancient Patriarchy," 71.

63. Bartchy, "Undermining Ancient Patriarchy," 70–73.

for others."⁶⁴ He demonstrates from Paul's teaching that love sometimes involves actions that entail relinquishing one's rights and comfort. It might even require us to suffer for the sake of others or the community's benefits. Paul's first letter to the Corinthians is filled with such examples.⁶⁵ For instance, in his reproach with regards to the lawsuits against believers (1 Cor 6:1–11), Paul teaches people to value the community's unity even if it means that they have to suffer losses. Another example can be seen in chapter 8 concerning food offered to idols. Paul's admonition to the Corinthians is for them to consider what will build up a "weak person" (1 Cor 8:11). In Thompson's read of Paul's instructions, we can see that Christian relationship is not merely a social relationship. As a covenantal kinship relationship, being brothers and sisters in Christ is a responsibility both to God and each other. To love each other as siblings means loving each other in the self-giving way God has loved us.

To love in a self-giving way cannot be achieved from following a set of rules. Thomas Ogletree indicates that in Paul's theology, God's grace is the very basis of our relationship. "The grace of God is what liberates peoples on all the earth from their compulsive attachments to their own norms of social order that they might be free to negotiate a common life with one another."⁶⁶ On our own, our sinfulness will lead us to value ourselves over others instead of putting others first. What we need is to acknowledge our need for God's grace and the Spirit's mediation in our relationships.

Ogletree further explains that living out a committed and loving relationship involves a continual renegotiation in a way that would allow diversity to remain and all to flourish.⁶⁷ What is required is for us to adopt "a stance of mutual recognition and regard instead of a mere tolerance of human oddities."⁶⁸ The negotiation would also involve reordering our priorities and putting others first with a commitment to build up others.⁶⁹ Ogletree again reiterates that it is the grace and love of Christ that frees us from selfish love and enables us to love God and love one another, thus grow together into Christ-likeness.⁷⁰

Understanding sibling love as founded on God's grace and sustained by the power of the Holy Spirit is essential in our learning to be a community

64. Thompson, *Moral Formation*, 160.
65. Thompson, *Moral Formation*, 161–66.
66. Ogletree, *Use of the Bible*, 158.
67. Ogletree, *Use of the Bible*, 158.
68. Ogletree, *Use of the Bible*, 159.
69. Ogletree, *Use of the Bible*, 135.
70. Ogletree, *Use of the Bible*, 168.

of love with people with profound autism. As all of us are dependent on the Spirit to enter into a loving relationship with each other, the way that we can love and be loved is not different from how Ellen and Dylan can love and be loved. All of us are lovable because each is created uniquely and lovingly by God. Furthermore, as we have seen in Ellen and Dylan's cases, autism may affect how they express love; it does not eliminate their ability to love. Living without autism also does not necessarily make us more loving. We can only commit to loving each other as siblings and see each other as more important than ourselves "out of reverence for Christ" (Eph 5:21). As we are summoned to be a community of God, we should receive each person, autistic or not, with the love of Christ, learning to give ourselves to each other and support each other to flourish in life.

Being with Others in Unity and Interdependence

Bringing people with different backgrounds together to form a church has never been easy. Division along ethnic, social-economical lines is evident in Paul's letters to various churches. He often had to address issues related to the inner dynamics and relationships within the church communities to bring unity to the church. To foster unity and harmony, Paul teaches Christians that they are all created differently, but all are equally valuable members of Christ's body.[71] However, there are different interpretations and applications of Paul's concept of the body of Christ.

Approaching Paul's epistles from the perspective of disability, Graham Monteith stresses that "equality is central to Paul's manifesto for the new church."[72] Monteith sees in Paul's teaching that every Christian is equal because of their shared faith. Every person is accepted into the body of Christ by faith through baptism. The same baptism that we receive commends the indispensability of all members in Christ's body.[73] With an equal standing in Christ, Monteith advocates that people with disabilities have the right to exercise their gifts and be given the opportunity to do so.[74]

Monteith explores the meaning of equality out of concern for the church's rejection of people with disabilities as members. His desire to argue for people with disabilities to be acknowledged with equal status in the body of Christ is admirable. However, Monteith's argument of equal rights carries

---

71. Banks, *Paul's Idea of Community*, 2.
72. Monteith, *Epistles of Inclusion*, 121.
73. Monteith, *Epistles of Inclusion*, 69.
74. Monteith, *Epistles of Inclusion*, 124.

a social and legalistic tone that is not necessarily part of Paul's vision for the Christian community.

Contrary to Monteith, John Elliot attests to the idea of Christians as "discipleship of equals."[75] He alleges that Paul's concern is not equality in political, economic, or social life, but "the inclusiveness of the believing community and oneness and unity of persons who are 'in Christ.'"[76] The oneness of all believers results from baptism that moves their belonging from the world to Christ. However, being in Christ does not eliminate the differences in a person's status (social, gender, and ability). What it does is giving Christians a new identity as children of God and siblings to each other.

What becomes evident through the dialogue with Elliot and Monteith is that social-political equality might not be the best way to look at Christian relationships. Following Paul's teaching, a better way to understand Christian relationships is to focus on what unites us despite our differences. Jean Vanier says, "We may be different in race, culture, religion, and capacities, but we are all the same, with vulnerable hearts, the need to love and be loved, the needs to grow, to develop our capacities, and to find our place in the world."[77] When we look at the basics of who we are as human persons, we can see what Vanier leads us to see. We can learn to be with each other in unity only through recognizing our sameness: We are all dependent, vulnerable people needing to be loved. We also need God and are dependent on God. At the same time, every person is equally loved and valued by God. As siblings, we do not seek our legal rights (1 Cor 6:1–11). We love each other because God first loved us (1 John 4:19).

Additionally, we do well to remember what Paul teaches us about Jesus's example of humility (Phil.2:68). Jesus, who is equal to God, does not use his equality with God as an advantage. Instead, he humbles himself and is obedient to the end; he even dies on the cross for all humanity's benefit. Dietrich Bonhoeffer explains this well: "[S]ince the love of God, in Christ's vicarious representative action, restores the community between God and human beings, so the community of human beings with each other has also become a reality in love once again."[78] Christ's willing self-emptying act should inform our thinking and actions towards one another. We can live in a way that is *with* each other when we seek to love like Christ in a self-giving way that is *for* others.

---

75. Elliot, "Jesus Movement," 174.
76. Elliot, "Jesus Movement," 174.
77. Vanier, *Becoming Human*, 153.
78. Bonhoeffer, *Act and Being*, 157.

In the discussion of self-giving, a related issue that needs to be explored is reciprocity. As we give, do we expect the receiver to give back in the same way that we give? In a situation that Thomas Reynolds calls economics of exchange, reciprocity "regulates interaction in a community."[79] To be expected to reciprocate in an exchange of social goods puts people with profound autism in a disadvantaged position because of a lack of social capital.[80] Reynolds advocates for affectionate reciprocity rooted in an economy of grace.[81] He describes this economy wonderfully: "All things have being insofar as they participate in a dance with other beings; and such interrelation connotes interdependence."[82] In dancing, the partners coordinate their steps and follow the rhythm of the music together. Similarly, in a Christian community, all members, regardless of their neurological status, depend on each other and support each other lovingly as they follow the rhythm of Christ's work in the world together.

The community of siblings is a community of people from diverse backgrounds and with varying abilities. The essential thing to keep in mind is that Dylan and Ellen, like all of us, are called by God into the community and gifted for the common good (1 Cor 12:7). Being united in the body of Christ does not eliminate the differences introduced by profound autism. When all of us, Dylan and Ellen included, can live with each other lovingly despite our differences, the unity arising from our love for each other offers opportunities for the body to grow in holiness.

Being for Each Other

Moving from "being with" to "being for," we need to revisit Paul's teaching on the purpose of the Christian community. As mentioned earlier in the chapter, James Thompson perceives that Paul's work of community building is based on God's covenantal promises. Therefore, he considers holy living in Christian communities as "the ultimate goal of Paul's work."[83] Attaining holiness is a process in which we need the Spirit's guidance, but also each other's support. If Thompson is right, then our being for each other has the individual and corporate growth in holiness as our goal.

Similar to Ogletree's idea of negotiation and renegotiation, Banks observes in Paul's teaching the need for constant realignment in the

---

79. Reynolds, *Vulnerable Communion*, 56.
80. Reynolds, *Vulnerable Communion*, 58.
81. Reynolds, *Vulnerable Communion*, 161–66.
82. Reynolds, *Vulnerable Communion*, 161.
83. Thompson, *Moral Formation*, 2.

relationships within a community for transformation and growth to occur within the community.[84] It is with a commitment to loving God and each other that we learn to adjust to each other, thus deepening our love for one another. The covenantal love of God flows into our relationship allowing all involved to grow and be transformed from one degree of glory to another (2 Cor 3:18).

If we recall what happened in the Red Hill community, we could see the transformation process that Banks mentioned. In chapter 3, I reported a weak ethos of belonging that existed at Red Hill and the growth of a sense of community at the end of the year. If we look at how the changes happened, we can see that the intentional engagement between Ellen and her Circle friends is the key. When Ellen and her Circle friends engaged with each other in a loving relationship, their being *with* each other became their being *for* each other. Ellen's Circle friends were certainly there with the idea of being for Ellen, but Ellen's being with them also brought revelatory changes. These changes did not come from what Ellen did that was specifically for her friends. They happened through a process of mutual learning and constant adjustments involved in the relationship.

Similarly, many people involved with the L'Arche communities reported experiences of transformation in and through being with others.[85] Jean Vanier shared with us how this transformation and growth happened. He says, "the secret of growth . . . comes from a gift of God which may pass through others."[86] However, it is not in doing things for others but in listening to others (which include people with intellectual disabilities and the other assistants) that people can discover this secret of growth.[87] Listening is not doing, because it is about being present with each other in a relationship in which we can be in touch with each other's emotions and needs.

The experience of the L'Arche community confirms the experience of Red Hill that it is through "being with others" in an attentive way that we are "being for others." We certainly might do things together and serve each other in some concrete ways. However, it is in and through being with each other and receiving the being of each other lovingly that our being for others can lead to growth in holiness. In other words, although Ellen and Dylan cannot *do* very much in terms of services to others, their being with others is serving as a being for others in a significant way that

---

84. Thompson, *Moral Formation*, 70–73.

85. See, for example, Greig, *Reconsidering Intellectual Disability*, 248; and Reimer, *Living L'Arche*, 53–54.

86. Vanier, *Community and Growth*, 42.

87. Vanier, *Community and Growth*, 142.

could bring transformation to the community and each individual involved in the relationship.

To conclude, kinship love is a love that desires to be with others and for others. It derives from the love that we receive from God in Christ. The love of Christ binds us together but being united in Christ does not eliminate our differences. Rather, the love of Christ enables us to live harmoniously together as one body despite our differences. In the relationship of covenantal siblinghood, we are committed to loving each other, which allows us to adjust and align with each other continually. This process leads to individual and corporate growth in holiness. Therefore, living out our call as siblings can be seen as a discipleship process.

Kinship as Discipleship

If we have been involved in a church community with people from diverse backgrounds, we will know that differences in opinions and practices are common. It can be messy to negotiate these differences in a community but committing to working through these differences is a discipleship process. To understand how a loving relationship with Ellen and Dylan might bring about transformation, I begin with Thomas Reynolds and Jean Vanier's experiences of transformation in living with people with disabilities. There we will see what resonates with The Cross and Red Hill's experiences and how the relationships in the church can be avenues for discipleship.

Thomas Reynolds uses the term "moral conversion" to describe the transformation arising from a caring relationship with his son, Chris, who has a mild form of autism and other medical conditions.[88] This experience leads him to explore how the intricate dynamics of vulnerability and love can bring about changes to people in relationships. Reynolds begins by suggesting that human beings are all vulnerable at heart. We seek to be loved and affirmed. "The basic question of human existence is whether there is welcome at the heart of things, whether we can find a home with others who recognize us, value us, and empower us to become ourselves."[89] To enter into a loving relationship requires that we accept our vulnerability and be willing to enter into a space of mutual giving and receiving created by God. The Holy Spirit draws us into this space and enables us to be open and welcoming towards God and with one another.[90] In this space, we encounter the presence of each other. This encounter demands our response. As each

---

88. Reynolds, *Vulnerable Communion*, 122.
89. Reynolds, *Vulnerable Communion*, 119.
90. Reynolds, *Vulnerable Communion*, 240–41.

of us makes a response and subjects ourselves to the other's vulnerability, it forces us to face our own vulnerability. In the process of opening ourselves to receive the other as a gift, we allow God's love to work in and among us, bringing us into communion with God and each other.

From living with people with intellectual disabilities for many years, Jean Vanier shares his view on the transformational process that has taken place at L'Arche. He advises that we need to be aware of the walls we have erected to protect ourselves. Having the courage to take down the walls is the necessary initial step for entering into a relationship with others in the community. Vanier describes the process of becoming a community as the way of the heart.[91] The heart, in Vanier's language, is "the very core of our being."[92] It is in the heart that one knows when one is loved. It is also where the sense of communion takes place. The way of the heart is thus the way of moving towards the communion of hearts, a deep relationship with one another. "The way of the heart implies a choice."[93] The willingness to learn and choose each other as people and not objects is the first essential step. What needs to happen next is the openness and vulnerability to share one's hopes and pain with one another.[94] However, reaching this point of openness is not easy. Vanier points out that we all carry the baggage of brokenness that might make us hate ourselves and hate others.[95] Moving towards communion with each other requires that we learn to forgive and receive forgiveness.[96]

What we can see in both Reynolds and Vanier's experiences of transformation is the need for openness and vulnerability. It is the first step that both sides of the relationship need to take to enter into a loving and transformative journey. This might explain why Lillian and Ellen's presentation to the congregation in Red Hill was instrumental to the subsequent changes that took place. In this instance, I can see openness on both sides: the church and the family.

The church's openness is evident in their invitation for Lillian and Ellen to present their thoughts to the church. For Lillian, the presentation was a deeply revealing experience. She mentioned that she always considered herself quite capable of soliciting help because she was well connected with service organizations. Having to ask church members to be Ellen's Circle

---

91. Vanier, *Community and Growth*, 88.
92. Vanier, *Community and Growth*, 85, 87.
93. Vanier, *Community and Growth*, 86.
94. Vanier, *Community and Growth*, 85.
95. Vanier, *Community and Growth*, 144.
96. Vanier, *Community and Growth*, 146.

friends made her realize that she was "not good in asking for help," at least not from the church she called a family. The presentation to the church further required Lillian to assume the vulnerable position of opening their family life to the whole church.

Some church members responded well to this gesture of vulnerability. These members acknowledged that they noticed Ellen's presence in the past but had never actively attempted to interact with her and understand her needs. These same people subsequently invited Lillian and Ellen to join them in social activities outside the church, such as the powwow ceremony at an Indigenous village nearby. They also supported Ellen to participate in some service activities (e.g., ushering, dishwashing) at the church. The gestures of openness offered by both sides welcomed the other in. Together they were embarking on a journey towards a deeper relationship with God and with each other.

In the case of The Cross, forgiveness might be what opened Vanessa's heart to the young people at the church. Vanessa mentioned that Dylan was rejected and mocked by some of the young people. To bring Dylan back to the group, Vanessa realized that she needed to forgive them. The support of the Circle friends in this journey was essential for the relationship to develop. Anna's openness to and friendship with Dylan made her a model of love for the group. Her persistent invitation for others to engage with Dylan made small but noticeable changes. Gradually, Vanessa noticed changes in the group. These young people no longer mocked Dylan. A couple of them were willing to interact with him towards the end of the project. Letting go of some of her negative feelings towards the group and learning to forgive them appeared to be what freed Vanessa to let down, or at least lower, the walls of protection. It opened the opportunity for change in the relationship between Dylan and the group.

With the introduction of the Circle of Friends program to The Cross and Red Hill, some people made an effort to engage Ellen and Dylan. The question is whether these relational changes could lead to the transformation of the hearts? Vanier says,

> We can only truly love people who are different, we can only discover that difference is a treasure and not a threat, if in some way our hearts are becoming enfolded in the heart of the Father, if somewhere God is putting into our broken hearts that love that is in God's own heart for each and every human being. For God is truly in love with people, and with every individual human being.[97]

---

97. Vanier, *Brokenness to Community*, 30.

Engaging in an open and vulnerable relationship, even with a familiar person, is not easy. Being open and vulnerable to a person that seems to be weaker in our sight is more challenging. Vanier's experience tells us that we need God to expand our hearts and sustain us in our relationships.

As children of God and imitators of Christ's self-emptying and self-giving gestures, in Reynolds's words, we are invited into the vulnerable space that God created for us to experience love. We can only experience transformation in this space when we relate to each other as brothers and sisters in Christ by the power and leading of the Holy Spirit. This, however, does not remove our responsibility and commitment to each other. Instead, to be children of God and siblings to each other, we are committed to loving God and one another. As Hanson suggests earlier, our desires to exercise righteousness and compassion flow from a worshipful heart towards God, who is the ultimate righteousness. Learning to be holy as God is holy is a journey of discipleship with Christ whose fidelity and obedience to his Father is our model. On this journey, we need to submit to Christ and the leading of the Spirit so that we can be transformed as we take each little step in faithfulness and obedience.

Stressing the importance of encountering Dylan and Ellen in Christ with humility and vulnerability brings us back to where we began in this chapter: to consider the nature of Christian relationships and how this relationship will help us recognize Ellen and Dylan as beings-with-and for-others. In my engagement with Paul's theology, I propose that Christian relationship is covenantal in nature and kinship in expression. As siblings bound by God's covenantal love, we relate to each other in the oneness of Christ's body. As such, our relationship with each other is not merely a social one. Instead, it is a relationship of commitment. God's covenantal faithfulness compels us to love God and each other. Christ's faithful response to God, who is with and for us, is our model. To imitate the self-giving love of Christ, we should also love each other in a way that is with and for others. This way of love does not seek to be equal but strives to live in a fashion that acknowledges each other's gifts and be interdependent of each other.

Dylan and Ellen may seem to be weak, but they are indispensable members of the family (1 Cor 12:22). Like everyone else, they belong to the church because they are brought into the family of God by Christ through the power of the Holy Spirit. Their identities as God's children and our siblings do not depend on their abilities but the work of God.

When we encounter with Ellen, Dylan, and others with profound autism in the relationship of covenantal kinship, we will be transformed in the process. This transformation happens gradually and only if we obediently follow the lead of the Spirit. The transformative journey begins when we are willing to be open and vulnerable with one another, welcoming each other into our hearts and allowing God to bind us together in love. The constant adjustments and realignments of relationships involved in living as a community with diversity will deepen our love for each other and unite the community.

As mentioned earlier, we are adopted as God's children through incorporation into Christ through baptism. Some churches, especially the evangelical churches like The Cross, make the profession of faith a criterion for baptism. This requirement is a significant barrier for Dylan, who has difficulties with communication, to become a member of the body of Christ. Even for Ellen, who was baptized as an infant, her ongoing need for discipleship has not been addressed. Without the opportunities to be discipled under Christ with their siblings in Christ, Dylan and Ellen cannot truly belong to Christ, grow with other church members, and exercise their gifts for the benefits of the community. I will, therefore, examine this issue in detail in the following chapter.

7

Entering and Growing in Life Together

> So then, just as you received Christ Jesus as Lord, continue to live your lives in him, rooted and built up in him, strengthened in the faith as you were taught, and overflowing with thankfulness.—Col 2:6

THIS BOOK IS ABOUT the belonging of people with profound autism, like Ellen and Dylan, to the church. Up to this point, I have shown that the recognition of Dylan and Ellen's belonging began by acknowledging that they are persons worthy of our respect and love. Like all of us, they are created in the love of God to live with and for others. I also illustrated that the ethos of belonging in the Christian community is covenantal in nature and kinship in expression. For Ellen and Dylan to belong to the church, they need to be acknowledged as our siblings in Christ and God's gifts for the community. What we need to consider now is how Ellen and Dylan can enter the covenant kinship community and grow spiritually with their siblings in Christ.

With a few exceptions, baptism generally is considered an essential rite of Christian initiation across denominations.[1] As Maxwell Johnson explains, Christian initiation rites are "about 'conversion' and 'faith.' They are about entering a *new* community to which one did *not* belong before, even by birth."[2] The indication is that a person may be attending a church regularly, but for that person to belong to the church community, she or he must be initiated into the community, often by means of baptism.

---

1. The Primitive Baptists practice foot washing as an ordinance of initiation (Olson, "Baptist View," 92). On the other hand, traditions such as Quakers and the Salvation Army do not see baptism and the Lord's Supper as necessary Christian practices (Bridge and Phypers, *Water That Divides*, 7).
2. Johnson, *Rites of Christian Initiation*, xix; emphasis original.

However, access to baptism has been denied to people with disabilities who are deemed to lack the ability to understand the content of the Christian faith.[3] We learn from Pastor George at The Cross that for Dylan to be baptized, he must demonstrate his faith in Christ by reciting at least some required Bible verses and understanding the fundamental doctrines. With Dylan's current abilities, it will be difficult, if at all possible, for him to meet these criteria. If the leadership of The Cross cannot affirm Dylan's faith in Christ, he will not be able to receive baptism.

The first task of this chapter is to unpack what is involved for Ellen and Dylan to be admitted to the membership at Red Hill and The Cross. We can see two issues. Firstly, the concept of faith is understood as a personal decision that can be demonstrated by biblical and doctrinal knowledge. The intellectual requirements mean that those who are unable to attain the knowledge will remain outside of the body of Christ. Secondly, while baptism is widely accepted as an initiation rite, an additional process is often required for admission to the local church membership. This process again requires cognitive abilities that would limit Ellen and Dylan's opportunities to be considered members of the church, thus belonging to the covenant community. If church membership is related to commitments to the local church covenant, discipleship, and discipline, denial of Dylan and Ellen's membership means that they are not given the opportunities to grow as Christ's disciples. It also goes against the Bible's teaching for the church to acknowledge the indispensability of all members in Christ's body.

My attempt to address these issues involves engaging the baptismal theology of Dietrich Bonhoeffer and his concept of the body of Christ. I argue that the church's responsibility is to walk alongside Ellen and Dylan and nurture their spiritual growth so that they can become disciples of Jesus. Their membership to the church should not be rejected based on a concept of faith as intellectual assent. Once Dylan and Ellen are baptized into Christ's body, they should have no restriction to full participation in the life of the covenant community. Without these valuable members, the body loses its fullness and richness of God's gifts. Conversely, supporting Ellen and Dylan to be contributory members will release the gifts of others in the body, bringing unity to the body and allowing it to grow into Christ's likeness.

---

3. Thinkers from different denominations have advocated for sacramental access for people with intellectual disabilities. See, for example, Foley, *Developmental Disabilities and Sacramental Access*; Whitt, "Baptism and Profound Intellectual Disability"; and Moon, *Engraved upon the Heart*.

Baptism

The theological positions that different Christian traditions hold regarding baptism have deeply divided the church, making it difficult for churches to recognize each other's baptism.[4] Theologians argue over issues such as elements of baptism (e.g., water, in the triune name), form (e.g., immersion, sprinkling), and who can be baptized (adults or infants). These positions ultimately reflect the ecclesiological understanding of the various traditions. They also affect how a person can fully belong to a church community.[5] This chapter does not intend to cover the whole range of issues concerning baptism. What is of interest is the relationship between baptism and the belonging of people with profound autism to the church.

My desire is to contribute an autism perspective to the ongoing debate on baptism-related issues. Consistent with the metaphor of using autism as a magnifying glass to examine the issues of belonging, my intent in tackling the question of baptism is to seek clarity for the place of people with profound autism in the church. I write as a member of an evangelical church with the hope of broadening our reflection on baptism and belonging as we consider the meaning of the church as one body in Christ with different members.

Keeping our focus on Ellen and Dylan's experiences, my reflection on baptism is limited to the denominations represented by The Cross and Red Hill. As Simon Jones points out, the way that churches practice Christian initiation is fundamental to the churches' understanding of their identity and mission.[6] Therefore, it is necessary to begin with a brief description of how the Baptist church and the United Church of Canada understand their denominational identity. Following that, I will describe their initiation and membership rules and practices and discuss how these practices impact Ellen and Dylan's belonging with their church community.

Baptism and Membership in the Baptist Tradition

It may be a stretch to describe the Baptist as one denomination. As Baptist theologian Roger Olson says, "there is no 'Baptist church,' there are only Baptist churches grouped in conferences and convention."[7] There is also no unifying Baptist statement of faith. The Baptists believe in the

---

4. Root and Saarinen, *Baptism and Unity*, 23.
5. Root and Saarinen, *Baptism and Unity*, 22–35.
6. Jones, *Celebrating Christian Initiation*, xi.
7. Olson, "Baptist View," 92.

autonomy of the local congregation. However, Olson alleges that the one doctrine that unites the Baptists is baptism. "Baptists insist on baptizing only persons old enough and willing to confess their faith in Jesus Christ for themselves."[8] Their insistence on believer baptism and refusal of infant baptism is a distinctive feature.

This rationale came to the Baptist church as a response to the indiscriminate admission of children and adults since Constantine's conversion.[9] According to John Hammett, the Baptist tradition was founded on the quest for a "pure church," meaning a church that is entirely comprised of regenerated people. Hammett finds support for the pure church ecclesiology in the Scripture. He argues that for the church to be a holy temple, the body of Christ needs to be made up of regenerated people who genuinely confess and practice their faith.[10]

Upholding the pure church ideology means that people being baptized into the church have to be believers. Therefore, people seeking baptism have to profess their faith in Christ. Baptists admitted that the profession of faith does not necessarily mean that all who confess Christ at baptism will remain believers. However, striving towards being a pure church is their "inexorable goal."[11] With the pure church ideology as the driving force behind the Baptist baptismal practice, several issues arise.

To find support for the practice of believer baptism, Baptist theologian Bruce Ware argues that confession of faith before baptism is the practice of the early church.[12] Ware reviews the baptisms described in Acts to say that baptism is only for those who have repented of sin (Acts 2:38–39) and who have come to faith in Christ (Acts 2:41). He also refutes using household conversion narratives to support infant baptism as he sees no clear evidence that the infants or young children were baptized with the adults. Ware insists that the infants and children who would not have been able to understand the apostles' teaching and were unable to profess their faith could not have been included in the household's baptism.[13] Appropriating this biblical principle, Ware further argues that infants and children who do not have the capacity to understand and confess their faith cannot be considered true believers. Therefore, they are not allowed to be baptized until they reach an age or a level of ability to declare their faith independently.

---

8. Olson, "Baptist View," 93.

9. Hammett, "Regenerate Church Membership," 24–25.

10. Hammett, "Regenerate Church Membership," 22–23.

11. Brewer, *Distinctly Baptist*, 7.

12. Ware, "Believer's Baptism," 21–40.

13. Ware, "Believer's Baptism," 29–34.

Unintentionally, this position means that people with profound autism, who cannot understand the propositional truths and do not have the language abilities, are also not accepted for baptism.[14]

Brian Brewer, a Baptist expert in sacramental theology, says, "Baptists . . . have understood that no person is born Christian or made Christian by any ritual or ceremony. Additionally, no person can have proxy faith for another."[15] This means that the individual must decide for faith on his or her own. The faith that an individual believer must demonstrate for baptism includes an intellectual assent to a set of truth claims and a personal commitment to identify himself or herself with Christ's life, death, and resurrection.[16] What is problematic in this model of faith is the idea that faith is a decision one makes based on one's understanding of doctrinal knowledge. To be fair, Brewer does talk about the Christian's ability to make a personal decision to follow Christ as "an endowment from God."[17] Nonetheless, Brewer's description of intellectual assent and personal decision as essential elements of faith gives individual believers too much control over their salvation.

Along with the personal decision model of faith, Mark Heim (1998), a Baptist theologian at Yale Divinity School, asserts that the Baptists view baptism as an act of obedience and public confession. In this sense, what Christians offer to their Lord is "our response, carried out at our initiative."[18] This "we" or "our" focus is clearly demonstrated in how Brian Brewer describes as what happens during baptism. Referring to Paul's teaching in Rom 6 on baptism as uniting with Christ in his death and resurrection, Brewer asserts that in baptism, "we are identifying ourselves with Christ . . . we declare ourselves as his, turning from our old lives . . . We are raised as like Christ to live new lives with our Lord when we place our love, our lives, and our faith in him."[19] What concerns me in these statements is the strong focus on the human efforts in the act of baptism. My point is not to suggest that we are totally passive in baptism. We do need to respond to God's grace and calling and thus be willing to submit ourselves to the Holy Spirit's leading to a new life in Christ. However, the initiative comes from God, not from us. Paul teaches that it is the Spirit who works in the baptismal water to baptize us into one body with Christ (1 Cor 12:13). Our

---

14. Whitt, "Baptism and Profound Intellectual Disability." 60.
15. Brewer, *Distinctively Baptist*, 2.
16. Brewer, *Distinctively Baptist*, 2.
17. Brewer, *Distinctively Baptist*, 24.
18. Heim, "Baptismal Recognition," 153.
19. Brewer, *Distinctively Baptist*, 139.

union with Christ cannot be our declaration to be his. Instead, it is Christ's gracious acceptance of us to be his own.

The Baptists' baptismal theology, as described above, came from a desire to offer an alternative ecclesiology that emphasizes the church as a community of committed disciples of Christ.[20] Incongruously, in many Baptist churches, baptism does not make the recipient an automatic member of the baptizing congregation, which supposedly is the community of committed disciples of Christ. A separate act of reception is commonly required.[21] According to Mark Heim, through baptism, believers are baptized into the body of Christ. However, their union with Christ and other Christians is a spiritual union, which is different from the visible union with the local church.[22] This position means that to be accepted into the local church fellowship, a baptized Christian has to demonstrate her or his commitment to Christ again. Additionally, the Christian needs to agree with the statements of faith and regulations of the local church.

We can see in this brief review of Baptist's baptismal theology and membership practice that if Dylan desires to be baptized and becomes a member of The Cross, he faces many challenges. The cognitive requirements for understanding the fundamental doctrines and memorizing Bible verses are beyond Dylan's current capability. Without baptism, Dylan can continue to attend The Cross. However, he will never be able to be brought into the oneness with other believers and be recognized as a member of the body of Christ.

Baptism and Membership in the United Church of Canada

In contrast to the Baptists' loose structure, the United Church of Canada (referred to as "UCC" from here on) is a well-structured ecclesial body governed by national policies and regulations. The UCC was established in 1925 as an ecclesial body formed by a merger of the Methodist Church in Canada, the Congregational Union of Canada, and 70 percent of the Presbyterian Church of Canada.[23] These churches came together to form the UCC during the Canadian Social Gospel movement. Since then, the UCC has strived to be a "Justice Seeking / Justice Living Church."[24]

---

20. Heim, "Baptismal Recognition," 152.
21. Heim, "Baptismal Recognition," 152.
22. Heim, "Baptismal Recognition," 155.
23. History of the United Church of Canada, para 3.
24. The United Church of Canada, *Theology and Inter-Church Relations*, 48.

As a result of the merger of churches from different backgrounds, the UCC has been on a journey to understand how the different traditions could come together and form a unified church with unique ecclesiology and liturgical practices.[25] In their official doctrine, UCC recognizes baptism as the sacrament of initiation into the church. Adopting the policy of infant baptism from its founding traditions, the UCC baptizes both children and adult converts.[26]

Since the 1980s, the UCC has been involved in ecumenical dialogues.[27] These dialogues brought changes to various practices of the church. For baptism, the UCC accepted the Baptists' criticism of indiscriminative baptism as a corrective. To ensure that the UCC churches would not entertain all requests for infant baptism indiscriminately, the directive is that baptism should only be administered to infants "where there is a reasonable expectation that the child will be brought up as a member of the Christian Church."[28] That being so, the UCC stands by their practice of infant baptism and asserts that it is "a sign of prevenient grace of God which answers our needs before we know of them."[29] What has changed is the requirement for the parents and godparents to profess their faith and promise to bring their child up in the faith. The church assumes greater responsibility by providing instructions for those who seek baptism for a child.

Without specifying an age, the UCC expects baptized children to participate in a confirmation rite at an appropriate age, usually in the teenage years. UCC does not recognize confirmation as a sacrament; rather, it is "a separate and independent rite, no longer part of Christian initiation, but almost a passage to Christian adulthood."[30] Notably, the preparation for confirmation follows a similar pattern to the Baptists' preparation for baptism. It includes instructions on doctrinal truths and requires a public profession of faith or the show of other visible evidence of conversion.[31] Correspondingly, adult believers will receive similar instructions with an expectation for the public profession of faith. The confirmands and adult believers also need to commit to the Christian way of life.[32] By incorporating some of the Baptist baptismal theology into their practices, the baptism and confirmation

---

25. Kervin, *Language of Baptism*, xviii.
26. The United Church of Canada, *Church Membership*, 10.
27. The United Church of Canada, *Ecclesiology*, 49.
28. The United Church of Canada, *Church Membership*, 10.
29. The United Church of Canada, *Church Membership*, 10.
30. Kervin, *Language of Baptism*, 234.
31. The United Church of Canada, *Church Membership*, 34.
32. The United Church of Canada, *Church Membership*, 35.

process at UCC entails cognitive demands that parallel the Baptist church's baptismal requirements. It, therefore, poses similar barriers to people who are not able to meet these demands.

However, the UCC maintains that although they have added an element of the personal decision to the initiation rites, they are taking a "middle way" in the matter.[33] "It emphasizes the importance of religious liberty and of personal decision, but it also believes that the church is the result not of human choices, but of God's will. It is his gift to men [sic]."[34] In practical terms, this position is used to support infant baptism, followed by confirmation. The UCC affirms that Christianity is for all kinds of people and not only for those who are mature in faith and perfect in conduct. It is also for "the weak, the doubting and immature, including small children."[35] They believe that God will apply the "judgment of charity" and forgive the sins of all people.[36] The "middle way" is an effort by the UCC to make compromises for different expressions of faith. However, it is difficult to see how it can be implemented in practice. If the doubtful are to be included, how can they be expected to profess their faith and be baptized? The church document also does not provide information on how the "weak and immature" may be supported to come to a personal decision or whether a personal decision is indeed required for all those who present themselves for baptism.

Besides, the UCC recognizes that while conversion can be momentous, it is a gradual process in most cases. They believe that the baptizands and confirmands do not come before them as people "who have already attained the full riches of Christ" but "as a little child" who will grow in the knowledge and experience of God.[37] In this process, personal faith finds its grounding in the faith of the church.[38] Again, the UCC document has not provided details on the relationship between personal faith and the church's faith. It is unclear if this refers to the parents and godparents' faith in the case of infant baptism. If this is so, how would the church's faith play a role in the confirmation of the teenagers and baptism of adult believers?

When the UCC changed their confirmation requirements, they added a new category of membership. Since baptism is the initiatory rite for incorporation into the body of Christ, all baptized individuals, children included, are accepted by the UCC as members of the church. However,

---

33. The United Church of Canada, *Church Membership*, 17.
34. The United Church of Canada, *Church Membership*, 17.
35. The United Church of Canada, *Church Membership*, 16.
36. The United Church of Canada, *Church Membership*, 17.
37. The United Church of Canada, *Church Membership*, 22–23.
38. The United Church of Canada, *Church Membership*, 22.

only those who are confirmed or baptized as adults can be accepted for full membership of the church and be involved in the church's operations locally and nationally.[39] This distinction again suggests that the church that one is baptized into is different from the local and national ecclesial body with which one is involved.

At the last interview with Pastor John of Red Hill United Church, he indicated an openness for Ellen to participate in a confirmation class. (The discussion went directly to confirmation because Ellen was baptized as a baby.) Having worked at a residential home for people with intellectual disabilities for two years, John understood the need to modify the curriculum to suit Ellen's learning style, which is concrete and practical. He was willing to explore what the curriculum might look like and the option of inviting Katie as her sponsor. John seemed confident that with Katie and Lillian's input, he would be able to structure the confirmation class in a way that would be suitable for all the young people while including Ellen in the class. As a justice-oriented church, Red Hill is an inclusion-focused community, and John was certain that the Session would have no objection to this accommodation. Therefore, the possibility for Ellen to find belonging at Red Hill seems promising.

Theological Issues in Baptism and Membership

As mentioned earlier, with faith being commonly linked to cognitive capacity, the possibility that people with profound autism might have the desire and ability for faith is often not readily recognized. Although the leadership at The Cross and Red Hill were willing to welcome Dylan and Ellen into the community, including them in the initiation rites (baptism for Dylan and confirmation for Ellen) did not cross the pastors' minds at both churches.

Profound autism is not a very descriptive term. Even within the more severe end of the autistic spectrum, the adjective "profound" covers a wide range of presentations. Some people with profound autism may have significant learning disabilities, but that does not mean that they cannot learn at all. People with learning disabilities just need to learn in ways uniquely suitable to their learning styles. When having a learning disability is mistaken to mean that the person cannot learn at all, the learning opportunity is often not provided. Sadly, this also means the church seldom addresses the spiritual needs of people with profound autism. Similarly, having a communication disability does not mean the person cannot communicate at all. As we have seen in chapters 2 and 3, Dylan and Ellen effectively communicated

---

39. The United Church of Canada, *Church Membership*, 20.

their desires and emotions and interacted with their friends with their specific communication modes.

As I pointed out, when both churches apply a cognitive definition to faith, people with learning and language difficulties will not meet the criteria for baptism or confirmation. The question then is whether this is an appropriate definition of faith. John Swinton comments:

> Certainly, our intellect and cognitive capacities help us to participate with God in ways relevant to our current understanding of reality. However, the essence of our relationship of grace is that it is initiated and sustained by God in a way that lies outside our current understanding, and as such, is independent of our cognitive capabilities.[40]

Accordingly, in Isa 55:9, God says quite plainly, "As the heavens are higher than the earth, so are my ways higher than your ways and my thoughts than your thoughts." No matter how intelligent people may be, God is beyond anyone's full comprehension.

Further, Paul makes it clear in Eph 2:8–9 that "For it is by grace you have been saved, through faith—and this is not from yourselves, it is the gift of God—not by works, so that no one can boast." We know God as God, as Swinton says, only by God's grace. The Divine initiates a relationship with us, thus allowing us to gain a knowledge of God. No one can attain faith, as Paul says, by our efforts. Therefore, the theological issue with accepting people for baptism lies not with people's capacity for faith but rather the understanding of faith as intellectual assent and personal decision.

What the Baptists want to do with their pure church ecclesiology is to define a clear boundary. As an entity instituted by Christ, the church does have a boundary, but it is one with a dotted line. The church, as the body of Christ, is bound by Christ. The boundary is thus tied to one's orientation to Christ. The issue then is not about defining fixed boundary markers but about considering how the church should responsibly support people to respond to Christ's call and develop a relationship with God. It is also required of us to explore how to responsibly administer the initiation rites without rejecting those Christ has called to be his own.

Lastly, the review of the baptismal practices reveals an issue with the understanding of the church as the body of Christ. Even though both denominations recognize baptism as an initiation rite that incorporates believers into the community, they both have an additional membership criterion. For the Baptist, it is the membership rite called the "right hand

---

40. Swinton, "Restoring the Image," 22.

of fellowship."[41] For the UCC, it is confirmation. For both, intellectual assent to propositional truth, a certain level of biblical knowledge, and an ability to publicly profess one's faith are essential criteria for membership or full membership. Although the church needs to have an institutional structure to guide the community's functioning, what needs to be clarified is the fundamental reality of the church as the body of Christ and the purpose of church membership. If we accept that the church is Christ's body and that each member is indispensable, we need to ask how our practices of belonging can reflect this reality?

The concern for how we can live out the reality of the church as the body of Christ is particularly pertinent when some people with profound autism, who have been baptized into the body of Christ are not admitted as full members of the church. Would they enjoy the right hand of fellowship and be considered brothers and sisters in Christ with the other church members? If the local church is a visible expression of the body of Christ, how can we ensure that every baptized person, who belongs to Christ, is invited to contribute to the church and be nurtured in faith?

To explore the theological questions raised in this reflection, I will engage with Dietrich Bonhoeffer's theology. Bonhoeffer has not written very much on disability-related theological issues. Still, his constant urging of the church to bear the image of the suffering Christ leads us to see the world from the perspectives "of the outcasts, the suspects, the maltreated, the powerless, the oppressed and reviled."[42] We will find him using the same perspective to approach infant baptism, from which we can draw some parallels to our discussion on the baptism of people with profound autism.

As discussed in chapter 5, Bonhoeffer's theology is one of sociality. To Bonhoeffer, Christ is revealed in the social reality of human existence in the context of the church community.[43] In this framework, faith as a gift is revealed in Christ's presence in the preaching of the Word, sacraments, and the life of the church community. This Christocentric view of faith offers a sound reason for rejecting the concept of faith as intellectual assent to propositional truths.

Recognizing faith as a gift does not allow the church to take it lightly. Bonhoeffer says, "Cheap grace is . . . baptism without the discipline of community."[44] With a high view on baptism as a sacrament, Bonhoeffer stresses the church's responsibility in discipling all believers. As it will

---

41. Heim, "Baptismal Recognition," 155 n.6
42. Bonhoeffer, *Letters and Papers*, 52.
43. Green, *Bonhoeffer*, 70–78.
44. Bonhoeffer, *Discipleship*, 44.

become clear as this chapter progresses, we can see once again how Bonhoeffer's theology of sociality is at play in his theology of baptism. By emphasizing the church community's role in the administration of baptism, Bonhoeffer shifts the focus from faith as intellectual assent to the community's practice of carrying each other in faith. It also changes faith from a personal and momentous decision to an ongoing journey of discipleship on which community members support and encourage each other to learn from Christ's examples.

Living out our faith in the community's life is an essential concept in Bonhoeffer's theology, but he also has a very realistic understanding of the church. Bonhoeffer alleges that the church is a divine reality, not an ideal.[45] We are to receive the church community as a gift of God and learn to live with others with love. He warns that those who love their dream of a Christian community more than they love the actual Christian community itself may end up destroying that very community they seek to serve.[46] We will see later how this understanding would help us live out the meaning of being the body of Christ with people with profound autism as a church with different members. Doing so will avoid the error of redefining the church with certain human ideals and requiring people to fit into socially defined standards.

Baptism and Faith

Bonhoeffer's baptismal theology is situated within his overall theological framework of radical discipleship. In *Santorum Communio*, Bonhoeffer describes the church's individualistic and consumeristic nature as nominal religious practices. He observes that "the church today has often become a religious theatre and auditorium . . . everyone is pleased to see many others who feel themselves exalted by the same spiritual enjoyment . . . But a common feeling, a knowledge of it, do not make a community."[47]

Bonhoeffer's thoughts against the mediocrity of Sunday Christianity and comfortable discipleship, which he calls "cheap grace," are also evident in *Discipleship*.[48] In the introduction to *Discipleship*, theologians Geffrey Kelly and John Godfrey assert that Bonhoeffer's thoughts in this book "are infused with a theology of the cross."[49] Bonhoeffer calls Christians to bear

---

45. Bonhoeffer, *Life Together*, 35.
46. Bonhoeffer, *Life Together*, 35.
47. Bonhoeffer, *Sanctorum Communio*, 16.
48. Bonhoeffer, *Discipleship*, 5.
49. Bonhoeffer, *Discipleship*, 6.

their crosses to follow the Lord in complete obedience. To do so, disciples have to die to the world and live to Christ. The dying and rising in the water with Christ in baptism is how Christ works through the Holy Spirit to effect our deaths to the world and our new life in him.

With the belief that Christ works through baptism to call people to be his own, baptism cannot merely be a sign for what has been accomplished, as some Baptists have proposed. For Bonhoeffer, baptism is a significant act of Christ. He says, "baptism thus implies a *break*. Christ invades the realm of Satan and lays hold of those who belong to him, thereby creating his church community."[50] With the use of a powerful militant language, Bonhoeffer impresses upon us that God acts in the water to rescue us from the power of the world.

> In baptism, we become Christ's possession. The name of Jesus Christ is spoken over baptismal candidates, they gain a share in that name; they are baptized into Jesus Christ (Rom 6:3; Gal 3:27; Matt 28:19). They now belong to Jesus Christ. Having been rescued from the rule of this world, they now have become Christ's own.[51]

Bonhoeffer's strong image of what happens in the baptismal water comes from a sacramental view of baptism. However, some Baptist thinkers also acknowledge baptism as more than a symbol of what has already been achieved.[52] For example, Stanley Grenz comments that in baptism, "we see ourselves as those who have passed from the rulership of sin and its condemnation into the fellowship of the people of God."[53] To Grenz, something significant happens in the baptismal water. More than the transfer of rulership from the world to God, believers also gain a new identity. Baptism, as spiritual birth, mediates to believers a new identity as children belonging to the family of God, who enjoy reconciliation with God and, therefore, with each other.[54]

Recognizing that God transfers a Christian's belonging in baptism from that of the world to Christ, Bonhoeffer emphasizes that baptism is not something that we offer to God. Instead, it is what Jesus Christ offers to us. Christ, by his sovereign will, calls his disciples to follow him into the water. After being baptized in the name of the triune God, believers belong to Christ's body,

---

50. Bonhoeffer, *Discipleship*, 207; emphasis original.
51. Bonhoeffer, *Discipleship*, 207.
52. Whitt, "Baptism and Profound Intellectual Disability," 61–62.
53. Grenz, *Theology for the Community*, 523.
54. Grenz, *Theology for the Community*, 523.

the church, as members. For the disciples, baptism is a step of obedience to Christ. God's gift is given freely, but God's grace is not coercive. By willingly receive the gift of baptism, the disciples rise with Christ to a new identity in Christ and are fully committed to obeying his teachings.

With baptism understood as an obedient response to Christ's call to die to our old self and rise into a new creation, Bonhoeffer does not eliminate the importance of faith. On the contrary, he affirms the connection between baptism and faith. Bonhoeffer agrees that faith must be present for baptism to occur. Faith itself is, therefore, not the issue; the meaning of faith is what requires clarification.

Bonhoeffer asserts that the predominant definition of faith as "personal faith" and as "personal decision for Jesus" is foreign to the biblical concept of faith.[55] He argues that Paul has never used the term "my faith" or "I believe" in his writings. He iterates:

> The formulations "faith came" and "faith was revealed" (Gal. 3:23, 25) are particularly striking. Faith is therefore first of all to be conceived objectively as revelation, event, grace, gift of God or Christ, through which the self is entirely superseded.[56]

As explained earlier, humanity cannot develop a knowledge of God by our intellectual efforts. What we can know of God is contingent on divine revelation. Faith is, thus, a gift to be received.

For Bonhoeffer, God is revealed in Christ, and Christ is revealed in the Word and the sacraments.[57] Since the preaching of the Word and administration of the sacraments happen in the church community, the revelation of Christ is communal in nature. The emphasis on community as where Christ is revealed and where faith is to be received is reflected in Bonhoeffer's well-known phrase: "Christ existing as church community."[58] His explanation of how Christ is revealed in the church community, as explained below, is complex, but it helps us acknowledge that our faith is resting upon God's grace, not our cognitive abilities. As such, Bonhoeffer's theology opens a space for people with profound autism to receive faith as a gift and baptism as an initiation into the body of Christ.

In chapter 5, I explained Bonhoeffer's concept of Christ as being the vicarious representation of humanity. As such, Christ is always with us and for us. The idea that Jesus has freely given himself to us and bound himself

---

55. Bonhoeffer, "Theological Position," 722.
56. Bonhoeffer, "Theological Position," 722.
57. Green, *Bonhoeffer*, 219.
58. Bonhoeffer, *Sanctorum Communio*, 141.

to the church community is significant to our understanding of Christ's self-revelation in the church community. In his Christology lecture, Bonhoeffer explains the three forms of Christ's presence: Word, sacraments, and church community.[59] For the convenience of relating his ideas to the concept of faith for people with profound autism, I am separating Bonhoeffer's theology of revelation through Word and sacraments from the revelation in the church community here.

Christ Revealed in Word and Sacraments

Christ, who is the Word of God, is present in the word of the church.[60] People encounter Christ and receive faith as a gift through the proclamation of God's Word in the church community. When Christ is present in the word of the church, "the community of faith does have the word of forgiveness at its disposal . . . As the Christian church, the congregation may declare in sermon and sacrament that 'you are forgiven.'"[61] The reason Bonhoeffer includes the sacrament as a proclamation with the power of forgiveness is that "The Word in the sacrament is the Word in bodily form."[62] Bonhoeffer is quick to point out that this does not mean Christ's presence changes the elements physically. Following the Lutheran tradition, Bonhoeffer emphasizes the concept of the sacramental union of Christ and the believers. To Bonhoeffer, the effects of the sacraments come from Christ's word of institution.[63] The sacraments are the Gospel enacted in the rites. Similar to Jesus's revelation of himself to the disciples on the road of Emmaus (Luke 24:13–35), when the bread is broken with the proclamation of Christ's death, Christ is revealed. In the sacraments, Christ encounters us bodily and makes us participants in the community of his body.[64]

What is revealed needs to be received by faith. Since faith is a gift, the awakening of it requires the work of the Spirit. Bonhoeffer explains that "the objective spirit is bearer and instrument of the spirit of the church of Christ . . . The objective spirit . . . is both the object and the means of the Holy Spirit's work."[65] The Holy Spirit works in an interrelated fashion with the human spirit to enable the church to encounter and receive Christ.

59. Bonhoeffer, "Lectures on Christology," 274–81.
60. Bonhoeffer, "Lectures on Christology,", 277.
61. Bonhoeffer, *Act and Being*, 112.
62. Bonhoeffer, "Lectures on Christology,", 277.
63. Bonhoeffer, "Lectures on Christology," 279.
64. Bonhoeffer, *Sanctorum Communio*, 228.
65. Bonhoeffer, *Sanctorum Communio*, 216.

Acknowledging that faith is the work of the Spirit is significant, as it again reinforces the idea that faith does not depend on human capacity. The Spirit works internally in each person in the church community as Christ is revealed, bringing them to the knowledge of Christ and faith in Christ. If faith is the work of the Spirit, human capacity does not come into consideration. People with profound autism, same as each of us, can come to faith because it is not by our efforts but by the work of the Spirit of Christ.

Christ Revealed in the Church Community

In Bonhoeffer's theology, humans are historical, social-ethical beings that always exist in relationship with others.[66] The person develops the concept of God in the encounter of others in an I–Thou relationship. "God, or the Holy Spirit, comes to the concrete Thou, only by his action does the other become a Thou for me, from which my 'I' arises. In other words, every human Thou is an image of the divine Thou."[67] Thus, the other person that the "I" encounters embodies Christ and reveals Christ to me. As we encounter each other, the other serves as an ethical barrier, which is the divine limit of God. Through these concrete ethical encounters, the "I" experiences the transcendence of God.[68]

Bonhoeffer further explains how God acts through encountering humanity in Christ. As God relates with us through Christ, Christ, as our mediator, reties "the cord between God and human beings" that has been severed by Adam's disobedience.[69] "By revealing God's own love in Christ, by no longer approaching us in demand and summons, purely as Thou, but instead by *giving God's own self as an I, opening God's heart. The church is founded on the revelation of God's heart.*"[70] Bonhoeffer wants to impress upon us that God is the one who takes the initiative to approach us in relational encounters. The Eternal God opens the divine heart towards us and invites us to respond to the marvelous revelation of love. Faith, understanding it this way, is what we receive experientially in and through God's relationship with us.

If it is true that faith is a gift of God for all people who are willing to receive the divine grace, then people with profound autism can also receive God's gift through relationships. As we encounter each other in the love of

---

66. Bonhoeffer, *Sanctorum Communio*, 47.
67. Bonhoeffer, *Sanctorum Communio*, 55.
68. Bonhoeffer, *Sanctorum Communio*, 49–52.
69. Bonhoeffer, *Sanctorum Communio*, 145.
70. Bonhoeffer, *Sanctorum Communio*, 145; emphasis original.

Christ, we experience God, who is love. We also learn our limits in these ethical encounters so that we know what is pleasing to God and what is against God's will. Similarly, we experience God's mercy in the forgiveness we receive from others. In these experiential encounters, the presence or absence of a certain level of cognitive capacity is of no relevance. We receive faith in our experience of God through loving relationships, not intellectual assent to propositional truths. What this experiential learning also indicates is that faith development is a process. The transcendent experience of God is present only because Christ is present in the church community. Therefore, we need each other in the church community on our journey of faith.

Carried by the Community of Faith

In the theological position paper on infant baptism, Bonhoeffer argues that baptism as an act of God's grace does not depend on personal conditions. "Rather, the entire weight falls on the power inherent within the sacrament in its performance instituted by Christ, a power dependent on no human conditions, and on the entire church community, the body of Christ, to whom this sacrament belongs."[71] Stressing that baptism is a gift of God's acceptance of us, Bonhoeffer indicates that it does not depend on the child's ability to understand doctrinal concepts and trust in Christ. It is God's power that effects salvation in the child. However, the church community needs to carry the child with "vicarious faith."[72]

Bonhoeffer uses the concept of vicarious faith to counter the Baptists' objection to proxy faith. He argues that faith is not a personal decision but rather always involves the church community and requires its faith. Bonhoeffer says, "the faith of the church community always precedes the faith of the individual."[73] As faith is revealed in the church community, faith is received by the church community before the individuals receive their faith.

The church, as a faith community, is also the context where baptism occurs. The faith community administers the baptism with the belief that the baptizand is acceptable to Christ. They intercede for the baptizands and, in the process, also receive faith from Christ as he answers their prayers. Thus, Bonhoeffer says, "The faith of the church community baptizes the child not on the strength of the church community's faith or the child's faith but on the strength of the word of Christ."[74] Here, Bonhoeffer

---

71. Bonhoeffer, "Theological Position," 721.
72. Bonhoeffer, "Theological Position," 724.
73. Bonhoeffer, "Theological Position," 725.
74. Bonhoeffer, "Theological Position," 725.

mentions "the child" but follows this comment by suggesting that the church community cannot see the hearts of adults any better than they can see the hearts of children—and for that matter, hardly the hearts of people with profound autism.

With the recognition of the costliness of grace, Bonhoeffer does not take lightly the church community's responsibility in carrying those who are seeking baptism. He strongly urges the church to take its responsibility seriously in what he calls "baptismal discipline."[75] For infant baptism, this entails the church community, ensuring that the child will be nurtured by believing parents and godparents who sincerely seek to bring up the child in the faith. If baptism is being sought for reasons other than faith, Bonhoeffer's advice is that the request should be refused.

Bonhoeffer's idea of baptismal discipline is worth considering in the case of baptism for people with profound autism who cannot express their faith in words. For Ellen and Dylan, the question for their church community is not whether they could or should administer the sacraments of baptism or confirmation. The consideration should be how they could responsibly support Dylan and Ellen and carry them in faith, which is a question that I will address in the Catechesis and Discipleship section later in this chapter.

Baptism and God's Care for the Lowly

On the subject of infant baptism, proponents often cite the Gospel pericopes of Christ blessing the children (Luke 18:15–17; Mark 10:13–16) as support for their position.[76] Often, the argument points to the quality of children (e.g., dependence, trust) as what makes them admissible to the kingdom of heaven.[77] Bonhoeffer offers a different and deeper meaning to Jesus's acceptance of the children in these Gospel accounts. He points out that Jesus's reference to the kingdom of heaven is to point to the eschatological significance of accepting the lowly in society. Bonhoeffer compares Jesus's reproach of the disciples' for blocking the children from approaching him with his responses to society's rejection of the blind, lame, and the poor.[78] Jesus's acceptance of the children and the marginalized, to

---

75. Bonhoeffer, "Theological Position," 731.

76. Ferguson, "Infant Baptism," 108. However, credobaptists refute the use of these pericopes for the support of infant baptism. For example, Charles Spurgeon argues on an exegesis basis that these pericopes do not address the issue of infant baptism ("Children Brought to Christ," 581–88).

77. Ferguson, "Infant Baptism, 108.

78. Bonhoeffer, "Theological Position," 720.

Bonhoeffer, is a demonstration of "the miracle of God, who humbles the lofty and raises up the lowly."[79]

In his theology, Bonhoeffer pays special attention to Christ's image "as one who suffers and is rejected."[80] As "Christ existing in community," the church should learn to see the world from the perspective of the suffering, the perspective "of the outcasts, the suspects, the maltreated, the powerless, the oppressed and reviled."[81] In fact, the resurrected Christ may indeed be encountered in our interactions with people who are rejected by society. Bonhoeffer warns that,

> The exclusion of the weak and insignificant, the seemingly useless people, from everyday Christian life in the community may actually mean the exclusion of Christ; for in the poor sister or brother, Christ is knocking at the door. We must, therefore, be very careful on this point.[82]

Bonhoeffer's warning is serious. The implication is that Christ is not only present in people who are cognitively and linguistically capable; he is also present in people with profound autism. It is a grave mistake to assume that people with profound autism do not belong to the church community because they look and act differently from others in the church. The body of Christ is a unity in diversity. It consists of people with different abilities individually gifted by God. We cannot reject or hinder anyone from being part of the body that Christ calls to his own possession. Otherwise, we risk rejecting God at the door.

In sum, I demonstrated by engaging Bonhoeffer's theology that the requirement of intellectual assent to propositional truths as an indication of faith is a mistaken concept. Faith is a gift of God. It is revealed and received in the Word, sacraments, and the church community. Faith comes to an individual in and through the community by the work of the Spirit. No one can know about God simply by their cognitive efforts. Therefore, cognitive capacity is of no concern for faith.

As Christ exists as church community, the church community is where the presence of Christ is revealed and received. Since it is the community that receives faith, the community's faith is what carries all those who present themselves for baptism. Adults, children, and people with profound autism alike need to receive their faith in and with their church community.

---

79. Ferguson, "Infant Baptism," 720.
80. Bonhoeffer, *Discipleship*, 84.
81. Bonhoeffer, "Letters and Papers," 52.
82. Bonhoeffer, *Life Together*, 33–34.

The church is called into being by Christ. It consists of people with different skills and gifts. All who love Christ belong to him regardless of their capacities. Jesus's command to the church is for us to make disciples of all nations, baptizing them, and teaching them to follow his commandments (Matt 28:20). Therefore, the church's job is to support and nurture the faith of all who respond to Christ's call and desire to be part of his body.

Catechesis and Discipleship

When it comes to catechesis and discipleship for people with profound autism, a misguided perception is the presumption of their incompetence for learning. Douglas Biklen and Jamie Burke, who work extensively with children with autism, advocate for teachers to take a stance of "presumed competence."[83] To presume competence is not the same as blindly affirming competence. What Biklen and Burke want to encourage is to maintain an openness and a trust for potentiality in people with profound autism for learning and communicating. As we have seen with Dylan and Ellen, they are definitely capable of learning. Through the modeling of their Circle friends, Dylan learned to participate in group games, and Ellen learned to serve as an usher. Those in positions of supporting and teaching need to trust their learning abilities and be willing to explore creative and innovative ways suitable for their learning styles.

In terms of Ellen and Dylan's abilities to communicate their willingness to follow Christ, we learned from Lillian and Vanessa that they have strong preferences for what they want to do. If going to church was not what they wanted to do, neither Dylan nor Ellen would have continued to attend church. Their Circle friends, who intentionally engage with them in relationships, also testified to how they could understand Dylan and Ellen's emotions and opinions through the short phrases that they expressed or through actions or gestures.

Specific to guiding a person with autism to communicate a commitment to Christ, Hartmut Kramer-Mills provided a helpful example. Walter, who has a non-verbal form of autism, showed up one day in the church where Kramer-Mills was a minister. The church recruited a small group of people to support Walter. The leadership was committed to disciple Walter. Without any prior knowledge in working with someone with autism, they sought outside support from people with professional backgrounds. With help, the leadership learned how to communicate with Walter and developed teaching materials suitable for his learning style. Although it

---

83. Biklen and Burke, "Presuming Competence," 166.

took time and effort, Kramer-Mills's team worked with Walter for many years, guiding him from receiving baptism to confirmation. From their interactions with Walter, the church leadership recognized that Walter had a deep emotional attachment to the church and a teachable spirit. They accepted Walter as a member, recognizing that membership is "constituted by God's call and the corresponding confession, but not by the ability to vote."[84] With a willingness to "hear" Walter's confession of faith in practices, Kramer-Mills's church showed us what is required and attainable for people with profound autism to be accepted as church members. The process, as Kramer-Mills indicated, transformed the church.

In guiding Ellen and Dylan to faith, we need to remember that faith, as a gift of God, is not something that human teachers can provide. Describing catechesis as a craft, theologian Petroc Willey and associates reckon the Holy Spirit as the ultimate craftsman, who works in the interior of people's lives to guide them to Jesus.[85] Catechesis is a craft because it is not about convincing people of a set of propositional truths. It is about bringing the whole person of the catechumen into participation in the work of grace.[86] By focusing on the relational rather than cognitive aspect of faith contents, there are many options for catechesis suitable for people with all abilities.[87]

For example, theologian Gregory Jones developed a catechesis for baptism based on Augustine's catechesis but adapted with Stanley Hauweras's attention to character formation and Alistair McIntyre's emphasis on the formative significance of Christian practices. Rather than focusing on forming the mind, Jones aims to direct the catechumens' hearts "towards the enjoyment of fellowship with the triune God."[88] Through involving the catechumens in community practices, Jones wants to form a habitus to shape their minds.[89] No additional verbal instruction, other than listening to the homilies, is included. Sponsors are assigned to the catechumen. They are exemplars who model the practices of faith and Christian living. Interpretation of Scripture and the teaching of doctrines are located within the context of Christian living.[90] Jones proposes that God must be placed at the

---

84. Kramer-Mills, "Walter's Ingress," 276–77.

85. De Cointet et al., *Catechism*, 1.

86. De Cointet et al., *Catechism*, 1.

87. For example, Brian Godawa advocates for the use of pictures to tell the stories of God (*Word Pictures*). Mary Therese Harrington demonstrates how sponsors should use their affectivity to express God's love, and symbols to communicate the stories ("Affectivity and Symbols," 116–29).

88. Jones, "Baptism," 154.

89. Jones, "Baptism," 166.

90. Jones, "Baptism," 164.

center of Christian practices, thinking, and relationships.[91] When God is at the center, both the sponsor and the catechumen, who is apprenticing his or her faith, are on a learning journey together.[92] The learning is a joint inquiry into "what it means to love God and enjoy Him [sic] and what it means to be known and loved by God."[93]

Jones developed this practical approach of catechesis for all Christians. It is not an adapted curriculum for people with disabilities. However, by emphasizing the practical aspect of faith development with the assignment of sponsors, Jones's model can apply to people with profound autism. Its use is also not limited to preparation for baptism. Journeying together in faith is a shared discipleship process for both the sponsor and the learner. Take Ellen as an example: her Circle friends function quite similarly to Jones's sponsors. They modeled and supported Ellen's participation in worship and church activities so that she can learn how to become a member at Red Hill. At the same time, these friends were learning about what God was doing in their community through Ellen. As such, the journey was mutually beneficial. The church, as reported in chapter 3, also grew in their sense of community.

What is worth considering in expanding Jones's model is the role of the community. In chapter 4, I discussed how the ethos of belonging in the two church communities could impact Dylan and Ellen's belonging. Similarly, Ann Casson, a Christian educator, noted the impact of what she called the "Christian ethos" on students' spiritual development in Christian school communities.[94] Casson and her team conducted a two-year longitudinal study in ten Christian secondary schools. They found that communities that demonstrated a Christian ethos in its "connection to God" positively influenced students' spiritual development.[95] When the community modeled the "virtue of hospitality, inclusivity, and nurture of each other," both staff and students learned the foundations of Christianity from each other, thus spiritually developing together.[96] These educators' findings help us appreciate the importance of the community's embodiment of faith for its members' spiritual development. When the community can live out its connection with God, all in the community will grow in faith through their relationships with God and each other.

91. Jones, "Baptism," 162.
92. Jones, "Baptism," 168–69.
93. Jones, "Baptism," 171.
94. Casson, "Sense of Belonging," 169.
95. Casson, "Sense of Belonging," 170.
96. Casson, "Sense of Belonging," 173.

Bonhoeffer says, "Formation occurs only by being drawn into the form of Christ . . . This does not happen as we strive 'to become like Jesus as we customarily say, but as the form of Jesus Christ himself so works on us that molds us, conforming our form to Christ's own (Gal. 4:9).'"[97] Try as we may, human efforts are not able to form a Christian. The formation is the work of the Spirit of Christ. The Spirit works to bring each of us into the truth of Christ and forms us into one body in Christ. Our job is to obediently and faithfully follow the Spirit's leading and to encourage each other on the journey.

Up to this point, I have shown how Dylan and Ellen should be supported and nurtured in faith, so that they can be baptized into Christ and confirmed as his followers. Along the way, I have explained how the church should be faithful to our responsibility of discipleship and walk with Ellen and Dylan on their journey of faith. The next topic that needs to be dealt with is their membership to the church and how we should acknowledge them as contributory and needed members in the body of Christ.

Indispensable Members of the Body of Christ

Bonhoeffer says, "The church is the present Christ himself."[98] With this statement, he reminds us that the church is not an institution, a building, but "a *person* with a body."[99] The reality of the church as the body of Christ is based on the incarnation of the Son of God, who bore humanity upon himself on the cross, died, and was raised again. Consequently, the incarnate Son of God exists as the representative of the new humanity.[100] Christ's continual existence on earth is in the church community, in which people "will participate not merely in his teaching, but also in his body."[101] Significant in Bonhoeffer's understanding of the body of Christ is that the church is not an institution that functions like a human body. The church *is* the body of Christ with individual believers incorporated into it through baptism.

It is instructive to note that Bonhoeffer uses Paul's concept of putting on Christ in Gal 3:27 to describe the believers' oneness in the body of Christ. Having put on Christ in baptism, believers become one in Christ. "[T]*he church is one; it is the body of Christ. At the same time, it is the multiplicity*

---

97. Bonhoeffer, *Ethics*, 93.
98. Bonhoeffer, *Discipleship*, 218.
99. Bonhoeffer, *Discipleship*, 218; emphasis original.
100. Bonhoeffer, *Discipleship*, 215.
101. Bonhoeffer, *Discipleship*, 266.

and community of its members."[102] The oneness in Christ eliminates the socially defined differences. Therefore, there is neither Greek nor Jew, neither free nor slave, neither neurotypical nor autistic. By emphasizing the unity in diversity, Bonhoeffer underlies Paul's teaching that all members are necessary for the body of Christ. We do not attempt to make a hand an eye, nor change an eye into an ear.[103] Instead, whether we are a hand, an eye, or an ear, we are brought into the body by God for divine purposes and the common good. People who are made uniquely and differently are united as one body in Christ by his Spirit. Each of us belongs to Christ and his church, not by any worldly defined worth or values, but by God's grace and the work of the Spirit.

Members of the Local Expression of the Body

Bonhoeffer says, "The body of the exalted Lord is also a visible body in the shape of the Church."[104] That is to say, our belonging to Christ is expressed in our belonging to a local church community that makes Christ visible to the world. The church is where corporate worship takes place, the Word is preached, the sacraments of baptism and the Lord's Supper are celebrated, and where believers enjoy their fellowship with each other. Our membership to a local church matters because without which we cannot participate in the functions of the body.

Further, Bonhoeffer indicates that the goal of all Christian community is for us to meet one another as bringers of the message of salvation.[105] As explained previously, in Bonhoeffer's concept of the church as the collective person of Christ, we encounter the divine Thou as we encounter each other in the community. Through these encounters we grow spiritually individually and corporately. However, the corporate growth requires that we receive what God gives us with a thankful attitude. "The more thankfully we daily receive what is given to us, the more surely and steadily will fellowship increase and grow from day to day as God pleases." Therefore, we need to treasure Christian fellowship and receive each other as God's gracious gift. Every person God has brought to the community enriches our experiences of Christ. The vitality and growth of the body depend on the full participation of all its members.

---

102. Bonhoeffer, *Discipleship*, 220; emphasis original.
103. Bonhoeffer, *Discipleship*, 220.
104. Bonhoeffer, *Discipleship*, 249.
105. Bonhoeffer, *Life Together*, 23.

Bonhoeffer's emphasis on the full participation of *all* members indicates that Ellen and Dylan, once baptized, should enjoy the same privileges as all baptized believers. He alleges that it is a "terrible distortion of the New Testament view" to allow a baptized Christian to participate in the worship service and the Lord's Supper but not the community's life. Actually, Bonhoeffer has some strong words against this kind of practice: "to refuse to have community with them (baptized brothers [sic]) in everyday life, and to abuse them and treat them with contempt, is to become guilty against the body of Christ itself."[106] To live truthfully as one body in Christ, we must not allow any preconceived ideas of autism to prevent us from welcoming Ellen and Dylan into any part of the community life. Once baptized into the body of Christ, Dylan and Ellen should have no restriction on the participation in church activities and discipleship opportunities.

On their parts, Ellen and Dylan once baptized into the church and confirmed as church members, are not exempted from fulfilling their membership commitments. As members, Stanley Grenz explains that we "share a story, a vision, and a mandate" with a local congregation.[107] For the church to be the visible presence of Christ, we also need to share a mutually binding promise to help each other grow spiritually. On the side of the church, the leadership promises to give oversight to the discipleship of church members, and that should include Dylan and Ellen. Equally, they need to promise to gather with and submit to the church.[108]

Some might ask if Ellen and Dylan can contribute to the church's vision and mission and receive oversight of the church on spiritual matters. As explained earlier, thes kinds of questions come from the common mistake of assuming incompetence. Contrary to doubting Ellen's abilities to be a contributing member, Katie offers her observations that support Ellen's commitments and contributions. When the question of Ellen's confirmation was discussed with the leadership at Red Hill, Katie commented that many young people who have gone through the confirmation classes did not attend the church regularly nor participated in the church's ministry. Conversely, Ellen has demonstrated her commitments to Red Hill by her regular attendance and dedicated services to the church. Therefore, Katie felt that Ellen has better fulfilled what was required to be a member at Red Hill than others who understood the requirements but did not put them into practice.

---

106. Bonhoeffer, *Discipleship*, 234.

107. Grenz, *Theology for the Community*, 234.

108. Jamieson, *Going Public*, 148

The example at Red Hill again illustrates that learning to be a member of the church community does not necessarily depend on one's cognitive ability, but relationships and regular practices in the community. What is crucial for us to note is that once baptized into the body of Christ, Ellen, Dylan, or others with profound autism ought to be recognized and supported to be contributory members of the church, the local expression of Christ's body. Katie's comments tell us that those who are willing to accompany people with profound autism on their faith journey will recognize their abilities in making commitments and contributions to the church. What is required is for the sponsors to model for them what it means to be participating in the church's missions and offer opportunities for them to join the church's ministries.

Contributory Members of the Body

With a chain analogy, Bonhoeffer describes each member of the church community as an "indispensable link . . . Only when even the smallest link is securely interlocked is the chain unbreakable."[109] Each piece of the link is essential for the wholeness of the body. Without even the smallest link, the body is broken. At the same time, Bonhoeffer's chain analogy conveys the purposefulness of God's design for the body. The Spirit enables each member of the body to perform specific tasks so that the community can remain healthy and strong.

In recognizing each member's gift, Bonhoeffer also indicates that each person is responsible for making contributions to the community. Therefore, there should be no idle member in the church. "A community which allows unemployed members to exist within it will perish because of them."[110] Bonhoeffer's strong statement comes from his book *Life Together*, inspired by his experience in the community of Finkenwalde. The expectation for each member to contribute to the community may sound reasonable at first. However, is that still reasonable for members with profound autism or other profound disabilities? What kind of contributions can be reasonably expected from these individuals? Are they truly indispensable if they are not able to contribute in the traditional sense? Ellen, who can serve as an usher and a kitchen helper with support, is undoubtedly making contributions. Dylan, who has not been given an opportunity to serve, appears to be unable to contribute. With profound autism presenting with a wide range of abilities, it is possible that a person with profound autism

---

109. Bonhoeffer, *Life Together*, 96.
110. Bonhoeffer, *Life Together*, 96.

may be dependent on others for personal care and daily activities. How then are we to understand his or her role in the community?

To answer these questions, we need to look again at how the body is made up. With a careful exegesis of 1 Cor 12:4–11, theologian Brian Brock points out the givenness nature of the body.[111] He asserts that every member of the body is gifted and appointed to their roles by divine design. Therefore, the composition of the body is "non-negotiable" and "non-re-arrangeable."[112] The implication is that being a member of the body of Christ involves accepting all its members as gifts. We are tempted to think in favor of those who appear stronger while considering some members who seem to be weak as not needed. Yet the wholeness and overall health of the body depends on us enjoying one another, welcoming each other as members given by God, and working together for the common good. When we understand the body this way, people with profound autism, who are among us, are gifts from God, and thus indispensable members of the body. Rejecting any one of them will mean that the body will lose its wholeness. It also means that we would not have the full set of gifts God has prepared for the body.

What about a member with profound autism who requires much care and cannot "do" anything for the church community? Can receiving care be a contribution? Jesse Zink, principal of Montreal Diocesan Theological College, explains that if the diversity within the body exists by God's purposeful design, then the presence of all members that God brings to the community allows the community to know and experience the richness of God.[113] A mature Christian community that accepts the diversity in its membership is also "one in which everyone is working steadily to release the gifts of others."[114] If Zink is right, the contribution of people with profound autism, at the very least, is the enrichment of the community's experience of God's providence of gifts. They also contribute by releasing others' gifts, such as the gift of caring and the gift of hospitality.

Other than bringing wholeness to the body of Christ and releasing the gifts of others, if we turn to the communities of Red Hill and The Cross, we can see the indispensability of people with profound autism in the transformation that happened in the communities. Following Bonhoeffer's idea of transformation in the "I–Thou" encounters, church members at The Cross and Red Hill encountered Christ in and through their encounters with Dylan

---

111. Brock, "Theologizing Inclusion," 354–55.
112. Brock, "Theologizing Inclusion," 355.
113. Zink, "Patiently Living," 223–41.
114. Zink, "Patiently Living," 227.

and Ellen. The Spirit of Christ transformed all who engaged in relationships, including Ellen and Dylan, and brought the community closer together. Further, acknowledging that Ellen and Dylan are bearers of God's image, their presence gives us a more expansive view of God and a deeper understanding of Gods' creative purpose for humanity.

Whether we think about the relationships within the body of Christ as an interlocking chain or one that is similar to a human body, the interdependence and interconnectedness of the members are what bind the body together. Every person, autistic or otherwise, is a needed member brought to the body by God. If any person is missing, the disconnected body loses its wholeness and strength. The spiritual gifts that each person is endowed by the Spirit to bring to the interconnected body strengthen the body and allow the body to grow collectively into the full measure of Christ.

Bonhoeffer's suggestion that each member should be encouraged to contribute to the community is only right if we can broaden the idea of contribution as the work of the Spirit in and through each member of the body. In this case, the church's responsibility is discerning and supporting its member to exercise their gifts. Someone like Dylan might be able to contribute to the group if he were supported in tasks such as handing out cookies at the end of the class. To release Dylan's gifts requires that the community honors him as a gift-bearer and be ready to receive him as a gift of God.

Respecting and honoring Dylan and Ellen as gifts of God and acknowledging them as valuable members of the body is what will bring the church community into the interlocking relationship that Bonhoeffer describes. When we can interlock with each other in loving relationships, it brings a sense of belonging and wholeness to the body, as well as the opportunity for the whole body to grow into Christ-likeness.

Being Together as One Body

Thus far, in light of the discussion of the church as the household of God, I have demonstrated that for Ellen and Dylan to be accepted into God's family, they have to be baptized into the body of Christ and confirmed as members of the local church. Like all of us, it is in Christ and through the Holy Spirit that "we cry out 'Abba, Father'" (Rom 8:15). In the body of Christ, each member is endowed with specific gifts for the benefits of the body. Without people with profound autism, like Ellen and Dylan, we will miss the unique gifts they bring to the church. On the other hand, their participation in the body enhances our experience of the richness of God's gifts.

Looking at the difficulties Ellen and Dylan faced in receiving the sacraments of baptism or confirmation, I demonstrated that the preconceived ideas about autism are the major barriers. The stereotypical understanding of people with profound autism as people who cannot develop the faith in Christ deprives them of discipleship opportunities. A misconstrued value system that esteems appearance, intelligence, and competence leads to difficulties in seeing Dylan and Ellen's indispensability to the church. Yet, those engaged with them intentionally and supported them in the participation of church activities gained a different view of their abilities. Anna found Dylan to be an incredible communicator. Katie saw Ellen's commitments to the church and her eagerness to be part of the church community.

God desires to summon all peoples, Dylan, Ellen, and other people with profound autism included, to a reconciled relationship in and through Christ. The church, as the body of Christ, cannot reject those who respond to God's call to come into the kinship community. Therefore, the question we need to answer is not if the church should accept Ellen and Dylan as members, but how to be one body in Christ with them.

In this chapter, I have argued that the church should be a nurturing body that, by faith, carries each person seeking to belong to Christ. The community of believers is on a journey of discipleship together. On this journey, the first thing we must do is to trust that every person belongs to Christ, and everyone can learn to know Christ because it is the Spirit who leads all of us to the truth of Christ. Profound autism presents no difficulties to the work of the Spirit. Therefore, we should not doubt if Dylan and Ellen can come to faith in Christ. Our job is to support them, paying attention to their specific needs and unique learning styles. As we trust in the Spirit's work in our hearts, we should be able to recognize Dylan and Ellen's faith. Being in Christ together, the Spirit opens our hearts for each other, God's transformative power will work in our relationships, enabling us to grow together.

As illustrated in the previous chapter, the bond between Christians is a kinship bond. In Bonhoeffer's chain analogy, we can only maintain our integrity as a Christian community by treasuring every member. Missing any piece of the chain, the community will fall apart. Conversely, recognizing the indispensability of members such as Dylan and Ellen, as experienced at Red Hill, strengthens the sense of community.

Being with each other and negotiating differences in the body, as discussed in detail in the last chapter, is never easy. Bonhoeffer's advice is that we need to love one another with spiritual love. He differentiates human love, which is a self-centered love, from the spiritual love that is brought about by the Holy Spirit. "Self-centered love constructs its own image of other persons, about what they are and what they should become. It takes the life of the other person into its own hands."[115] Self-centered love expects Dylan and Ellen to fit into one's ideal of the body of Christ. It rejects Ellen and Dylan instead of welcoming and supporting them to be who God has called them to be. Conversely, "spiritual love loves the other for the sake of Christ."[116] Spiritual love loves Dylan and Ellen as who they are—beloved of God. Spiritual love seeks to be for others, just as Christ is for us. To be for others is to put others first, serve them, and care for them. As such, spiritual love does not reject Ellen and Dylan but love them just as Christ would. It is only with the spiritual love that we can view each person, autistic or not, as an indispensable member of Christ's body. The remaining question for us to explore is how to put the theological concepts developed in this book into practice.

---

115. Bonhoeffer, *Life Together*, 44.
116. Bonhoeffer, *Life Together*, 42.

8

Practicing Kinship Solidarity

> Finally, all of you, be like-minded, be sympathetic, love one another, be compassionate and humble. —1 Pet 3:8

EVEN IN THE EARLY church, we can see how differences in racial backgrounds, gender, and social status could divide the church. A divided church is incompatible with what the church is called to be. Therefore, Paul worked tirelessly to bring about unity in the church. His strategy was to remind the church of their shared identity as God's children and urge them to live out their kinship relationship in community life. Applying the same principle to becoming a united body with Ellen, Dylan, and other people with profound autism, we need to practice our kinship relationship and seek solidarity with them.

Acknowledging that the kinship relationship is what Paul wants to use to formulate the ethos of Christian communities, David Horrell identifies establishing a "'corporate solidarity' with impulses towards egalitarianism" as Paul's primary goal.[1] As explained in chapter 6, the equalizing effect comes from the common identity of all Christians as children of God. I also mentioned that the centrality of love is what characterizes Paul's teaching of the sibling relationship. Therefore, Paul's idea of an egalitarian community is a community of siblings who are equally loved by God, and similarly loving towards each other.

Just as God's love is the basis of equality among siblings, "the value of corporate solidarity has a fundamentally Christological basis," says Horrell.[2] What Horrell is referring to in this comment is Paul's emphasis for Christians to imitate Christ's self-giving love. Paul indicates that Christ's love is for all people but particularly for those rejected by the world: lepers,

---

1. Horrell, *Solidarity and Difference*, 109.
2. Horrell, *Solidarity and Difference*, 218.

women, tax collectors, the sick, and the disabled. To imitate Christ's self-giving love, Paul teaches that we need to adopt an "other-regard" attitude.[3] Siblings should treat each other in the way that Christ views and receives each person, regardless of their social backgrounds and abilities, with love. Recognizing each person as a beloved and valued brother or sister is what will bring solidarity to the community.

In her study of how the church, as the body of Christ, should stand in solidarity with black women oppressed by society, theologian Shawn Copeland offers a reflection on the meaning of solidarity. She suggests that to be in solidarity is to adopt the gestures of "recognition and regard, mutual openness and obligation."[4] The principles that Copeland proposes parallel much of what has been discussed in chapter 6. To be in solidarity with others means demonstrating recognition of the humanity of others regardless of human differences. Mutual openness involves an eagerness to "receive the other and to be received by the other in a mutual relationship."[5] Our willingness to sincerely welcome each other and be open to inviting others into our lives is challenging but necessary. However, we need to be careful with the idea of obligation. As I have explained in chapter 6, loving God and loving others is not an obligation in the legal sense. To accept human differences as a legal obligation, as discussed previously, may lead to inclusion but not belonging. Nevertheless, being in a covenantal kinship relationship does carry with it a sense of responsibility. Like the covenant of marriage, the covenant of siblinghood in Christ commits us to love each other deeply. Jesus has modeled for us what it means to be obedient to the command of love in his solidarity with humanity. What we need is to follow Jesus's examples and do likewise.

In chapter 5, I discussed Dietrich Bonhoeffer's theology and explained that God is a being-with-us and a being-for-us. God's being with us is most prominently revealed in Jesus, the Emmanuel—God with us. He is present with us and for us in love, and He sets us free to be with and for others in love. Therefore, I will discuss kinship solidarity practices under these two categories: being *with* others and being *for* others. Acknowledging that our solidarity with each other finds its source in the solidarity of Christ with humanity, what follows is a reflection on how we can participate in Jesus's being with and for us in our practices of being Christ's presence and bringing Christ's love to each other.

---

3. Horrell, *Solidarity and Difference*, 218.
4. Copeland, "New Anthropological Subject," 37.
5. Copeland, "New Anthropological Subject," 37.

Being with Others: Practicing the Presence of Christ

Theologian William Reiser advises that the Gospel of Mark provides valuable theological pointers on Jesus's practice of solidarity with the people of God.[6] In Mark's account of Jesus's life and ministry, we can see how he lived and died in solidarity with his people. His love for people is not selective. Jesus loves all those who are brought before him (children, the rich young man, the blind, the deaf, and others with disabilities), but he immerses himself particularly "in the lives of men and women forced into poverty and other dehumanizing conditions."[7] In Reiser's exegesis of the Gospel of Mark, he identifies the essence of Jesus's solidarity with his people in how he willingly "tak[es] their weight upon himself . . . which is above all a matter of love."[8] Jesus's love for people is "concretely reflected in the attitude and response of Jesus on countless occasions: in his compassion, in his healing and exorcizing, in his fidelity to his mission."[9] If Reiser is correct, our response to Jesus's call to follow him should be standing in solidarity with him in welcoming and caring for the very people he loves.

Extending a Radical Welcome

Noting that believers come from all different backgrounds and abilities, Paul exhorts the Romans to follow the example of Christ in their welcome for each other (Rom 15:1–7). According to New Testament scholar Thomas Schreiner, this exhortation of Paul is an integral part of the theological center of the epistle.[10] Just as Christ, who did not please himself, we, the seemingly strong, should learn to please the seemingly weak among us and strive to live in harmony with one another. Paul says, our welcome for one another in this way will bring glory to God.

To Paul, the resolution of division in the church is "crucial, for it relates to God's saving purposes and promises." We welcome each other, not because other members are naturally pleasing. We welcome each other "because Christ welcomed us despite our hostility to him, in order to bring glory to God."[11] Put differently, since Christ has accepted us unconditionally, our welcome for others should be the same. Profound autism should present no difficulties for

---

6. Reiser, *Jesus in Solidarity*, ix.
7. Reiser, *Jesus in Solidarity*, ix.
8. Reiser, *Jesus in Solidarity*, 27.
9. Reiser, *Jesus in Solidarity*, 27.
10. Schreiner, *Romans*, 704.
11. Schreiner, *Romans*, 754.

our welcome for Ellen and Dylan because Jesus welcomes them. Our presence to and with them is, in fact, necessary because Christ graciously invites us into his presence even when we were hostile to him.

Welcoming requires more than opening the door of a building and laying out tea and refreshments. To welcome others like Christ has welcome us requires a radically different way of accepting each other. Daniel Homan and Lonni Collins Pratt of the Benedictine order call this kind of welcome radical hospitality.[12] Acceptance is not tolerance. "When we accept, we take an open stance to the other person. We stand in the same space, and we appreciate who they are, right now at this moment, and affirm the Sacred in them."[13] To accept is to simply love without question. One does not have to be beautiful or smart or anything else to be accepted. This way of welcome reflects the welcome we receive from God—an unconditional welcome. What is required then is for us to see each other through Christ and recognize that we were all strangers to God before Christ came to redeem all of humanity. In Christ, Ellen and Dylan are no longer strangers but the beloved children of God, welcomed by Christ into God's household. Therefore, they are our siblings in Christ to be welcomed and loved in the same way we welcome anyone else.

The space that we are welcoming each other into, according to Jean Vanier, needs to be our hearts. He says to welcome is "to give space to someone in one's heart, space for that person to be and to grow; space where the person knows that he or she is accepted just as they are."[14] In a simple sentence, Vanier describes for us the demanding nature of welcoming. To open our hearts puts us in a vulnerable position, with the potential to be rejected or hurt. Welcoming someone into our hearts requires clearing inner space to make room for others. And the space that we need to prepare, as Vanier suggests, should be large enough to allow others to grow. We also need to accept without judgment, welcoming them as they are without attempting to change them. Putting all these requirements together seems to make welcoming a daunting task. But what makes this possible, as I have explained in chapter 6, is the presence of Christ in our hearts. If the heart space is the space where Christ is present, welcoming each other into that very space is to come into the presence of Christ together. The Holy Spirit brings us into the hospitality of Christ, which opens our hearts towards each other and enables us to welcome each other.

---

12. Pratt and Homan, *Radical Hospitality*, xxi.
13. Pratt and Homan, *Radical Hospitality*, xxvii.
14. Vanier, *Community and Growth*, 264.

When we consider Dylan's experience, what we see is that The Cross did not welcome him much more than to open the physical doors of the church. It took a long time before he was even offered any cookies at the end of the Awana sessions, something all the other children automatically received without having to ask. In discussing the need for the church to move from inclusion to belonging, John Swinton says, "to belong one needs to be missed."[15] To be missed, one has to occupy a space in the hearts of people in the community or else the absence may not be noticed. In some unfortunate cases, as we have now seen, one's absence may even have been welcomed. To belong, Dylan must be welcomed into the hearts of people at The Cross as a beloved brother in Christ. Only then will his absence stimulate a sense of emptiness, and his presence to be longed for.[16]

One more point that I want to make is the mutuality of welcoming. We can see this idea of reciprocity in Paul's teaching when he says that we should welcome *each other*. One-sided welcoming will not bring us into solidarity and may even be coercive. In the discussion of Christian relationship as kinship in chapter 6, I mentioned the mutual openness and vulnerability required to enter into a relationship of love. An excellent example of this is Lillian inviting others into her and Ellen's life and the church's response to opening itself to receive Lillian and Ellen as valuable members. What I want to emphasize here is that without the mutual opening of hearts, solidarity is impossible. Just as Dylan and Ellen desire to have relationships with people at the church and their families are ready to return to the community, the church community needs to open their hearts to receive them. When we welcome each other into our heart spaces where Christ is present, God can work to bring solidarity into our relationship.

Being Present

Having talked about the need to welcome Dylan and Ellen into Christ's presence, we need to think about what it means to be present to each other. John Swinton says, "To be present to others is not simply to be alongside them; it is to recognize them for who they are and to learn what it means to love them."[17] Being present in the same room without being acknowledged, according to Ilan Wiesel and Christine Bigby, researchers in disabilities studies, could lead people with disabilities to feel rejected

---

15. Swinton, "Inclusion to Belonging," 183.
16. Swinton, "Inclusion to Belonging," 183.
17. Swinton, "Who is God?" 287.

and excluded.[18] Wiesel and Bigby call the non-interactive and tolerated presence of people with intellectual disabilities a "passive acceptance."[19] A hospitable exchange of a smile or a friendly gesture, such as a nod, a wave, or a high-five, acknowledges others' presence. However, a meaningful encounter often requires more. It entails an intentional interaction to get to know the person.[20] In fact, developing a relationship with a person with profound autism is not very different from establishing a relationship with other people. All healthy relationships require multiple intentional engagements so that both parties can get to know each other and build upon that knowledge to further their relationships.

The difference between physical presence and relational encounter is quite clearly visible in the case of The Cross. Initially, Dylan's presence at Awana was rarely acknowledged. Even when Anna invited others to greet him with something as non-committal and straightforward as a high five, the children at Awana were unwilling to do so. But as people gradually learned to interact with Dylan over a year, especially in the games sessions, they slowly became acquainted with him. Increasingly, they began to acknowledge him as a person worthy of attention, if not love. At the same time, Dylan also began to realize who cared about him and responded to them warmly and cheerfully.

We cannot develop a relationship with anyone unless we encounter them with an intent to know them personally. David Benner, psychologist and spiritual coach, alleges that "presence involves honouring the sacredness of whatever or whomever you seek to be present to."[21] I mentioned earlier the need for recognition and regard in a relationship of solidarity. To develop a relationship of equal siblinghood, we need to truly recognize that we belong to Christ together because of Christ's love and God's grace. No one in the household of God is more superior than another. All are beloved of God. This way of perceiving each other is how we can see each other as "sacred" as Benner says.

Moreover, Benner explains that when we treat our encounter with each other as a "sacred encounter," we will also encounter the Eternal God.[22] His idea is an expansion of Martin Buber's "I and Thou" concept. In an "I-It" relationship, the other person is regarded as an object (It). As an "It", the person is to be utilized or known for some purposes. In an "I-Thou"

---

18. Wiesel and Bigby, "Being Recognised," 1755.
19. Wiesel and Bigby, "Being Recognised," 1755.
20. Wiesel and Bigby, "Being Recognised," 1755.
21. Benner, *Presence and Encounter*, 78.
22. Benner, *Presence and Encounter*, 79.

encounter, we engage the Thou in its entirety and enter into a relationship with the person. In such an encounter, both the I and the Thou are transformed by the relationship.[23] Explicating Martin Buber's I and Thou concept for Christian encounters, Benner says,

> Every "It" can become a "Thou." And you hold the key to this transformation. That key is the way you engage it. Engage it with honour and its otherness will be revealed to you through an encounter with a "Thou" But engage with anything less than this, and you simply meet an "It."[24]

To encounter each other as a "Thou" requires acknowledging that every person is made in God's image. The key to experiencing the presence of a person with profound autism is the same. We must honor Ellen and Dylan's personhood and belovedness before we can truly be present with them and engage them in a sibling relationship.

An additional requirement to encounter a person with profound autism is to believe that they can enter into a relationship. In chapter 1, I discussed that people commonly presume that people with profound autism do not want social relationships due to difficulties in social interaction. I have demonstrated that this is false. The problems arise from the unrealistic expectations of people with profound autism to engage in social interactions in the same way that others do. When we recognize that people with profound autism want and can relate to others in their own way, we can also see that engagement with them requires the same intentionality that predetermines any other social engagement acts.

Ellen and Dylan's engagements with their communities illustrate this perfectly. We have seen that they want to have relationships with others and can sustain such relationships. What is necessary is people's willingness to engage them in "dialogues" that do not involve speech. When Ellen and a church member made up a game of pushing a glass back and forth between them at the pub, they encountered each other in a mutual and reciprocal relationship. Through this game, this church member recognized that Ellen is a fun-loving young woman like anyone else her age. For Ellen, she experienced a valuable moment of acceptance by this member and the others around the table who bore witness to this insight into Ellen, and a social transaction that many probably did not think was possible.

---

23. Buber, *I and Thou*, 31–32.
24. Benner, *Presence and Encounter*, 78.

Presence in Silence and Slowness

The intention to be present in our encounter with a person also involves being attentive and responsive to the person's interests, wishes, and needs. As an attendee at a church with many young adults, I often find myself "excluded" when their conversations focus around certain youth cultures entirely foreign to me. To be present with a person with profound autism requires attentiveness to this sort of situation. If loving a person involves honoring the person and respecting their uniqueness, we need to take time to be with them, do things that they will be comfortable with, and engage them in activities that will release their gifts.

Commonly, when we think about being present with someone, we think about having a meeting, a conversation, or a dialogue with him or her. Not relying on spoken words for communication is difficult for many of us. Coming from a contemplative tradition, Stephen Rossetti asserts that "perhaps true communication does not consist in the skillful use of words or in their abundance. Rather, it is an exchange of hearts."[25] He suggests that silence is a better way—in fact, "a golden way" of communicating love.[26] As we open our hearts to each other in silence, we receive each other "with respect and cherish it."[27] In the contemplative practice of being in God's presence, silence is undoubtedly an essential spiritual discipline. But that is not the only thing Rossetti wants us to understand. He uses an example of an older married couple sitting together in quietness to illustrate his point. Silence "is not merely an absence of words but rather a communion beyond the mind and heart; it is a communion of souls."[28] It is also how we can truly be present and encounter each other heart-to-heart.

Without much ability to use words to express their thoughts, sitting in silence with Dylan and Ellen is sometimes what it means to be present with them. Simply sitting together to enjoy each other's presence may require practice. In Rossetti's explanation, we see the echo of needing to open our hearts and welcome each other into our heart space. Indeed, welcoming each other into a space where God is present, where we can be open, heart to heart, is how we can appreciate the presence of others in silence. Theologian John Gillibrand and his son, Adam, who has profound autism, understand this beauty

---

25. Rossetti, "Pure Gold of Silence," 75.
26. Rossetti, "Pure Gold of Silence," 71.
27. Rossetti, "Pure Gold of Silence," 75.
28. Rossetti, "Pure Gold of Silence," 76.

of silent companionship. Gillibrand states that the time he spends sitting in silence with Adam is when he can most feel solidarity with him.[29]

At times, silence could also mean doing something together without exchanging words. Dylan's Circle friend Lydia demonstrates this well. She noticed that Dylan always brought a basketball to Awana. Although she was not athletic, Lydia engaged Dylan by passing the basketball back and forth between them. It was a simple game, but it often brought a smile to Dylan's face. Without speech, he understood and appreciated Lydia's love demonstrated by this simple ball game. The examples of interactions between Dylan, Ellen, and their Circle friends above speak to each participant's intentionality in being present to each other. These speechless games (passing a glass across a table or a basketball on the court) also speak to the friends' willingness to spend time with Dylan and Ellen in silence. Their desire to be present with Dylan and Ellen this way moved them towards kinship solidarity.

God's time is "slow" when considered within our fast-paced efficiency-minded context. But God's "slowness is in fact the speed of love."[30] To love others as Christ loves us, Swinton encourages us to learn to live in God's time.[31] Dylan's Circle friend Anna demonstrates the joy of being in God's presence with Dylan most beautifully. As a sporty young woman, Anna was very competitive during Awana's games. However, Anna was very gentle and patient with Dylan. She took the time to show Dylan the rules and take him by hand to participate in the games. It took them much longer to finish one set of hurdles because Dylan could not run, but the joy of friendship was evident when they walked around the obstacles. The joy on their faces was probably what drew others, especially the leader of the games, to pay attention to Dylan's particular needs. When Dylan's participation lengthened or slowed the game, she encouraged him to complete the games and changed the games to accommodate his needs. Perhaps, as Swinton says, it was in these acts of slowness that all who were present were drawn into God's loving presence.[32]

To conclude, I want to emphasize that to be with others begins with treasuring each other's presence. It means regarding others as beloved brothers and sisters, welcoming them into our hearts, and loving them. To do so requires that we look beyond human differences, including those manifested by profound autism. Being with one another requires not only

29. Gillibrand, *Disabled Church*, 66.
30. Swinton, *Becoming Friends*, 58.
31. Swinton, *Becoming Friends*, 73.
32. Swinton, *Becoming Friends*, 71.

the physical presence but also intentional engagement and willingness to spend time together. This intentionality includes being together in silence to enjoy each other's company. For many of us, remaining silent requires practice and extra time, but doing so reflects Christ's love and solidarity with us. When we can faithfully practice being with each other in more profound and meaningful ways, the Spirit will draw us into solidarity with Christ and each other.

Being for Others: Practicing the Love of Christ

Just as being *with* others flows from Jesus's being with us, our being *for* others is also rooted in Jesus's being for us. Dietrich Bonhoeffer explains this with the concept of vicarious representation, which I explained in chapter 5. Briefly, Christ is the vicarious representative for humanity because Jesus has taken the sin of humanity upon Himself on the cross. "In Christ . . . humanity has been brought once and for all . . . into community with God."[33] What concerns us here is how the church can follow Jesus's example to be vicarious in our practices of being-for-others. Clifford Green's explanation of Bonhoeffer's theology is helpful for this consideration.

> Christ's presence in church community transforms sin into the co-humanity of love which actively wills, affirms, serves, and bears the other; sin is overcome in "active being-for-one-another" where love voluntarily and vicariously identifies with and suffers for others, intercedes for others and forgive others.[34]

To be for others requires a recognition that we are co-humans with each other in the body of Christ. Being members of one body, we become "active being-for-one-another" because of the intimate connection within the body. It allows us to feel and share one another's joys and sufferings. The love we have for each other comes from Christ, whose love flows freely in the body, moving each member to love and care for each other.

Caring for One Another

To be with and for a person with profound autism will unavoidably involve personal support and care. When we look to Jesus for instructions on how we should practice our love for our siblings, we will see that Jesus's

---

33. Bonhoeffer, *Sanctorum Communio*, 146.
34. Green, *Bonhoeffer*, 55.

love is self-giving and entirely for others. Going to Judea to care for Mary, Martha, and Lazarus despite the Jews' hostility against him is an example (John 11: 5–8). To love like Jesus then is to think about others as more important than ourselves and care for them out of sibling love. When we love each other as Christ has loved us, his love flows into our relationship, eliminating the distinction between the carer and the cared for, thus drawing us into solidarity.

When we experience the presence of Christ in our caring relationship, we will see "caring" quite differently. In his study of Jean Vanier's theology, Benjamin Wall explains that Vanier considered caring as worship. When Christ is placed at the center of a caring act, the care we have for others becomes an expression of faith and a worshipful act. It is so because caring expresses the belief that God's divine action is breaking in through the "presence of Christ who claims the carer, sick, poor, and vulnerable."[35] It is an act of worship because Christ will receive our care for "the least" as care that is done to him (Matt 25:40).

To care is to love one's siblings in Christ. When we care, we acknowledge that the person we care for is a sibling, given to us as a gift. As loving siblings, we rejoice in our sibling's presence, thus stirring a desire to respond to their needs supportively. The caring act, performed out of love in the body of Christ, draws all closer to God, who in turn will transform us and deepen our relationship with each other.

As members of the body of Christ who are intimately joined together, one member's suffering becomes the entire body's suffering. As such, we should be aware of the stresses that primary caregivers experience from the demanding nature of care for those with profound autism. To express our concern, we can offer respite. John Swinton says, "Respite is a deeply timefull practice."[36] It is so because if we acknowledge time as a gift of God, then "giving away the gift to those who care is central to living faithfully" as Jesus's disciples.[37] When Ellen was young, Lillian received the gift of respite from a woman at the church, allowing Lillian to participate in worship once a month. To this day, Lillian is very grateful for this generous gift that made a huge difference in her life and Ellen's.

Although those who receive care may feel grateful, we should remember that caring is not pitying. Jesus says that as we respond to his call to care for those with needs, we care for him (Matt 25:40). When we meet each other in caring relationships in the presence of Christ, as many carers

---

35. Wall, *Welcome*, 88.
36. Swinton, *Becoming Friends*, 210.
37. Swinton, *Becoming Friends*, 210.

have testified, we receive as much, if not more, than we give. The presence of Christ in the caring relationship is transformative. As many assistants working at L'Arche have testified: Those who have learned to care often experience the love of Christ in many profound ways. Some reported gaining wisdom, new life, and new energy, but all found the community they yearned for.[38]

Carrying Each Other's Burden

Lillian and Vanessa talked about the difficult times, especially in Dylan and Ellen's early years. They both stated that encountering God in prayers gave them the strength to handle difficulties. To help Dylan, who experienced rejection and mocking frequently, Vanessa taught him to pray to Jesus. She observed that after prayers, Dylan regained peace and was able to forgive those who mocked him.

Using the psalmist in Psalm 22 as an example, Ann Fritschel (2002), Old Testament scholar, explains that in the face of dissonance and disorientation, one needs to bring their lament before God for a firm grounding of the situation.[39] In bringing one's suffering from profound autism in lament to God, one acknowledges the chaos in life brought upon by the experience of profound autism, the loneliness and injustice that comes from rejection by society, and the sense of helplessness in the situation.

Being a loving community, Fritschel suggests that we need to stand in solidarity with those lamenting. The communal lament expresses the community's loving care for them in two ways. First, the community embodies the presence of the seemingly absent God to the person with profound autism and his or her family. "The corporate presence both incarnates God's presence and enables individuals to find ways to relate to the lamenter."[40] Second, the community also "believe in God" for the lamenter.[41] By naming the pain as their own, the community depends on God with the lamenter, bringing them back to trust and hope in God.

John Swinton agrees. He further explains the idea of lamenting in solidarity by stressing the importance of adopting a "we" posture.[42] Swinton points out that "lament has a purpose and an endpoint beyond the simple

---

38. See, for example, Greig, *Reconsidering Intellectual Disability,* 248; and Vanier, *Community and Growth*, 131–34.

39. Fritschel, "Psalms," 24.

40. Fritschel, "Psalms," 28.

41. Fritschel, "Psalms," 28.

42. Swinton, *Raging with Compassion*, 113.

expression of pain, which is reconciliation with and a deeper love of God."[43] When people's lives are in turmoil, they may not see beyond their current situations. The lamenting community that takes a "we" approach carries them and sustains them during such times.

Recognizing the need for a lamenting community is vital for our love for individuals with profound autism and their families. As mentioned earlier, many families experienced rejection at the church. They either kept switching churches to find an accepting one or stopped attending church altogether. Their absence from church often went unnoticed. Without support, many families struggle to manage life with profound autism. Roberta Woodgate and her healthcare researchers team identified "living in a world of our own" was the primary experience of Canadian families with children with autism.[44] If we believe that the church is the body of Christ and members of the body are dependent on each other, we need to sincerely learn to be a loving and caring community and share each other's burdens.

By being with individuals with profound autism and their families, the church community's loving presence brings the healing power of God, helping them to trust and depend on God. The experience of God's love, in and through the community, is vital for them to navigate the complicated life of profound autism and experience joy and peace that surpass understanding.

Sharing Each Other's Joy

Having lived with people with intellectual disabilities for many years, Jean Vanier understood their struggles and shared their pain. Vanier also knew the importance of celebrating lives with disabilities. Instead of being seen as problems, people with significant intellectual disabilities "need laughter and play; they need people who will celebrate life with them and manifest their joy of being with them."[45] To have one's life celebrated is to know that one's life is worth living. Being in solidarity with people with profound autism, caring for them, and sharing their pain is not enough; we need to celebrate them and rejoice over them. With simple celebratory acts, we can communicate a love that reveals their value, a love that acknowledges them as a source of joy.

To celebrate, we need to be attentive and responsive to what is happening in our brother or sister's life. Lillian talked about this in one of her interviews. She experienced joy with each little milestone that Ellen passed. It

---

43. Swinton, *Raging with Compassion*, 111.
44. Woodgate et al., "Living in a World," 1078.
45. Vanier, *Becoming Human*, 26.

came from Ellen being able to say good morning to people without prompting, or something as simple as when Ellen was able to put away her iPad gently. No matter the size of the accomplishment, they brought joy to Lillian's heart. When Lillian praised Ellen for doing a good job, that validation brought a big smile to Ellen's face, which clearly indicated her joy.

Some members of Red Hill understood this idea of celebration. Once they became more comfortable communicating with Ellen, they commended her for serving as an usher. They also congratulated her on how well she did the job. These might be small gestures, but they went a long way in affirming Ellen, giving her confidence and helping her believe that she had a role in the community. At the same time, the joy in these small successes was mutual. Katie, one of Ellen's Circle friends, was delighted to see how Ellen could serve the church. The mutual appreciation and celebration not only brought joy but also deepened their relationship.

This experience in Red Hill demonstrates that in becoming siblings with persons with profound autism, we share in their successes in life, no matter how big or small. "Being for" involves taking time to join our brother or sister in their activities. Our interest in sharing what brings delight to their hearts is an act of celebration. It communicates an affinity and an affirmation that they are sources of our joy. At the same time, celebrating their successes brings joy to our hearts and further deepens the kinship love.

In sum, being for others is to be with others for their sake and on their terms. God calls us to be in solidarity with one another so that we can be a source of strength for each other. When our brother or sister needs attention, we provide care out of sibling love. In difficult times, we lift each other up in prayers of laments. In times of celebration, we rejoice with each other. To be present for others does not mean that we are better than others but instead says that we want to practice the love and compassion of Christ in our lives together. We acknowledge that people with profound autism are not objects of charity, but a source of joy and a gift of life. They are valuable siblings, just like all others in the body of Christ.

Kinship Solidarity

As an apostle tasked to establish Christian communities in the gentile world, Paul understood deeply the need to bring people with different backgrounds together as a community. To do so, Paul showed the early Christian communities (and us today) the Christians' identities as children of God, which forms the basis of our solidarity as siblings in Christ. As Horrell mentions, the kinship community expresses our solidarity in imitating

Christ's self-giving love for all peoples, but most profoundly in his love for the people living in dehumanized conditions.[46]

Unlike the Jewish teachers of his time, Jesus associated himself with people marginalized, oppressed, and abandoned by society. People were astonished that he would eat with the sinners (Mark 2:16) and touched the untouchable (Luke 5:13). Against the common view of his world, Jesus showed the Jews then, and us now, that his presence is to be experienced most profoundly on the margins of society. In his parting instructions to the disciples, Jesus taught them to immerse their lives with the least among them. Jesus says, "Truly I tell you, whatever you did for one of the least of these brothers and sisters of mine, you did for me" (Matt 25:40). Unexpectedly, solidarity with the least among us is the most life-giving thing we should do. If we desire to be in the presence of Jesus now and in eternity, we need to immerse ourselves in the lives of those who are forced to live on the margins of society.

Christ's love for humanity, regardless of who we are, teaches us to see Dylan, Ellen, and other people with profound autism more correctly as brothers and sisters and treat them with sibling love. Christ's love opens the doors of our hearts to welcome each other in and be truly present to each other. This deep connection builds us into a community of siblings that live in solidarity with Christ and each other.

Being in solidarity as one body in Christ does not eliminate individual differences. On the contrary, we celebrate our differences. In learning to practice kinship solidarity, we strive to be present to each other in the way that Jesus lived with and for us. When we do that, the Spirit joins us to Christ and brings us into solidarity with Christ and each other. In the oneness of the body, we share each other's joy and suffering. As such, the kinship community lives in a radically different fashion to that of the world. Instead of valuing power, appearance, and intelligence, we value each person regardless of their backgrounds or abilities. Our solidarity as a kinship community with people with all differences, including those living with profound autism, is how we can bear witness to Christ's love to the world and speak to Christ's solidarity with humanity.

---

46. Horrell, *Solidarity and Difference*, 218.

Conclusion

Proclaiming God's Holiness in Community Life

> But you are a chosen race, a royal priesthood, a holy nation, a people for his own possession, that you may proclaim the excellencies of him who called you out of darkness into his marvelous light. —1 Pet 2:9

THERE IS NO DENIAL that belonging is an issue for the church in Western countries like Canada. Dylan, Ellen, and their families were not the only people who needed help to find belonging at the church. However, as part of a group of people who are least likely to receive welcome and support at the church, Ellen and Dylan's perspectives offered us a magnified view of the issues of belonging at the church. As expected, they met with barriers that prevented them from belonging to the church as valued members. As explained in chapter 4, their experiences concurred with the issues of belonging identified by young Canadians. What their views from below offered is a deepened understanding of these issues.

Looking into why young people left the church, James Penner and associates found that these young people wanted "to be desired, pursued, valued, and celebrated. They want to know that they are missed in their absence and appreciated in their presence."[1] Four primary reasons for their leaving are hypocrisy (not practicing what was preached), judgmentalism (judgmental against certain behaviors), exclusivity (not giving a place and a voice to certain individuals), and failure (considered to be failing the church's expectations).[2] Similarly, Barna researchers David Kinnaman and

---

1. Penner et al., *Hemorrhaging Faith,* 63.
2. Penner et al., *Hemorrhaging Faith,* 58–65.

CONCLUSION: PROCLAIMING GOD'S HOLINESS IN COMMUNITY LIFE

Aly Hawkins reported that young Canadians "are a generation prepared to be not merely hearers of doctrine but doers of faith; they want to put their faith into action, not just to talk."[3] The title of their book, *You Lost Me*, summarizes these young Christians' dissatisfaction with the "talking heads" who did not live out what they preached.[4]

Not putting their faith into actions, incidentally, summarized the issues at Red Hill and The Cross. While members of both churches acknowledged that the church should be a family, they were not relating to each other in ways that reflected that belief. To be recognized as family members, Lillian and Vanessa should be supported when the church was aware of their needs. When Lillian and Ellen left the church, the absence of these family members would have been missed. When Ellen and Dylan arrived at the church, their expectations were similar to the young people mentioned above. They wanted "to be desired, pursued, valued, and celebrated," instead of being ignored and rejected.[5]

Reflecting on Dylan and Ellen's experiences of belonging, I suggest what needs to happen now is for the church to reconceptualize Christian relationships and reconsider the concept of the church as the household of God. As explained in chapter 6, the church is a people called by the covenanting God to live as a holy nation in this world. The covenanted people's faithful response to God's call to holiness is to love God and each other. God faithfully fulfilled the covenantal promise in and through the life and redemptive work of Jesus. Christ's example of living with and for people, especially those marginalized by society, gives believers a model for what life as God's faithful children should look like.

As a holy people called by God, we live in the world but separate from the world. The separation is an essential characteristic of what John Stott calls radical discipleship. Living out an alternative vision of community life is what sets us apart from the world. It is also a testimony to God's holiness. Stott says,

> The church has a double responsibility in relation to the world around us. On the one hand, we are to live, serve, and witness in the world. On the other hand, we are to avoid becoming contaminated by the world. So we are neither to seek to preserve our holiness by escaping from the world nor to sacrifice our holiness by conforming to the world.[6]

3. Kinnaman and Hawkins, *You Lost Me*, 11.
4. Ault et al., "Congregational Participation," 58.
5. Penner et al., *Hemorrhaging Faith*, 63.
6. John Stott, *Radical Disciple*, 17.

In a world that often views autism as a defect to get rid of, rejection and oppression of people with profound autism are common. The church should strongly resist becoming influenced by the worldly ideas of human values. Instead of honoring intelligence, appearance, and competence, the church has a responsibility to present a radically different view that cherishes people with profound autism as indispensable members of the community.

Acknowledging Ellen, Dylan, and others with profound autism as indispensable members begin with accepting that every human life has intrinsic value. The love of the Creator God defines the value of each of us. Each person is created in the image of God to live freely with and for God and each other. As such, Ellen and Dylan are free to be with and for others, in the same way that each human person is created to be. The church needs to respect their created freedom. Instead of requiring Dylan and Ellen to make changes and fit into how most people live, they should be supported to live their lives just as they are.

The experiences of The Cross and Red Hill showed us that without intentional encounters with Dylan and Ellen, people could not see beyond the autism label and know them as persons with their unique skill set. The relationships the Circle friends and some church members established with Ellen and Dylan helped them discover their gifts, personalities, and needs. Knowing Dylan and Ellen as a person triggered the subsequent changes that led Ellen and Dylan deeper into the church community. Put differently, encountering Ellen and Dylan with the trust in their abilities and desires to communicate and be involved in the community is the first step towards bringing them into the community as valuable members.

Given that church members' recognition of Dylan and Ellen's personhood arose from their relationships in the church context, we need to pay attention to the church's ethos of belonging. At best, with a community ethos of a school, Dylan could relate with others only as a student. Functioning as a community center, Ellen belonged to Red Hill as a member of its many activity clubs. These relationships were not deep enough for the two communities to live out the family relationships they claimed to have.

To truly belong as a family of God, we need to realize the covenantal nature of our kinship relations. Christians cannot choose to belong to Christ. Rather, Jesus summoned each of us to follow him. As each person responds to Jesus's call obediently, they are baptized into the body of Christ and become children of God. Recognition of the givenness nature of each member of the body is vital for us to receive each other as gifts of God and value each other as beloved siblings. When we can welcome Dylan and Ellen into the kinship community and engage with them as siblings in God's love, the Spirit corrects our misconception that they were dispensable because of their seeming weakness. With the Spirit's help, we can see them correctly as equally valuable members of God's household.

For Ellen and Dylan to belong to God as children in the divine household, they need to be incorporated into the body of Christ through baptism. Earlier, I have demonstrated that faith is a gift of God, not an intellectual assent. The acceptance of Dylan and Ellen is by the grace of Christ. The church's responsibility is to carry every person who desires to belong to Christ and commits them to the leading of the Spirit. Church members also need to dedicate their efforts to be companions on their discipleship journey.

Here we can see again the need to trust Ellen and Dylan's abilities to learn and communicate. Without the belief that Dylan and Ellen can learn, a discipleship pathway will not be considered. Although Christ is summoning them to his church, and they might believe in Christ, the bias against people with autism often leads to an assumption of incompetence. Reversing that, we need to acknowledge that the onus is on us, who have been given the gifts of understanding, to design a discipleship program suitable to Ellen and Dylan's unique learning styles.

Stanley Hauerwas says it well, "The mark of a truthful community is partly seen in how it enables the diversity of gifts and virtues to flourish. Therefore, the church is not only a community of character but also a community of characters, since we are convinced that God rejoices in the diversity of spirits who inhabit his church."[7] The church cannot claim to be a faithful community of Christ without rejoicing over the differences that exist in the church as God's gifts. Living as a community of loving siblings is not only the right thing to do as Christians. Our being a community of characters reflects God's holy character. The love that we have for one another, especially for those who seem to be weak, expresses the love of Christ that is with and for the world.

All of us, autistic or not, is valuable because God has lovingly and uniquely created each of us. We are brought together in the body of Christ by the Holy Spirit. When missing even one small part of the body, it will fail to be whole; it will lose the fullness of gifts that God sent to the community. Conversely, when we faithfully embody our calling as a mutually supportive sibling community and practice Christ's presence and love in how we live with and for each other, we will grow individually and corporately to become more holy like Christ.

---

7. Hauerwas, *Community of Character*, 14.

A Christian community with people of different characters living together as a loving family is a powerful proclamation of God's holiness. In his earthly ministry, Jesus showed us how he stands in solidarity with people with various disabilities against the society that oppressed them. In our world, people with disabilities continue to be oppressed and forced into poverty. Living out Christ's love by welcoming people with profound autism into the fabric of the community, standing in solidarity with them as they navigate the complicated life of autism, is what we must do as followers of Christ. When we obediently embody the holiness command of God in our community life, loving those with profound autism and others who are abandoned and oppressed by society, we testify to the world that all creatures of God are made uniquely and differently. Still, all can and should live harmoniously and lovingly together.

Bibliography

Aasgaard, Reidar. "Brotherhood in Plutarch and Paul: Its Role and Character." In *Constructing Early Christian Families: Family as Social Reality and Metaphor*, edited by Halvor Moxnes, 166–82. New York: Routledge, 2002.

Altiere, Matthew J., and Silvia von Kluge. "Searching for Acceptance: Challenges Encountered while Raising a Child with Autism." *Journal of Intellectual and Developmental Disability* 34 (2009) 142–52.

American Psychiatric Association. *Diagnostic and Statistical Manual of Mental Disorders (DSM-5®)*. Washington, DC: American Psychiatric Publishing, 2013.

Anagnostou, Evdokia, and Margot J. Taylor. "Review of Neuroimaging in Autism Spectrum Disorders: What Have We Learned and Where We Go from Here." *Molecular Autism* 2 (2011) 1–9.

Augustine, of Hippo, Saint. *The Trinity*. Translated by Edmund Hill. Edited by John E. Rotelle. New York: New City, 1991.

Ault, Melinda Jones, et al. "Congregational Participation and Supports for Children and Adults with Disabilities: Parent Perceptions." *Intellectual and Developmental Disabilities* 51 (2013) 48–61.

Ault, Melinda Jones, et al. "Factors Associated with Participation in Faith Communities for Individuals with Developmental Disabilities and Their Families." *Journal of Religion, Disability & Health* 17 (2013) 184–211.

Baglieri, Susan. *Disability Studies and the Inclusive Classroom: Critical Practices for Creating Least Restrictive Attitudes*. New York: Routledge, 2012.

Banks, Robert J. *Paul's Idea of Community: The Early House Churches in their Cultural Setting*. 2nd ed. Peabody: Hendrickson, 1994.

Barclay, John M. G. "An Identity Received from God: The Theological Configuration of Paul's Kinship Discourse." *Early Christianity* 8 (2017) 354–72.

Bartchy, S. Scott. "Undermining Ancient Patriarchy: The Apostle Paul's Vision of a Society of Siblings." *Biblical Theology Bulletin* 29 (1999) 68–78.

Barth, Karl. *Church Dogmatics*, Vol.≠≠ III: *The Doctrine of Creation*. Edited by G. W. Bromiley and T. F. Torrance. Translated by J. W. Edwards et al. Edinburgh: T. & T. Clark, 1958.

Beckwith, Roger T. "The Unity and Diversity of God's Covenant." *Tyndale Bulletin* 38 (1987) 93–118.

Bell, Valerie. *2017 Annual Report*. Streamwood, IL: Awana International, 2017.

Benner, David G. *Presence and Encounter: The Sacramental Possibilities of Everyday Life*. Grand Rapids: Brazos, 2014.

Biklen, Douglas, and Jamie Burke. "Presuming Competence." *Equity & Excellence in Education* 39 (2006) 166–175.

Birge, Mary Katherine. *The Language of Belonging: A Rhetorical Analysis of Kinship Language in First Corinthians*. Leuven: Peeters, 2002.

Bogdashina, Olga. *Sensory Perceptual Issues in Autism and Asperger Syndrome: Different Sensory Experiences - Different Perceptual Worlds*. London: Jessica Kingsley, 2016.

Bölte, Sven. "Is Autism Curable?" *Developmental Medicine & Child Neurology* 56 (2014) 927–31.

Bonhoeffer, Dietrich. *Act and Being: Transcendental Philosophy and Ontology in Systematic Theology*. Translated by H. Martin Rumscheidt, edited by Wayne Floyd Jr. Dietrich Bonhoeffer Works in English 2. Minneapolis: Fortress, 2009.

———. *Creation and Fall: A Theological Exposition of Genesis 1–3*. Translated by Douglas S. Bax. Edited by John W. de Gruchy. Dietrich Bonhoeffer Works in English 3. Minneapolis: Fortress, 1997.

———. *Discipleship*. Translated by Barbara Green and Reinhard Krauss. Edited by Geffrey B. Kelly and John D. Godfrey. Dietrich Bonhoeffer Works in English 4. Minneapolis: Fortress, 2003.

———. *Ethics*. Translated by Reinhard Krauss et al. Edited by Clifford J. Green. Dietrich Bonhoeffer Works in English 6. Minneapolis: Fortress, 2005.

———. "Lectures on Christology." In *The Bonhoeffer Reader*, edited by Clifford J. Green and Michael P. De Jonge, 274–81. Minneapolis: Fortress, 2013.

———. *Letters and Papers from Prison*. Translated by Isabel Best, et al., edited by John W. de Gruchy. Dietrich Bonhoeffer Works in English 8. Minneapolis: Fortress, 2010.

———. *Life Together: Prayerbook of the Bible*. Translated by Daniel W. Bloesch and James H. Burtness. Edited by Geffrey B. Kelly. Dietrich Bonhoeffer Works in English 5. Minneapolis: Fortress, 1996.

———. *Sanctorum Communio*. Translated by Reinhard Krauss and Nancy Lukens, edited by Clifford J. Green. Dietrich Bonhoeffer Works in English 1. Minneapolis: Fortress, 2009.

———. "Theological Position on the Question of Baptism." In *The Bonhoeffer Reader*, edited by Clifford J. Green and Michael P. De Jonge, 717–32. Minneapolis: Fortress, 2013.

Bonker, Elizabeth M., and Virginia G. Breen. *I Am in Here: The Journey of a Child with Autism Who Cannot Speak but Finds Her Voice*. Grand Rapids: Baker, 2011.

Boyd, Brian A., et al. "Sensory Features and Repetitive Behaviors in Children with Autism and Developmental Delays." *Autism Research* 3 (2010) 78–87.

Brewer, Brian C. *Distinctly Baptist: Proclaiming Identity in a New Generation*. Valley Forge, PA: Judson, 2011.

Bridge, Donald, and David Phypers. *The Water That Divides: A Survey of the Doctrine of Baptism*. Fearn, UK: Christian Focus, 1998.

Broady, Timothy R., et al. "Understanding Carers' Lived Experience of Stigma: The Voice of Families with a Child on the Autism Spectrum." *Health & Social Care in the Community* 25 (2017) 224–33.

Brock, Brian. "Augustine's Hierarchies of Human Wholeness and their Healing." In *Disability in the Christian Tradition*, edited by Brian Brock and John Swinton, 65–100. Grand Rapids: Eerdmans, 2012.

———. "Theologizing Inclusion: 1 Corinthians 12 and the Politics of the Body of Christ." *Journal of Religion, Disability & Health* 15 (2011) 351–76.

Brower, Kent. *Living as God's Holy People: Holiness and Community in Paul*. Milton Keynes, UK: Authentic Media, 2014.

Browning, Don S. *A Fundamental Practical Theology: Descriptive and Strategic Proposals*. Minneapolis: Fortress, 1995.

Brueggemann, Walter. *Theology of the Old Testament: Testimony, Dispute, Advocacy*. Minneapolis: Fortress, 1997.

———. *An Unsettling God: The Heart of the Hebrew Bible*. Minneapolis: Fortress, 2009.

Buber, Martin. *I and Thou*, Translated by R. Gregory Smith. Edinburgh: T. & T. Clark, 1958.

Casson, Ann. "A Sense of Belonging: Spiritual Development in Christian-Ethos Secondary Schools." In *Christian Faith, Formation and Education*, edited by Ros Stuart-Buttle, and John Shortt, 165–80. London: Springer, 2018.

Chennattu, Mary J. Rekha. *Johannine Discipleship as a Covenant Relationship*. Peabody, PA: Hendrickson, 2006.

Comensoli, Peter A. *In God's Image: Recognizing the Profoundly Impaired as Persons*, edited by Nigel Zimmermann. Eugene, OR: Cascade Books, 2018.

Copeland, M. Shawn. "The New Anthropological Subject at the Heart of the Mystical Body of Christ." *Proceedings of the Catholic Theological Society of America* 53 (1998) 25–47.

Cortez, Marc. *Theological Anthropology: A Guide for the Perplexed*. Edinburgh: T. & T. Clark, 2010.

Cox, Jennifer Anne. *Autism, Humanity and Personhood: A Christ-Centred Theological Anthropology*. Newcastle upon Tyne: Cambridge Scholars, 2017.

Cross, Frank Moore. "Kinship and Covenant in Ancient Israel." In *From Epic to Canon: History and Literature in Ancient Israel*, 3–21. Baltimore: Johns Hopkins University Press, 2000.

David, E. J. R., and Annie O. Derthick. "What Is Internalized Oppressions, and So What?" In *Internalized Oppression: Psychology of Marginalization*. Edited by E. J. R. David. New York: Springer, 2013.

Dawson, Geraldine, and Kathleen Zanolli. "Early Intervention and Brain Plasticity in Autism." In *Autism: Neural Basis and Treatment Possibilities*, edited by Gregory Bock and Jamie Goode, 266–80. Chichester, UK: Wiley, 2003.

De Cointet, Pierre, et al. *Catechism of the Catholic Church and the Craft of Catechesis*. San Francisco: Ignatius, 2018.

Deidun, Thomas J. *New Covenant Morality in Paul*. Rome: Gregorian Biblical Press, 2006.

Dinishak, Janette, and Nameera Akhtar. "A Critical Examination of Mindblindness as a Metaphor for Autism." *Child Development Perspectives* 7 (2013) 110–14.

Donnellan, Anne M., et al., "Rethinking Autism: Implications of Sensory and Movement Differences for Understanding and Support." *Frontiers in Integrative Neuroscience* 6 (2013). https://www.ncbi.nlm.nih.gov/pmc/articles/PMC3556589/.

Duffy, John, and Rebecca Dorner. "The Pathos of 'Mindblindness': Autism, Science, and Sadness in 'Theory of Mind' Narratives." *Journal of Literary & Cultural Disability Studies* 5 (2011) 201–15.

Dunn, James D. G. *The New Perspective on Paul*. Grand Rapids: Eerdmans, 2007.

Dunning, David. *Social Motivation*. East Sussex, UK: Psychology, 2011.

Dykens, E. M., and M. Lense. "Intellectual Disabilities and Autism Spectrum Disorder: A Cautionary Note." In *Autism Spectrum Disorders*, edited by David Amaral et al., 261–69. Oxford: Oxford University Press, 2011.

Earls, Aaron, "Churches Believe They Are Welcoming to Those with Disabilities." https://lifewayresearch.com/2020/03/10/churches-believe-they-are-welcoming-to-those-with-disabilities/.

Eastman, Susan. "Oneself in Another: Participation and the Spirit in Romans 8." In *"In Christ" in Paul: Explorations in Paul's Theology of Union and Participation*, edited by Michael Thate, et al., 103–25. Heidelberg: Mohr/Siebeck, 2014.

Elliott, John H. "The Jesus Movement was not Egalitarian but Family-Oriented." *Biblical Interpretation* 11 (2003) 173–210.

Erickson, Millard J. *Christian Theology*. Grand Rapids: Baker Academic, 1998.

Falvey, Mary, et al. *All My Life's a Circle: Using the Tools-Circles, MAPS and PATH*. 2nd ed. Toronto: Inclusion, 2015.

Farajallah, Peiling Su. "Coping Styles and Stress Levels of Chinese-American Mothers of Disabled Children." PhD diss., University of Arizona, 1996.

Ferguson, Sinclair. "Infant Baptism View." In *Baptism: Three Views*, edited by David F. Wright, 77–112. Downers Grove: IVP Academic, 2009.

Frederickson, Norah, and Jane Turner. "Utilizing the Classroom Peer Group to Address Children's Social Needs: An Evaluation of the Circle of Friends Intervention Approach." *Journal of Special Education* 36 (2003) 234–45.

Frith, Uta. *Autism: Explaining the Enigma*. Oxford: Blackwell, 2003.

Fritschel, Ann. "The Psalms: Individual Laments as Communal Hymns." In *The Difficult but Indispensable Church*, edited by Norma Cook Everist. Minneapolis: Fortress, 2002.

Furnish, Victor Paul. *Theology and Ethics in Paul*. 3rd ed. Louisville: Westminster John Knox, 2009.

Gaventa, William. "Learning from People with Disabilities: How to Ask the Question." In *The Paradox of Disability: Responses to Jean Vanier and L'Arche Communities from Theology and the Sciences*, edited by Hans Reinders, 103–12. Grand Rapids: Eerdmans, 2010.

Gay, David A., and John P. Lynxwiler. "Cohort, Spirituality, and Religiosity: A Cross-Sectional Comparison." *Journal of Religion and Society* 15 (2013) 1–17.

Gillibrand, John. *Disabled Church–Disabled Society: The Implications of Autism for Philosophy, Theology and Politics*. London: Kingsley, 2010.

Godawa, Brian. *Word Pictures: Knowing God through Story and Imagination*. Downers Grove, IL: InterVarsity, 2009.

Goode, David. *A World without Words: The Social Construction of Children Born Deaf and Blind*. Philadelphia: Temple University Press, 1994.

Green, Clifford J. *Bonhoeffer: A Theology of Sociality*. Grand Rapids: Eerdmans, 1999.

Greig, Jason Reimer. *Reconsidering Intellectual Disability: L'Arche, Medical Ethics, and Christian Friendship*. Washington, DC: Georgetown University Press, 2015.

Grenz, Stanley J. *Theology for the Community of God*. Grand Rapids: Eerdmans, 2000.

Grudem, Wayne A. *Bible Doctrine: Essential Teachings of the Christian Faith*, edited by Jeff Purswell. Grand Rapids: Zondervan, 1999.

Hafemann, Scott. "The Covenant Relationship." In *Central Themes in Biblical Theology*, edited by Scott Hafemann and Paul R. House, 20–61. Grand Rapids: Baker Academic, 2007.

Hacking, Ian. "Humans, Aliens & Autism." *Daedalus* 138 (2009) 44–59.

Hahn, Scott. *Kinship by Covenant: A Canonical Approach to the Fulfillment of God's Saving Promises*. New Haven: Yale University Press, 2009.

Hammett, John. "Regenerate Church Membership." In *Restoring Integrity in Baptist Churches*, edited by Thomas White et al., 21–44. Grand Rapids: Kregel Academic, 2008.

Hammond, George C. *It Has not Yet Appeared What We Shall Be: A Reconsideration of the Imago Dei in Light of Those with Severe Cognitive Disabilities*. Phillipsburg: P&R, 2017.

Hanson, Paul D. *The People Called: The Growth of Community in the Bible*. 2nd ed. Louisville: Westminster John Knox, 2001.

Harrington, Mary Therese. "Affectivity and Symbols in Catechesis." In *Developmental Disabilities and Sacramental Access: New Paradigms for Sacramental Encounters*, edited by Edward Foley, 116–29. Collegeville, MN: Liturgical, 1994.

Hassall, Richard. "Does Everybody with an Autism Diagnosis Have the Same Underlying Condition?" In *Rethinking Autism: Diagnosis, Identity and Equality*, edited by Katherine Runswick-Cole et al., 49–65. London: Kingsley, 2016.

Hauerwas, Stanley. *A Community of Character: Toward a Constructive Christian Social Ethic*. Notre Dame: University of Notre Dame Press, 1991.

———. "Suffering the Retarded: Should We Prevent Retardation?" In *Critical Reflections on Stanley Hauerwas' Theology of Disability: Disabling Society, Enabling Theology*, edited by John Swinton, 87–112. Binghamton: Haworth Pastoral, 2005.

Hauerwas, Stanley, and Jean Vanier. *Living Gently in a Violent World: The Prophetic Witness of Weakness*. Downers Grove, IL: InterVarsity, 2010.

Heim, S. Mark. "Baptismal Recognition and the Baptist Churches." In *Baptism and the Unity of the Church*, edited by Michael Root and Risto Saarinen, 150–163. Grand Rapids: Eerdmans, 1998.

Higashida, Naoki. *Fall Down 7 Times Get Up 8*. Translated by K. A. Yoshida and David Mitchell. Toronto: Knopf. 2017.

Hodge, Caroline Johnson. *If Sons, Then Heirs: A Study of Kinship and Ethnicity in the Letters of Paul*. Oxford: Oxford University Press, 2007.

Hodge, Nick. "Schools without Labels." In *Rethinking Autism: Diagnosis, Identity and Equality*, edited by Katherine Runswick-Cole et al., 185–203. London: Kingsley, 2016.

Hollin, Gregory J. S., and Alison Pilnick. "Infancy, Autism, and the Emergence of a Socially Disordered Body." *Social Science & Medicine* 143 (2015) 279–86.

Horrell, David G. *Solidarity and Difference: A Contemporary Reading of Paul's Ethics*. 2nd ed. London: T. & T. Clark, 2015.

Huntly, Alyson C. *Open Hearts: Resources for Affirming Ministries in the United Church of Canada*. http://ause.ca/wp-content/pdf/OpenHearts.pdf.

Jaarsma, Pier, and Stellan Welin. "Autism as a Natural Human Variation: Reflections on the Claims of the Neurodiversity Movement." *Health Care Analysis* 20 (2012) 20–30.

James, Alistair, and Gerv Leyden. "Putting the Circle Back into Circle of Friends: A Grounded Theory Study." *Educational and Child Psychology* 27 (2010) 52–63.

Jaimeson, Bobby. *Going Public: Why Baptism Is Required for Church Membership*. Nashville: Broadman & Holman, 2015.

Johnson, Maxwell E. *The Rites of Christian Initiation: Their Evolution and Interpretation*. Collegeville, MN: Liturgical, 2007.

Jones, L. Gregory. "Baptism: A Dramatic Journey into God's Dazzling Light: Baptismal Catechesis and the Shaping of Christian Practical Wisdom." In *Knowing the Triune God: The Work of the Spirit in the Practices of the Church*, edited by James Buckley et al, 147–178. Grand Rapids: Eerdmans, 2001.

Jones, Simon. *Celebrating Christian Initiation: A Practical Guide to Baptism, Confirmation and Rites for the Christian Journey*. London: SPCK, 2016.

Kanner, Leo. "Autistic Disturbances of Affective Contact." *Nervous Child* 2 (1943) 217–50.

Kaylor, R. David. *Paul's Covenant Community: Jew and Gentile in Romans*. Louisville: Westminster John Knox, 1988.

Kervin, William. *The Language of Baptism: A Study of the Authorized Baptismal Liturgies of the United Church of Canada, 1925–1995*. Lanham, MD: Scarecrow, 2003.

Kinnaman, David, and Aly Hawkins. *You Lost Me: Why Young Christians Are Leaving Church and Rethinking Faith*. New York: Baker, 2011.

Kinnear, Sydney H., et al., "Understanding the Experience of Stigma for Parents of Children with Autism Spectrum Disorder and the Role Stigma Plays in Families' Lives." *Journal of Autism and Developmental Disorder* 46 (2016) 942–53.

Kramer-Mills, Hartmut. "Walter's Ingress: How a Young Man Transformed a Church." *Journal of Religion, Disability & Health* 14 (2010) 269–78.

Macaskill, Grant. *Union with Christ in the New Testament*. Oxford: Oxford University Press, 2013.

Mak, Winnie W. S., and Yvonne T. Y. Kwok. "Internalization of Stigma for Parents of Children with Autism Spectrum Disorder in Hong Kong." *Social Science & Medicine* 20 (2010) 2045–51.

Martens, Elmer A. *God's Design: A Focus on Old Testament Theology*. 4th ed. Eugene, OR: Wipf & Stock, 2015.

McCormack, Bruce. "Misuse of Imago Dei." Paper presented at Los Angeles Theology Conference, 3 Feb. 2015. https://postbarthian.com/2015/02/24/bruce-mccormack-misuse-imago-dei-image-god/.

McDonaugh, Patrick. "Autism and the Age of Empathy." In *Worlds of Autism: Across the Spectrum of Neurological Difference*, edited by Joyce Davidson and Michael Orsini. Minneapolis: University of Minnesota Press, 2013.

McGuire, Anne. *War on Autism: On the Cultural Logic of Normative Violence*. Ann Arbor: University of Michigan Press, 2016.

McNair, Jeff. "Christian Social Constructions of Disability." *Journal of Religion, Disability & Health* 11 (2007) 51–64

Ne'eman, Ari. "The Future (and Past) of Autism Advocacy or Why the ASA's Magazine, The Advocate, Wouldn't Publish This Piece." *Disability Studies Quarterly* 30 (2010). http://dsq-sds.org/article/view/1059/1244.

Mengestu, Abera M. *God as Father in Paul: Kinship Language and Identity Formation in Early Christianity*. Eugene, OR: Pickwick Publications, 2013.

Monteith, William Graham. *Epistles of Inclusion: St. Paul's Inspired Attitudes*. Tolworth, UK: Grosvenor, 2010.
Mukhopadhyay, Tito Rajarshi. *I'm not a Poet but I Write Poetry: Poems from My Autistic Mind*. Bloomington: Xlibris, 2012.
Müller, Ralph-Axel, and Inna Fishman. "Brain Connectivity and Neuroimaging of Social Networks in Autism." *Trends in Cognitive Sciences* 22 (2018) 1103–16.
Nordahl-Hansen, Anders et al. "Mental Health on Screen: A DSM-5 Dissection of Portrayals of Autism Spectrum Disorders in Film and TV." *Psychiatry Research* 262 (2017) 351–53.
Nordahl-Hansen, Anders et al. "Pros and Cons of Character Portrayals of Autism on TV and Film." *Journal of Autism and Developmental Disorders* 48 (2018) 635–36.
Nouwen, Henri J. M. *Adam: God's Beloved*. Maryknoll, NY: Orbis, 2012.
Nouwen, Henri J. M. et al. *Compassion: A Reflection on the Christian Life*. New York: Imagebooks/Doubleday, 2006.
O'Farrell, Kevin. "Profound Intellectual Disability and the Grammar of Baptism." *Journal of Disability and Religion* 23 (2009) 387–406.
Ogletree, Thomas W. *The Use of the Bible in Christian Ethics*. Louisville: Westminster John Knox, 2003.
Olivas, Bernice M. "What I Mean When I Say Autism: Re-Thinking the Roles of Language and Literacy in Autism Discourse." Master's thesis, University of Nebraska, 2012.
Olson, Roger. "The Baptist View." In *The Lord's Supper: Five Views*, edited by Gordon T. Smith, 91–108. Downers Grove, IL: IVP Academic, 2010.
Owens, Janine. "Exploring the Critiques of the Social Model of Disability: The Transformative Possibility of Arendt's Notion of Power." *Sociology of Health & Illness* 37 (2015) 385–403.
Penner, James et al. *Hemorrhaging Faith: Why & When Canadian Young Adults Are Leaving, Staying & Returning to the Church*. Toronto: EFC, 2011.
Persico, Antonio M., and Thomas Bourgeron. "Searching for Ways Out of the Autism Maze: Genetic, Epigenetic and Environmental Clues." *Trends in Neurosciences* 29 (2006) 349–58.
Post, Stephen G. "Drawing Closer: Preserving Love in the Face of 'Hypercognitive' Values." In *The Paradox of Disability: Responses to Jean Vanier and L'Arche Communities from Theology and the Sciences*, edited by Hans Reinders, 27–36. Grand Rapids: Eerdmans, 2010.
Pratt, Lonni Collins, and Daniel Homan. *Radical Hospitality: Benedict's Way of Love*. Brewster: Paraclete, 2011.
Pridmore, Eric. "The Christian Reformed Church as a Model for the Inclusion of People with Disabilities." *Journal of Religion, Disability & Health* 10 (2006) 93–107.
Prince, Dawn Eddings. "An Exceptional Path: An Ethnographic Narrative Reflecting on Autistic Parenthood from Evolutionary, Cultural, and Spiritual Perspectives." *Ethos* 38 (2010) 56–68.
Rapin, Isabelle. "Introduction: Autism Turns 65—A Neurologist's Bird Eye View." In *Autism Spectrum Disorders*, edited by David Amaral, et al., 3–14. Oxford: Oxford University Press, 2011.
Reimer, Kevin Scott. *Living L'Arche: Stories of Compassion, Love and Disability*. Collegeville, MN: Liturgical, 2009.

Reinders, Hans S. *Receiving the Gift of Friendship: Profound Disability, Theological Anthropology, and Ethics.* Grand Rapids: Eerdmans, 2008.

Reiser, William E. *Jesus in Solidarity with His People: A Theologian Looks at Mark.* Collegeville, MN: Liturgical, 2000.

Rendtorff, Rolf. *The Covenant Formula: An Exegetical and Theological Investigation.* New York: Bloomsbury Academic, 1998.

Reynolds, Thomas E. *Vulnerable Communion: A Theology of Disability and Hospitality.* Grand Rapids: Brazos, 2008.

Root, Michael, and Risto Saarinen. *Baptism and the Unity of the Church.* Grand Rapids: Eerdmans, 1998.

Rossetti, Stephen. "The Pure Gold of Silence." In *Spiritual Traditions for the Contemporary Church*, edited by Robin Maas and Gabriel O'Donnell, 73–82. Nashville: Abingdon, 1990.

Runswick-Cole, Katherine. "Understanding This Thing Called Autism." In *Rethinking Autism: Diagnosis, Identity and Equality*, edited by Sami Timimi, et al., 19–29. London: Kingsley, 2016.

Sacks, Oliver. *An Anthropologist on Mars: Seven Paradoxical Tales.* New York: Vintage, 1995.

Sarrett, Jennifer C. "Trapped Children: Popular Images of Children with Autism in the 1960s and 2000s." *Journal of Medical Humanities* 32 (2011) 141–53.

Scherr, Jessica F. et al., "Stranger Fear and Early Risk for Social Anxiety in Preschoolers with Fragile X Syndrome Contrasted to Autism Spectrum Disorder." *Journal of Autism and Developmental Disorder* 47 (2017) 3741–55.

Schlieder, Mary et al. "An Investigation of "Circle of Friends" Peer-Mediated Intervention for Students with Autism." *Journal of Social Change* 6 (2014) 27–40.

Schreiner, Thomas R. *Romans.* Grand Rapids: Baker Academic, 1998.

Shute, Nancy. "Desperate for an Autism Cure." *Scientific American* 303 (2010) 80–85.

Silberman, Steve. *Neurotribes: The Legacy of Autism and the Future of Neurodiversity.* New York: Avery, 2015.

Singer, Judy, and Sally French. "Why Can't You Be Normal for Once in Your Life?" In *Disability Discourse*, edited by Mairian Corker and Sally French, 59–67. Buckingham, UK: Open University Press, 1999.

Singer, Peter. "Twenty Questions." *Journal of Practical Ethics* 4 (2016) 67–78.

Smith, Duane Andre. "Kinship and Covenant in Hosea 11: 1–4." *Horizons in Biblical Theology* 16 (1994) 41–53.

Spurgeon, Charles. "Children Brought to Christ, not to the Font." In *The Metropolitan Tabernacle Pulpit*, 581–88. London: Passmore & Alabaster, 1865.

Stott, John R. *The Radical Disciple: Some Neglected Aspects of Our Calling.* Downers Grove, IL: InterVarsity, 2012.

Stubblefield, Anna. "Knowing Other Minds: Ethics and Autism." In *The Philosophy of Autism*, edited by Jani Anderson and Simon Cushing, 143–66. Lanham, MD: Rowman & Littlefield, 2008.

Swinton, John. *Becoming Friends of Time: Disability, Timefullness, and Gentle Discipleship.* Waco, TX: Baylor University Press, 2016.

———. "The Body of Christ Has Down's Syndrome: Theological Reflections on Vulnerability, Disability, and Graceful Communities." *Journal of Pastoral Theology* 13 (2003) 66–78.

---. "From Inclusion to Belonging: A Practical Theology of Community, Disability and Humanness." *Journal of Religion, Disability & Health* 16 (2012) 172–90.
---. *Raging with Compassion: Pastoral Responses to the Problem of Evil*. London: SCM, 2018.
---. "Reflections on Autistic Love." *Practical Theology* 5 (2012) 259–78.
---. "Restoring the Image: Spirituality, Faith, and Cognitive Disability." *Journal of Religion and Health* 36 (1997) 21–28.
---. "Who Is the God We Worship? Theologies of Disability; Challenges and New Possibilities." *International Journal of Practical Theology* 14 (2011) 273–307.
Swinton, John, and Harriet Mowat. *Practical Theology and Qualitative Research*. 2nd ed. London: SCM, 2016.
Tanner, Kathryn. "Trinity, Christology, and Community." In *Christology and Ethics*, edited by F. LeRon Shults, and Brent Waters, 56–74. Grand Rapids: Eerdmans, 2010.
Thompson, James W. *Moral Formation according to Paul: The Context and Coherence of Pauline Ethics*. Grand Rapids: Baker Academic, 2011.
United Church of Canada. *Church Membership: Doctrine and Practice in the United Church of Canada*. Toronto: Church Union Office Collection, 1963.
---. Theology and Inter-Church Inter-Faith Committee *Ecclesiology Report*. Toronto, 2012.
Vanier, Jean. *Becoming Human*. Rev. ed. New York: Paulist, 2008.
---. *Community and Growth*. Mahwah, NJ: Paulist, 2006.
Verhoeff, Berend. "What Is This Thing Called Autism? A Critical Analysis of the Tenacious Search for Autism's Essence." *Biosocieties* 7 (2012) 410–32.
Vorstman, Jacob A. S. et al. "Autism Genetics: Opportunities and Challenges for Clinical Translation." *Nature Reviews Genetics* 18 (2017) 362–76.
Vukov, Joseph. "Personhood and Natural Kinds: Why Cognitive Status Need not Affect Moral Status." *Journal of Medicine and Philosophy* 42 (2017) 261–77.
Wadell, Paul J. *Happiness and the Christian Moral Life: An Introduction to Christian Ethics*. Plymouth: Rowman & Littlefield, 2016.
Wall, Benjamin S. *Welcome as a Way of Life: A Practical Theology of Jean Vanier*. Eugene, OR: Cascade, 2016.
Wang, Peishi, et al., "Stresses and Coping Strategies of Chinese Families with Children with Autism and Other Developmental Disabilities." *Journal of Autism and Developmental Disorders* 41 (2011) 783–95.
Ware, Bruce. "Believer's Baptism View." In *Baptism: Three Views*, edited by David F. Wright, 19–50. Downers Grove, IL: IVP Academic, 2009.
Watermeyer, Brian, and Tristan Görgens. "Disability and Internalized Oppression." In *Internalized Oppression: The Psychology of Marginalized Groups*, edited by E. J. R. David, 253–80. New York: Springer, 2013.
Webb, Marsena Williams. "A Study of Churches as a Source of Support for Families with Children on the Autism Spectrum." Ed.D. diss., University of Tennessee, 2012.
Webb-Mitchell, Brett. *Beyond Accessibility: Toward Full Inclusion of People with Disabilities in Faith Communities*. New York: Church, 2010.
Welch, Christie, et al., "Autism Inside Out: Lessons from the Memoirs of Three Minimally Verbal Youths." *Disability and Rehabilitation* 41 (2019) 2308–16.
Weiss Block, Jennie. *Copious Hosting: A Theology of Access for People with Disabilities*. New York: Bloomsbury Academic, 2002.

Whitehead, Andrew L. "Religion and Disability: Variation in Religious Service Attendance Rates for Children with Chronic Health Conditions." *Journal for the Scientific Study of Religion* 57 (2018) 377–95.

Whitt, Jason. "Baptism and Profound Intellectual Disability." *Christian Reflection: A Series in Faith and Ethics* 45 (2012) 60–67.

Wiesel, Ilan, and Christine Bigby. "Being Recognised and Becoming Known: Encounters between People with and without Intellectual Disability in the Public Realm." *Environment and Planning A: Economy and Space* 46 (2014) 1754–69.

Woodgate, Roberta L. et al. "Living in a World of Our Own: The Experience of Parents Who Have a Child with Autism." *Qualitative Health Research* 18 (2008) 1075–83.

Wright, N. T. *Climax of the Covenant: Christ and the Law in Pauline Theology*. London: T. & T. Clark, 2004.

Zink, Jesse. "Patiently Living with Difference: Rowan Williams' Archiepiscopal Ecclesiology and the Proposed Anglican Covenant." *Ecclesiology* 9 (2013) 223–41.

Index

Augustine, 82–83, 149
Affirming Ministries, 53–54
autism, 11–27
    as a disorder, 12–16
    as a bio-sociological phenomenon, 20–25
    as a human difference, 19–20
    as a social construction, 17–18
    cultural bias, 8, 31
    DSM-5, 12
    evil spirits, 30–31, 91
    language and communication, 23–24
    mindblindness, 24–25
    profound autism, 6
    sensory-motor difficulties, 21–23

baptism, 90–91, 128–42, 157, 177
    believer baptism, 132–34
    Bonhoeffer on baptism, 140–48
    incorporation into Christ, 110–12
    infant baptism, 135–36
    initiation rite, 129–30, 138
Barclay, John, 110–12
Bartchy, S. Scott, 118
Barth, Karl, 84–85
being for others, 122–24, 160, 168, 172
    caring, 168–70
    celebrate life, 171
    lament, 170–71
being with others, 120–22, 160–61
    being present, 163–65
    radical welcome, 161–63
    silence and slowness, 166
belonging, 129, 152, 175
    eye-opening experience, 45–46, 59, 61, 69
    from inclusion to belonging, 2–4, 163
    intentional engagements, 59, 72, 76, 95, 164
    issues of belonging, 71–75
    mutually enriching journey, 63–64, 77–78, 150
Biklen, Douglas, 88, 148
Bonhoeffer, Dietrich, 95–96, 130, 139
    cheap grace, 139–40
    Christ exists as church community, 147
    definition of faith, 138, 142
    freedom, 97–98
    I-Thou, 101, 144
    spiritual love, 157–58
    theology of baptism, 139–40
    theology of sociality, 95, 97, 139
    vicarious representation, 99, 102–3, 142, 168
Brock, Brian, 83, 155
Brower, Kent, 107–8
Brueggemann, Walter, 107, 113
Buber, Martin, 164–65

catechesis, 146, 148–50

INDEX

celebrating differences, 17, 36, 90–91, 160, 164, 173
church, 120, 174–77
    body of Christ, 2, 74–75, 110, 122, 151–58
    covenant community, 105–7
    divine reality, 140
    household of God, 4, 9–10, 74, 110–11, 176
    kinship community, 108–11
community relationship, 72–74, 119
Comensoli, Peter, 88–89
covenant, 105–8, 129–30, 160
    covenant formula, 113
    covenanted people, 115–17
    covenanting God, 113–14

Deidun, Thomas, 107–8
discipleship, 77, 127–28, 130, 157, 175, 177

Eastman, Susan, 109
Elliot, John H., 111, 121
ethos of belonging, 108, 129, 150, 176
    community center, 49–51, 72
    religious theatre, 140
    school, 32–35, 70, 104

faith, 40, 47, 70, 112, 157, 177
    carried by the community, 145
    gift of God, 138–40, 142–51, 149
    intellectual assent, 10, 74, 130, 133, 147
fear, 15, 27, 41–42, 69, 91
Fleischman, Carly, 21
forgiveness, 40, 125–26, 145

Goode, David, 87
Grenz, Stanley, 141, 153

Hacking, Ian, 20
Hammond, George, 85, 90–91
Hanson, Paul D., 115–16
Hauerwas, Stanley, 89, 177
Higashida, Naoki, 21
Horrell, David, 159–60, 172

image of God, 81–82, 176
    freedom, 97–100, 102–3
    functional view, 82–83, 85
    relational view, 84–85
    substantive view, 82–83, 88, 92
inaction encourages injustice, 42–44
inclusion
    denominational influence, 59, 131
    fear and discomfort, 27
    legislation, 1–2
    mainstreaming, 3
    on the margins, 173
    segregation, 3, 18
    specialized program, 2, 31
indispensability
    contributory members, 9, 71, 130, 154
    indispensable members, 73–75, 77–78, 127, 151–52, 176
    wholeness of the body, 154–56
internalized oppression, 38

Johnson Hodge, Caroline, 110–12
Jones, Gregory, 149–50

Kanner, Leo, 11
kinship, 105, 117
    as discipleship, 124–28
    covenantal kinship, 112–13, 116–17, 160
    kinship in Christ, 108–12
    kinship (sibling) love, 114, 118–20, 124, 169, 172–73
    solidarity, 43, 110, 159–61

lament, 170–71

Macaskill, Grant, 108–9
membership, 38, 73–75, 130, 152–54
    Baptist, 134, 155
    United Church of Canada, 136–37
Monteith, Graham, 120
mutuality, 59–61, 117, 150, 153, 163, 177

Nouwen, Henri, 43, 87

INDEX

openness, 40, 51–52, 125–26, 148, 160
other-regard, 119, 158, 160

participation studies
    Earls, Aaron, 2, 28
    Jones Ault, Melinda, 5
    McNair, Jeff, 2
    Whitehead, Andrew, 5
personhood, 79–81, 89, 102–4, 165, 176
    dignity and sacredness, 3, 71–72, 94, 97
practical theology, 7
presence, 10, 89, 124, 155–56
    being the presence of Christ, 147, 160–71
presumed competence, 148
pure church, 132, 138

Reynolds, Thomas
    cult of normalcy, 4
    economics of exchange, 122
    moral conversion, 124
    vulnerable communion, 4, 122, 124
radical discipleship, 140, 175
Reinders, Hans, 26, 45, 86
Rendtorff, Rolf, 113

Silberman, Steve, 14
social withdrawal, 42
spiritual development, 150
Swinton, John
    autistic love, 7
    Christian vocation, 63
    faith, 138
    from inclusion to belonging, 163
    lamenting community, 170–71
    being present, 163
    respite, 169–70
    slowness, 167
    transvaluation, 101

Tanner, Kathryn, 85
Thompson, James, 118, 122
transformation, 69, 123–27, 155, 165

union with Christ, 108–9, 134
unity in diversity, 95, 119–22, 147, 152

Vanier, Jean
    beloved of God, 72
    caring as worship, 169
    celebrate lives, 171
    journey of belonging, 45–46, 48, 63, 78
    listening, 123
    relational walls, 27
    the way of the heart, 125–26, 162
    vulnerable hearts, 121
vulnerability, 124–27, 163

Webb-Mitchell, Brett, 3
Weiss Block, Jennie, 3
welcome, 124, 128, 153, 155, 161–63, 166

www.ingramcontent.com/pod-product-compliance
Lightning Source LLC
Chambersburg PA
CBHW051741230426

43670CB00012B/2117